RESEARCHING VOLUNTARY ACTION

Innovations and Challenges

Edited by
Jon Dean and Eddy Hogg

First published in Great Britain in 2022 by

Policy Press, an imprint of
Bristol University Press
University of Bristol
1-9 Old Park Hill
Bristol
BS2 8BB
UK
t: +44 (0)117 954 5940
e: bup-info@bristol.ac.uk

Details of international sales and distribution partners are available at
policy.bristoluniversitypress.co.uk

© Bristol University Press 2022

British Library Cataloguing in Publication Data
A catalogue record for this book is available from the British Library

ISBN 978-1-4473-5668-4 hardcover
ISBN 978-1-4473-5671-4 ePub
ISBN 978-1-4473-5670-7 ePdf

Cover design by Qube Design
Front cover image: iStock.com
Bristol University Press and Policy Press use environmentally responsible
print partners
Printed and bound in Great Britain by CPI Group (UK) Ltd,
Croydon, CR0 4YY

FSC
www.fsc.org
MIX
Paper from
responsible sources
FSC® C013604

Contents

List of figures, tables and boxes

Figures

Tables

Boxes

Notes on contributors

Ellen Bennett is Senior Lecturer at Sheffield Hallam University. Her research focuses on voluntary action, with a particular emphasis on the relationships between the state and voluntary organisations, and voluntary sector policy analysis. Ellen is a qualitative researcher, with expertise in participatory and discursive methodologies.

Abhishek Bhati is Assistant Professor in political science at the Bowling Green State University. His research focuses on fundraising techniques used by non-profit organisations and international nongovernmental organisations to raise donations and engage with donors. His work uses both qualitative and quantitative research methodologies.

James Bowles is a PhD student at the Third Sector Research Centre, University of Birmingham. His research looks at the use of spatial data and geographic information systems by third sector organisations in the UK from a social constructionist perspective.

Georgina Brewis is Associate Professor in the history of education at University College London. Her research explores the interlinked histories of voluntary action, humanitarianism and education. She campaigns to raise awareness of the value of voluntary organisations' archives and records and to support their preservation.

Carolyn Cordery is Professor of Charity of Accounting and Accountability at Aston University. Her research focuses on how community and voluntary sector organisations are regulated as well as the impact of resource constraints on their future viability. Much of her work is based on international comparisons.

James Davies has a PhD from the University of Strathclyde. His research looks at youth volunteering and examines how possibilities for participation develop in the context of group norms and social settings. He currently works for the UK Civil Service.

Jon Dean is Associate Professor of politics and sociology at Sheffield Hallam University. His research examines inequalities within the charity sector, and charity's role in wider society and culture. His research makes use of innovations in qualitative methods, and highlights the role of reflexivity in the collection and analysis of data.

Angela M. Eikenberry is D.B. and Paula Varner Professor in the School of Public Administration at the University of Nebraska at Omaha. Her research focuses on the social, economic and political roles of philanthropy, voluntary associations and non-profit organisations in democratic governance; often using critical qualitative methods.

Triona Fitton is Lecturer in sociology at the University of Kent. Her research interests include charity retail, philanthropic history and pedagogy, and social inequalities in access to higher education. She is primarily a qualitative researcher, specialising in ethnographic methods.

Eddy Hogg is Senior Lecturer in social policy at the University of Kent. His research looks at volunteering and voluntary action, with a particular focus on the role of voluntary action in the delivery of public services. His work uses a mix of qualitative and quantitative research methodologies.

Rose Lindsey is Senior Research Fellow at the University of Southampton. Her research uses mixed methods to examine volunteering and voluntary action over time. She specialises in the use of secondary qualitative data and is particularly interested in methodological issues that relate to its use.

Danielle McConville is Senior Lecturer (education) in accounting at Queen's University Belfast and a Chartered Accountant. Her research interests include not-for-profit regulation in the UK and internationally, with qualitative and quantitative research into the performance reporting practices of UK charities and the implications of this for accountability and trust.

Diarmuid McDonnell is Research Fellow at the Third Sector Research Centre, University of Birmingham. His research focuses on the regulation and financing of non-profit organisations. His work leverages large-scale, open administrative datasets and employs quantitative research methodologies.

Hans-Peter Y. Qvist is Assistant Professor at the Department of Sociology and Social Work at Aalborg University. His research explores the causes and consequences of volunteering over time and in different contexts. His work draws on survey and administrative register data and uses quantitative methods.

Alasdair C. Rutherford is Professor of social statistics at the University of Stirling. His research focus is the analysis of administrative and survey data in the fields of health and the third sector. He has also been involved in initiatives to build data analysis skills among third sector practitioners.

Xiaowei Song is a doctoral candidate in the School of Public Administration at the University of Nebraska at Omaha. His research focuses on the role of governance structures in capital and infrastructure finance, performance budgeting and management, and citizen participation in the budget process. His work aims to advance practice-relevant scholarship.

Diarmuid Verrier is Senior Lecturer in psychology at Sheffield Hallam University. His research looks at individual differences such as personality and motivation across many different domains, including education, social media use and volunteering. His work is primarily quantitative in nature.

Kimberly Wiley is Assistant Professor of Nonprofit Leadership and Community Development in the Department of Family, Youth, and Community Sciences at the University of Florida. She engages qualitative methodologies to study publicly funded non-profit organisations and societal perceptions of voluntary action.

Acknowledgements

This volume would obviously not have been possible without the commitment and passion of the authors who have contributed chapters. To have done so during a global pandemic enhances that achievement. Thank you. We would also like to express gratitude to the amazing team at Policy Press, without whom research into voluntary action would not exist to anywhere the level that it does. And to series editor John Mohan, and the reviewers who took the time to provide critical feedback on the text, we are very grateful. Finally, we are both indebted to our families for their continued love and support.

Series editor's foreword

John Mohan

The world of voluntary action is a complex one. Scholars in the field study actions by individuals that are not reducible to considerations of financial return or personal gain, and organisations that occupy hybrid spaces in the interstices between communities, markets and states. We may expect relatively straightforward results from commercial or statutory organisations – goods supplied at market prices to those who can pay for them, or services delivered on a consistent basis to those in need of them. What we expect of voluntary organisations is much less clear: we expect them to provide direct benefits, certainly, but also latent and indirect ones in the form of benefits to society such as the promotion of social capital within communities. As Hogg and Dean observe, voluntary action is a difficult and complex field to investigate, straddling as it does the public and private spheres. It is therefore a field with a need for robust research that will offer clear and grounded insights.

Yet the field is one that to date has lacked a volume that brings together in one place a range of contributions from scholars researching voluntary action. That is the aim of the present edited collection. The chapters exemplify important challenges: the disjunctures between the academic and the common sense of everyday meanings of voluntary action by individuals; the complexities of relationships between researcher and researched, in situations in which individuals may have little to gain directly from participation; the need to give voice to research participants while at the same time not resorting to uncritical, hagiographic accounts of individuals struggling against impossible odds.

Given the diversity of voluntary action and of the settings in which it takes place, the diversity of sources and methods within this collection is a key theme. The studies encompass combinations of survey and administrative data, regulatory returns and text from annual reports, visual methods, participant observation, archives and autobiographical accounts by individuals. The topics themselves are also highly diverse but they are united by a shared concern with private action for the public good. The relationships that this entails, the meanings that people attach to their actions and the expectations that society invests in voluntary action are complex, and they impose a requirement for contextually specific, sensitive and appropriate research methods. The issues that this raises are discussed extensively in this volume.

The COVID pandemic commenced after this book was conceived. Immediate responses to the pandemic, and discussion of social reconstruction in the future, have laid great stress on the potential contribution of voluntary action and the third sector. High-quality research will be essential to determine whether those heightened expectations will be realised. This volume offers a vital guide to research in this area that will be of value to a wide range of practitioners and academics in the field.

Introduction

Eddy Hogg and Jon Dean

'Methodology is destiny', wrote Rooney, Steinberg and Schervish (2004). As a reflection on their finding that when individuals are given more detailed prompts they better recall their previous charitable giving and volunteering, their three-word phrase sums up a central point about social research: if you ask better questions, you get better answers. Do the methodological groundwork, think through the possibilities, *put more in*, and you get more out. More impact. More esteem. And, most importantly, more understanding of our social lives and worlds. It seems fascinating therefore, that within the study of voluntary action (more on that term shortly), while the phrase 'methodology is destiny' has been applied twice more in our field (Bekkers and Wiepking, 2006; Li, 2017), research into voluntary action rarely seems to engage directly with issues of methodology. Obviously, academic and research debate happens between scholars all the time – discussions around the most appropriate dataset to use, or the best coding software or the right way to phrase a question about giving in a national survey – but methodological debates in the non-profit and voluntary action research networks and published reflection and learning are, in our view, relatively scarce.

This surprising lack of attention was one of the inspirations for putting together this volume on researching voluntary action. While all researchers give focus to methodology when collecting data or conceptualising their studies, considered and detailed methodological reflection and advice is generally lacking in voluntary action research journals (although we note that in the two to three years during which this volume has been in development that landscape has started shifting, with developed Research Note sections and special issues). This matters. Good methodology is key. It is key to assessing data validity and making inferences as to the 'quality' of academic findings. It is key too to replicating studies to test for validity in different times or contexts, this being an issue that is becoming increasingly important, especially in specific social research disciplines like psychology and economics (Open Science Collaboration, 2015; Bell et al, 2020). But perhaps most importantly, it is key because voluntary action research often (rightly) positions itself as on the side of the angels, especially when our research involves evaluating or assisting a charity aimed at improving the world. For all of these reasons and more, thinking through the specifics of how methodological questions arise in our field specifically seems vital, particularly considering what innovations researchers see as beneficial and what challenges they encounter. This volume is a small contribution, from 18 authors, to our collective destiny.

Why is this book needed?

Voluntary action is different and raises unique methodological opportunities and challenges. This is because it takes place in the realm between public and private, it contains an often unimaginable diversity of activity, a multitude of meanings are attributed to it, the researchers are often embedded in the field in their own lives – and, for some reason, this knowledge is under-shared between researchers.

Voluntary action – in its broadest sense defined as private action for the public good (Payton and Moody, 2008; Davies, 2015) – is studied by scholars, students, practitioners and policy makers across the world. Researchers draw on a huge range of research methods, reflecting a diversity of epistemological positions, to seek to better understand each and every facet of voluntary action. In doing so, they – we – base our research on both tried and tested and new and experimental methodological approaches. Yet, as researchers and users of research, it is not always clear why we take the approaches we do, what strengths they bring and what compromises they necessitate.

Many of the initial studies of formal voluntary action that emerged in the 1970s and 1980s were undertaken by economists who wanted to understand why people gave their time and money for no obvious financial return and why organisations existed that were driven neither by compulsion (via taxation) nor by profit. From these studies, theories of 'warm glow' (Andreoni, 1990) in motivating individual giving and the problem of 'public goods' (Weisbrod, 1975) explaining the existence of voluntary organisations emerged. These foundational theories in the study of voluntary action start from the assumption that something – people giving for no financial return and organisations existing where no profit can be made – about voluntary action is inherently different. We start from the same belief, that voluntary action *is* different. While in many ways the actions of individuals, groups, organisations and even states that are studied by scholars of voluntary action are similar to those actions undertaken in other contexts – driven by intrinsic and extrinsic motivations, for example, or riven by wider structural inequalities – they are also different. The reasons why people do voluntary actions, the meanings they attribute to them and the way we as societies understand them are all subtly (and sometimes not so subtly) different. In particular, we argue that voluntary action is often a difficult field to research because it sits between the public and private realms. Is one's volunteering primarily about developing one's own personal biography and experience, or is it about a commitment to a person's wider community? Is a charitable donation a private choice or a public statement of values? And if both, how can methodology best penetrate both intimate and open arenas of personal and social life?

This unique situation means that contextually specific and contextually sensitive research methods are essential to conducting robust and reliable data collection and analysis. One size does not fit all, with voluntary work being understood through different conceptualisations and paradigms between and within cultures (Lyons et al, 1998; Rochester et al, 2010), and different legal frameworks for charitable organisations around the world (Picton and Sigafoos, 2020). Respondents understand terms in varying ways, due to everything from honest misunderstanding to cultural specificities (Hodgkinson, 2003). Take the example of 'volunteering', where we find people split on what counts and what does not count (Cnaan et al, 1996), with views that cut against legal definitions. The intricacies of non-profit organisations may be of interest to researchers but not particularly fascinating to the public (Hogg, 2018), and, connectedly, media narratives on charities and charitable giving are often based on a simplistic understanding of voluntary action not rooted in empirical reality. Because the work of voluntary sectors covers the whole gamut of human experience, trying to do the expected methodological work of categorisation and comparison becomes exhausting. As Damm and colleagues (2021) put it:

> To anyone doing research on the voluntary sector, or building services that help voluntary organisations, the size and diversity of activities that charities undertake is always staggering. From a large international charity building relations between Britain and Japan to a small trust maintaining a village playing field, the term 'voluntary sector' hides a huge amount of complexity.

Therefore, better understanding of the organisation of the data that we already have is a key concern of many of the contributors to this volume. In the chapters, we see the need for robust methods that can help to support a better public understanding of voluntary action through providing key stakeholders with clear and grounded insights.

And finally, emerging as a site of methodological study, are the (voluntary action) researchers themselves. The people doing the research in this sphere, the people reading the theories, applying the concepts, asking the questions and interpreting the data are undertaking and riven by the same public actions and private concerns as the people whose action they seek to understand. Harris (2001) asks, when so many voluntary action researchers are so engaged with charities, at donor, volunteer, staff, trustee level or in some other way, why do our own experiences rarely come to bear on our own work? How often are we actually taking our learning into the field, or our experiences of the field into our learning? This wider move towards reflexive work (Dean, 2017) asks not solely for us to consider the impact of a male researcher in majority-female research environments, for instance, but further epistemological questions about the doing of methodology, our choice of theory, the role of disciplinary expectations and practical concerns over how much time we have to devote to the study – even whether another researcher in a different mood would get different results. It is not surprising that many authors in this volume do critical reflexive work, but it is surprising that it hasn't been done to any great extent in our field before now.

Centring discussions of methodology within our field, rather than our respective (sub)disciplines, is particularly necessary because of the recent growth in the study of voluntary action around the world. The 2010s have seen an increase in the number of researchers and research centres undertaking the study of voluntary action in all its diverse forms, and these new and established researchers will all benefit from a comprehensive and high-quality compendium of case studies from experienced researchers who have published research on voluntary action in world-leading academic publications. Moving from the challenges of studying different cultures and communities using qualitative methods, to the opportunities and pitfalls involved in exploring large-scale data on charities and voluntary action, this book aims to provide researchers of all levels – from those who are well experienced to those who may be exploring the field for the first time – a compendium of disparate examples and analyses to help them through the process. Written in an accessible manner with short, focused and useable contributions, and guidance towards key readings in the area, the volume seeks to demystify and deepen our methodological ability to research voluntary action.

While obviously researchers tend to specialise in specific subfields and have favoured methodological practices and traditions, we do feel that all of the book's content will be of interest and use to all of those researching voluntary action in some way, especially in terms of opening up wider epistemological thinking and stimulating discussions around the possibility of mixed methods and multifaceted approaches to inquiry.

Closer to home, we both teach on undergraduate and postgraduate modules or courses concerning voluntary action, and also supervise undergraduate and postgraduate students undertaking independent study in dissertations on voluntary action issues. To date, we have never had a methods text to recommend to them that is specific to the topics they are studying. Given the increased prominence of non-profit and voluntary action studies, we are pleased to be able to help rectify this!

Finally, we are delighted that colleagues across the voluntary action research community have chosen to highlight and unpick the methodological and practical questions that have arisen in their research. Attending as we do many of the voluntary sector research conferences that occur worldwide, we know that these are challenges and issues that many researchers are facing, and see great value in intervening to see what the voluntary action research contribution to methodological debates is.

A note on terminology

One of the perils of research in our field is disambiguation. For example, in the US, the term 'non-profit sector' is most prevalent in describing the arena of society and the economy where voluntary action (more later on that problematic term) takes place, although of course voluntary action also takes place across the public or government sectors as well. Some prefer the term 'civil society' to cover all of this activity, although that generally has a broader remit. In the UK, the term 'voluntary sector' is probably the phrase most commonly used to describe the activity that occurs outside of the private and public sectors, although it is frequently used interchangeably with charity sector, third sector or voluntary and community sector. Former UK prime minister David Cameron tried to get the term 'first sector' used (Ainsworth, 2009), because voluntary action predates and is more fundamental to human life than government or private enterprise, but the idea never took hold. This use of different terms to mean generally the same thing extends to 'voluntary action'. For some, voluntary action often means volunteering, the giving of one's time to help others (see Chapter 14 for a full discussion). But for us, voluntary action is not limited to volunteering, and the chapters in this book try to provide insight into a wide range of activities and behaviours that make up that phrase, including volunteering, but also those in paid employment in charities and non-profits, the fundraising materials those groups rely on to generate donations and the regulatory frameworks that surround them. While 'voluntary action research' is a specific research approach in itself, centred on collaboration and applied to solving problems, we use the terms voluntary action research and research into voluntary action interchangeably.

Overview of the book

The 13 chapters that follow this introduction provide overviews of 13 distinct yet overlapping research methodologies. In each, the contributors reflect on a research project or programme of research looking at voluntary action and the methods that were used. They focus on why those methods were adopted and what particular value they bring to our understanding of voluntary action, as well as reflecting on the challenges that they, the contributors, have faced – and overcome – in using these methods. The book begins by looking at a broad range of qualitative methods, moves through more mixed-method content analysis and finishes with a selection of quantitative approaches.

In Chapter 2, James Davies kicks off the analysis with two stalwarts of qualitative methodologies – interviews and focus groups. Assessing his doctoral research project in Glasgow, Scotland, Davies reflects on his study of youth volunteering in deprived urban areas, using focus groups and follow-up interviews to explore the attitudes towards voluntary action of young people aged between 12 and 18. Focus groups have the potential to generate hugely rich data, due to the dialogue they stimulate between participants rather than just between researcher and participant, helping to address inherent power relations when researching young people. The project encountered challenges, however. Davies discusses the process of negotiating access and consent with 'hard to reach' participants, including non-volunteers, and emphasises the importance of gatekeepers – for better or for worse – in organisations.

Continuing the interpretivist theme, Chapter 3 sees Triona Fitton reflecting on her ethnographic 'participant observation' study of two charity shops in the north of England. Fitton was immersed in her research setting for over 360 hours, studying the reality that shop staff, volunteers and customers create and interpret through their social interactions. Ethnography, Fitton argues, makes no claim of 'completeness'. Rather, the ethnographer is looking for the important, the compelling or the concerning, with the aim of creating transformative, impactful research – as opposed to generalisable or replicable data – not that this is easy! Doing ethnography requires reflexivity about the ways in which even intentionally unobtrusive methods will influence the social interactions being studied. To combat this, Fitton emphasises the importance of being a 'participant-as-researcher' rather than an 'observer as participant'. Ethnography undertaken in this way relies on trust and cooperation – two fundamental elements of voluntary action.

Voluntary action is also a powerful agent for change, and in Chapter 4 Eikenberry and Song outline how research can contribute to this. Drawing on Eikenberry's research on Giving Circles in the US and UK, this chapter explores the use of a range of methods (including interviews, surveys, observation and participant observation, and document analysis) while addressing the tension of doing practically relevant research that is also critical and academically rigorous. Doing this is hugely important when researching a field such as ours that focuses squarely on the delivery of social benefit. Inevitably, addressing this tension comes with challenges, not least in overcoming positivist assumptions about 'truth' and 'rigour' that seek to delegitimise interpretivist approaches. There is also the need for researchers engaged in and with voluntary action to question assumptions and received wisdom, such as the extent to which Giving Circles democratise philanthropy, and to negotiate differences in motivations for research between academics and those working in practice.

These challenges appear again in Chapter 5, in which Ellen Bennett reflects on 20 years of peer-research projects within and alongside voluntary organisations. Like Davies, Fitton and a number of other authors in this collection, Bennett is concerned with power imbalances in research, and in this chapter outlines how peer research approaches seek to hand control and influence to non-academic researchers in order to create knowledge and change. Doing so, co-researchers are engaged in a meaningful way and research benefits come from the experience that stakeholders bring. Handing over power isn't easy, however. Even if academic researchers' egos can be put to one side – not always easy – it is rare that research starts from a blank canvas. Existing agendas may be in play, some fundamental details decided without peer engagement –and even when projects are up and running, questions nonetheless often remain about how decisions are taken on everything from research design to dissemination. And, just as Eikenberry and Song note in the previous chapter, different agendas can create tensions between different needs and priorities. Helpfully to those contending with such issues, Bennett finishes with a nine-step guide to the process of developing a successful peer-research programme.

The focus on participatory research approaches continues in Chapter 6, in which Bhati and Dean reflect on two pieces of research conducted using visual methods to explore representations of need in charity fundraising and advertising materials, one conducted in the UK and the other in India. Such methods have been underused in the study of voluntary action, something Bhati and Dean are keen to address. They argue that visual methods can offer creative alternative ways of understanding the role and successes of and the challenges facing the voluntary sector. They have particular value as a less formal and more inclusive way of gathering data, meaning that they offer a useful way of accessing those 'harder to reach' populations identified in Davies' chapter. They afford research participants the chance to tell their own story – particularly valuable when researching traditionally 'powerless' groups such as homeless adults and children. However, the visual's ability to break down power inequalities isn't a given, and indeed the method can serve to reinforce them.

Next, we move on to the first of two chapters which explore the use of archival methods. Once again, giving a voice to those whose voices are not often heard is a key aim. Chapter 7 draws on Georgina Brewis' experience of research using voluntary organisations' records and material culture across several historical and interdisciplinary research projects in the UK, including the British Academy-funded infrastructure project 'Archiving the Mixed Economy of Welfare'. Brewis outlines how historical records can form a source base to explore voluntary action and the role it has played in society in the past, present and future, and to amplify the voices of marginalised and vulnerable communities and individuals. To make use of these archival resources researchers must gain access to collections, many of which are privately held and for which access will need to be negotiated. To help with this, Brewis provides an example memorandum of understanding between a researcher and organisation whose archive they wish to access.

We stay with historical research in Chapter 8, in which Rose Lindsey reflects on work over a number of years studying the Mass Observation Project. Mass Observation has run in the UK since 1937, the first iteration running from then until the mid-1950s. It was then relaunched in 1981 and has run until the present. Lindsey explains how, when properly contextualised, this data can provide rich insight into the general public's lives and identities, with a focus on their attitudes to and participation in voluntary action. Further, it can enable researchers to explore how these attitudes and activities have changed over time. While there are concerns – returning again to power and representation – about how representative are the members of the public who volunteered to write for the Mass Observation Project, Lindsey concludes that what is most important is to know why the writers have chosen to contribute, which can be explored through occasional biographic responses to the Project.

From analysis of historical texts we move to analysis of a more contemporary kind of 'text' – television storylines. In Chapter 9, Kimberley Wiley reflects on her US-based study of 131 television storylines to explore how volunteering is portrayed, focusing on what volunteer managers can learn from television portrayals and capturing the paradox of coercive or mandatory volunteering. Television as a medium allows researchers to gain a broad and nuanced view of how the cultural industries present, debate, critique and poke fun at a topic. Studying the storylines of television series, Wiley explains, allows researchers to capture multiple views of voluntary action from the point of view of the volunteer, the volunteer supervisor and the beneficiary. While the storylines are of course fictional, they can be read as a text to make sense of how people – characters and viewers – experience the world. In a further methodological innovation, Wiley recruited undergraduate research assistants to gather the storylines by watching the television shows and recording their analysis of the content of the programmes in online codebooks, and a sample recruitment form for such a study is included.

Continuing the content analysis theme, in Chapter 10, Cordery and McConville look at the opportunities that content analysis of charities' annual reports offers to researchers, drawing on their research in Australia, New Zealand and the UK. They argue that the richness of the quantitative and qualitative data in these reports represents a 'potential goldmine' for those seeking to understand how voluntary organisations – in particular those formally constituted as charities – operate. The goldmine is indeed rich: these reports include narrative data and case studies of organisational success alongside performance and financial data, with some jurisdictions gathering this in a standardised way that allows for comparisons to be made. Cordery and McConville reflect on getting started in this research, including their initial reviewer feedback being rather mixed! Presenting a salutary lesson in the difficulties of researching with 'novel' methods or data sources, they explain how they refined their approach to include content analysis. They also reflect on the vast differences in information collected by regulators in annual reports and the different challenges this can present for researchers both when studying one jurisdiction and, most acutely, when engaging in comparative research. Nonetheless, they conclude that content analysis of freely (if not always straightforwardly) accessible data offers a huge opportunity for researchers to better understand the operation and impact of voluntary organisations.

At this point of the book, the use of regulatory data emerges as a clear theme, with Chapter 11 seeing McDonnell and Rutherford reflect on the methodological implications and challenges associated with using the large-scale datasets produced by and for charity regulators to study risk in the voluntary sector. They do so by drawing on a wide range examples from their ongoing research on charities in the UK and beyond. They emphasise the importance of understanding the 'biography' of administrative data and guide researchers through how to achieve this. However, they note that the use of such data poses both opportunities and challenges around: access to data; the coverage it provides; the quality of the data; the extent to which the data can (or cannot) capture reality; how timely the data is; how the data is gathered and measured; what level of detail the data captures; and how linked the data is to other administrative datasets. McDonnell and Rutherford provide examples from their work to illustrate how they have overcome these challenges. In doing so, they conclude that there is huge potential in the use of regulatory data to better understand risk in the voluntary sector – so long as researchers are aware of the challenges.

Staying with the analysis of large-scale datasets, in Chapter 12 Hans-Peter Qvist explores the huge opportunities that the 'mergeability' of different sets of longitudinal administrative data in the Nordic countries offers for researchers. This enables researchers to explore the possible benefits of volunteering by looking at data on participation alongside actual labour market and health outcomes. This, Qvist outlines, presents researchers with unique opportunities to relate people's volunteering behaviour to changes in their subsequent labour market and health trajectories. The benefits of this are obvious. Many studies that seek to explore the benefits of volunteering rely on self-reported health or labour market outcomes, on inferring causality from correlation in cross-sectional datasets or on longitudinal data collection methods with high attrition rates. Using state administrative data with unique individual identifiers alleviates many of these problems. However, it is not without its own issues. Using this data requires researchers to operate with sensitivity and to recognise that this data has not been gathered for their use – the data is a by-product of state systems. Therefore they will need to assess and modify the data before it is suitable for research purposes. Additionally, researchers need to be aware that even governments – maybe especially governments – change their methodology from time to time, meaning that longitudinal data may not be as stable as it seems. A helpful reminder that all data needs to be viewed with a critical eye.

In the penultimate chapter things get spatial, with James Bowles in Chapter 13 outlining the opportunities and challenges of a different use of regulatory data – mapping techniques that allow researchers to better understand the geographical nature of voluntary action. Reflecting on his doctoral research in the UK, Bowles explains how he has utilised regulatory data (a consistent theme in the more quantitative chapters in this collection) alongside local voluntary sector listings, grant-making data and local government data to explore the spatial distribution of voluntary action. By using spatial visualisation tools, Bowles adds spatial attributes to this data so that it can be visualised graphically. This is shown through rich maps of charity distribution in the UK. The opportunities are clear, as are the challenges – any map is a representation, not reality, and any data analysis requires the drawing of boundaries that include as much as they exclude. While maps are seductive in their ability to 'mirror' reality, they need to be treated as sceptically as any data source.

The final chapter takes a look at two familiar approaches for researchers in academia and charities – the survey. In particular, it focuses on an approach widely used in undergraduate research projects but perhaps underused in academic research more broadly – the (amended) restudy. In Chapter 14,Dean and Verrier explore their restudy of Cnaan, Handy and Wadsworth's (1996) influential study of how 'volunteering' is defined, reflecting on their experience of conducting a restudy of such an influential piece of work, 25 years on. Taking a sample of undergraduate students, Dean and Verrier reflect on their use of a new survey and of factor analysis to explore and make conceptual sense of the results. The value of restudies is made clear, both as a way of generating insightful and comparable data and as a way of critically examining one's own and peers' research practices.

Conclusion

What attendance at numerous non-profit and voluntary action research conferences, events, meetings, seminars and colloquia has taught us is that while methodologies are fundamentally important to how we understand the world, they aren't something that scholars of voluntary action talk about much in public. This book seeks to help change that. It cannot hope to be a collection of everything we know about researching voluntary action, and similarly if an issue is not focused on here that does not mean that we and our colleagues who have contributed chapters think it unworthy of attention: the volume is not meant to be the last word on researching voluntary action, but merely one of the first (see Conclusion).

Voluntary action and the sectors in which it occurs are distinct and different from other research fields, given its unique position in social life and the special set of meanings that people attribute to voluntary action. And the reasons that make voluntary action often a difficult field to research – sitting between the public and private realms, comprising a set of relations that can broadly be defined as private action for the public good, the deep meanings that people attribute to their own voluntary action and the expectations that society has of the role of voluntary organisations – mean that contextually specific and contextually sensitive research methods are essential to conducting robust and reliable data collection, and make more detailed methodological examinations in our sphere vital.

2

(Un)suitable methods and reflexive considerations: an interview and focus group study of youth volunteering

James Davies

Introduction

The methodological reflections in this chapter are based on a qualitative study of youth volunteering in deprived urban areas in Glasgow, Scotland conducted during my doctorate (2013–18). The research explored young people's understandings of volunteering, their routes to participation, the meanings they attributed to it and barriers to participation. Young volunteers and non-volunteers, aged 12–18, were recruited to focus groups and interviews from youth organisations and educational institutions. Interviews were also conducted with youth workers. The focus of this chapter, however, is on the methodological issues encountered during fieldwork with young people. The chapter explores the role of gatekeepers, the negotiation of access and consent, recruitment challenges and the combined use of focus groups and interviews. It reflects on my attempt to use participatory methods during the pilot study and examines what 'failed' interviews can teach us about the research process. The chapter takes a reflexive approach and considers how, due to demographic differences and varying meanings attributed to volunteering, 'outsider' researchers can encounter challenges when studying voluntary action.

The research and I

Before discussing the methods, I want to provide an account of my positionality and route to the research. Qualitative methods are associated with a constructivist epistemology that views research as a process of meaning-making. Discussions between researchers and participants are shaped by the histories and biographies each brings to the encounter. Accordingly, my reflections on the methods I employed are contingent upon the interactions I had in the field and, without a brief biographical sketch, something may be lost in the following account.

I was born into a middle-class family in the south-east of England. My parents, who met while studying at university, relocated from the north-west a few years before I was born. I attended an independent day school that offered a variety of extra-curricular activities to 'build character' and enhance university applications – the assumption being that pupils would attend university. Aside from a brief stint in a charity shop one summer, I had little engagement with volunteering until I was an undergraduate, studying sociology at the University of Liverpool. While studying, I volunteered with a variety of groups, including adults with learning difficulties, deaf and blind children, asylum seekers and other students. My participation in these activities was motivated by a variety of factors, including, a desire to help others, an impulse to socialise with friends and a module requirement. It was not, however, my experiences of volunteering that led me to study it during my doctorate. Rather, I applied for a studentship at the University of Strathclyde in Glasgow. The studentship was supported by Volunteer Scotland and focused on young people and volunteering. Having enjoyed studying as an undergraduate and possessing some experience of volunteering (as a young*ish* person), I was drawn to the opportunity and, shortly after applying, moved to Glasgow to start the project.

My experiences of growing up and volunteering differed from those of the young, working-class Glaswegian participants in the study. In the UK there is a history of middle-class intervention in working-class life and of conflict between England and Scotland (indeed, the fieldwork took place following the 2014 referendum on Scottish independence). Awareness of this macro context, in which the participants' and my personal trajectories met, is helpful to understanding how fieldwork encounters unfolded.

Negotiating access and consent

Recruiting participants is of obvious importance when conducting qualitative research and can create various challenges during the early stages of a project. One reason for focusing on youth volunteering in deprived urban areas was due to evidence highlighting comparatively lower levels of volunteering for this group than those in less deprived rural areas (Davies, 2018). From the outset it was anticipated that the recruitment of so-called 'hard-to-reach' participants, particularly as a researcher with no pre-existing connections to the study population, could prove challenging.

As the project focused on routes and barriers to volunteering, I needed to speak to current and non-volunteers. Recruiting non-volunteers presented itself as a challenge, due to their non-participation. Schools were initially selected as sites at which it was anticipated that both volunteers and non-volunteers could be recruited. Conducting research in educational settings can be a slow process, generating further obstacles for researchers

(Ellard-Gray et al, 2015). In addition to gaining ethical permission from my university's ethics committee, I applied to Glasgow City Council for permission to approach schools. Once approval was granted, I sent a letter to 14 educational institutions outlining the research and requesting their involvement. After a week or so of waiting and not hearing back, an intense period of attempting to contact relevant members of staff followed. In some instances, I was unable to reach beyond school receptionists. On the occasions when I did, three schools were quick to say they were unable to assist, while others expressed interest but highlighted the challenges of fitting the fieldwork into their schedules. In a number of cases, my efforts to follow up went dry and I considered it inappropriate to keep pushing. Of the 14 institutions approached, I conducted fieldwork with volunteers and non-volunteers in three secondary schools and one college. (In Scotland, secondary schools are for pupils aged 11–18 and are compulsory up to the age of 16. The college was a further education college offering vocational courses for students aged 16 and over.)

During this period, it became apparent that I would struggle to recruit a sufficient number of participants by focusing solely on schools. A number of youth-based organisations, providing sports, child- and youth-orientated activities, were identified following online searches. The sites were initially approached by e-mail and followed up with phone calls and visits. This period of correspondence, often with youth workers, provided the opportunity for them to ask questions about the research and for me inquire about the activities the organisation undertook and how they involved young people. Perhaps due to their comparatively smaller size and less bureaucratic structure than schools, I had greater success contacting the 'right' people and conducted fieldwork with volunteers and non-volunteers at 11 different sites.

Collins et al (2016: 507) emphasise the importance of identifying 'champions' in organisations who, due to their investment to the research, can help with recruitment. Many of the youth workers expressed interest in the project and a desire for the young people to have their voices heard. Unlike schools where volunteering was an extra-curricular activity, it was central to the day-to-day practices of youth organisations. As a way of enticing participation and seeking to give back to those who gave their time to the study, I stated from the outset that interim reports would be available from Volunteer Scotland's website and that a practitioner-friendly summary of the findings would be shared at the end of the research. Such an offer may have held greater significance for youth organisations than for schools.

In both the educational and youth-group settings, negotiating with gatekeepers was necessary to recruiting participants. While gatekeepers play an important role in protecting young people, an unintended consequence is that they can remove young people's right to make decisions for themselves (Collins et al, 2016), raising ethical issues about consent. In many of the schools I contacted, young people were denied the opportunity to join or to decline participation in the study, due to decisions made by gatekeepers. Yet, in circumstances where the 'gate was opened', there may have been instances where young people felt compelled to take part.

To address this, where possible, I endeavoured to meet and interact with participants prior to conducting fieldwork. The development of rapport is commonly noted in the literature on participant recruitment, particularly for hard-to-reach populations who may be wary of the research process (Ellard-Gray et al, 2015). At one youth organisation, for instance, I took part in a workshop with three young volunteers, two of whom I subsequently interviewed. Before the workshop started, we undertook a warm-up activity that involved jumping up and down and running in circles. I felt the activity reduced some of the social distance between us and led to relaxed interviews. Indeed, one participant contrasted our interview favourably with another she had undertaken, noting, 'see that wee guy that took about 15 minutes? This wans been better, I like talking' (Amy). Due to my having interacted beforehand and provided space for Amy to inquire about the process and me, she was better placed to consent to the study. The benefits of this can be seen in the more enjoyable experience she described and the appearance she gave of happily discussing her experiences for the hour that our interview lasted.

Yet, my efforts to develop rapport were not always as successful. At a similar organisation, I followed the same steps of introducing myself and sitting in on a workshop prior to conducting fieldwork. I held two focus groups with volunteers at this site, the first of which was characterised by a stifled discussion, the second more conversational. Despite the same organisational setting and pre-interview steps, the focus groups unfolded in contrasting manners. The comparative reticence of the first group may have been related to the fact that, although I had stated that participation was voluntary, they were acting out of compliance with the youth workers' request that they participate rather than their own desire to do so.

Negotiating access in research with young people does not end with gatekeepers. Accessing participants' reflections on their experiences requires researchers to create an environment in which participants are able to provide consent and feel comfortable sharing their views. Achieving this is made challenging by unequal power relations in the research process. The methods I selected, focus groups and interviews, were partly influenced by an attempt to address this imbalance.

Focus groups and interviews

Liamputtong (2011) describes how, despite being developed as an academic research method in the early 1940s, focus groups became synonymous with market research from the 1950s onwards. It was not until the 1980s, when researchers reorientated the method away from its more quantitative market research underpinnings, that it became more prevalent in the social sciences. A central characteristic of focus groups is the interaction between participants, which provides insights that would otherwise be inaccessible in one-to-one interviews. Focus groups facilitate a 'synergy that individuals alone don't possess' (Krueger and Casey, 2000: 24), making them an effective method for exploring how different groups experience a topic. As the method emphasises the interaction between participants and gives prominence to their points of view, it can enable researchers to 'pay attention to the needs of those who have little or no societal voice' (Liamputtong, 2011: 4). Accordingly, it was considered an appropriate method for researching youth volunteering in areas of deprivation.

In light of my 'outsider' status and the unequal power relations characterising research with young people, focus groups were considered suitable, due to the comfort participants can derive from a sense of 'safety in numbers' (Merryweather, 2010: 2.11). Focus groups, particularly if conducted with pre-existing friendship groups, can go some way to reducing power imbalances by virtue of the fact that participants outnumber the researcher (Gallagher, 2009). They are less invasive than individual interviews and can enhance participants' willingness to share opinions and experiences (Krueger and Casey, 2000), making them appropriate for research conducted across social divisions.

The foregrounding of the group interaction makes focus groups useful for exploring similarities and differences between groups. The expectations and experiences participants bring can have the effect of socially moderating the discussion, revealing normative views among the cohort in question (Hennink and Leavy, 2014). Discrete groups were sought based on participants' age (12–15 and 16–18), gender and status as (non-)volunteers. This approach complemented the theoretical framework adopted during the study. Pierre Bourdieu's (1990) concept of 'habitus' was employed to understand how individual and collective dispositions towards, and away from, volunteering were shaped by the social conditions in which participants were located. By conducting focus groups comprised of individuals with shared characteristics, it was anticipated that it would be possible to explore how experiences and understandings of volunteering were informed by the social positions of participants (Merryweather, 2010).

While the group dynamic in focus groups is beneficial for understanding how a particular cohort approaches an issue, it may lead some to avoid discussing personal information (Liamputtong, 2011). Furthermore, pre-existing group dynamics can negatively impact on the contributions participants feel willing to make (Gallagher, 2009). The differing dynamics of focus groups and interviews can make the latter more appropriate for exploring sensitive aspects of a topic (Michell, 1999). In light of such concerns, it was considered necessary to supplement focus groups with individual interviews.

Interviews have been described as 'professional' (Braun and Clarke, 2013: 77) conversations in which the interaction between researcher and participant constructs knowledge about a given topic. They can be advantageous, due to the depth that can be achieved when exploring participants' views (Legard et al, 2003). This was particularly valuable in light of the notion that focus group discussions do not necessarily represent the views of each participant (Hennink and Leavy, 2014). Group norms can prohibit participants from discussing topics that are not perceived to conform to peer expectations.

It was anticipated that, by conducting follow-up interviews with focus group participants, it would be possible to gain additional insights into how volunteering was experienced (Michell, 1999). Follow-up interviews further complemented the use of habitus as a way of understanding (non-)participation. While focus groups provided a way of analysing collective dispositions, interviews facilitated a more nuanced exploration of how individual trajectories towards or away from volunteering were formed in areas characterised by low levels of volunteering.

Piloting participatory approaches

Prior to conducting the main study, a pilot project was completed to test the suitability of focus groups and interviews. During the pilot, participatory approaches – a mapping exercise and photo-elicitation interviews – were trialled as ways of supplementing data collection. Participatory methods can provide young people with a greater role in the research process and were considered a pertinent way of engaging participants in the study.

The mapping exercise, used during focus groups, was intended to provide insight into how possibilities for volunteering were embedded in participants' local areas. Before each group, I printed a map of the area where the research site was located. During the focus group, participants were invited to discuss opportunities for volunteering and reflect on their (im)mobilities in the area. While some could pinpoint volunteer-involving organisations, others struggled to orientate themselves. Further, it transpired that a few travelled to the research sites and were not overly familiar with the areas depicted. Discussions tended to focus on distances between organisations and homes but did not go into greater detail about factors facilitating or inhibiting access to volunteering. Overall, it was felt that the mapping exercise did not significantly add to the study. Indeed, the time taken to set it up reduced the amount of time available to discuss the research themes. Resultantly, the activity was not taken forward.

In hindsight, alternative ways of using a mapping approach might have generated deeper insights. Rather than using pre-existing maps, a more fruitful approach may be to invite participants to create their own. Researchers have noted that this approach can enable young people to visually express their views and highlight places of significance (Darbyshire et al, 2005). Encouraging participants to create their own maps would have freed them from the constraints of geographic accuracy and allowed them to emphasise factors that they considered important in their (non-)volunteering. It might also have moved discussions on to the more social and cultural dimensions of their experiences. The time required to conduct such an activity, however, might make it better suited to individual interviews or circumstances where there are several researchers available to facilitate the activity.

In the period between focus groups and follow-up interviews, participants were invited to take photographs of things relating to their volunteering experiences to be used as discussion prompts. This approach is known as photo-elicitation interviewing and can lead to more relaxed interviews as participants have control over the images produced and can better anticipate what will be discussed (see Bhati and Dean, Chapter 6 in this volume).

Participants were asked to use their smartphones to generate images and send them via e-mail or a messaging application to a phone purchased for the study. Disposable cameras were purchased for those without smartphones but were not required. The brief was deliberately wide, so as to give participants autonomy over the images they produced (Darbyshire et al, 2005). Participants were asked to generate images of places, objects and items that they felt related to their experiences of volunteering. Unfortunately, when it came to the interviews, none of the participants had completed the task. When asked why, participants reported that they had forgotten about it. Researchers have noted that absenteeism and attrition can be prevalent among vulnerable groups, who may deprioritise the study against other worries in their lives (Ellard-Gray et al, 2015). Moreover, while research is highly significant for researchers, it can be inconsequential for those researched. Additionally, in light of my positionality, I may have given insufficient attention to potential concerns about the data costs associated with sending images by smartphone. Furthermore, a week had passed between the focus group and follow-up interview, perhaps providing too little (or, indeed, too much) time to engage with the activity. As the method had not been piloted, it was not used during the main study.

While multiple methods can deepen understandings of young people's worlds, they require greater input from participants. Participants must, therefore, be provided with the time, tools and support to complete tasks they are invited to undertake. Although the use of participatory methods was unsuccessful during the pilot, conducting follow-up interviews after focus groups generated additional insights. One participant, for instance, contributed little during a focus group but had much to say when interviewed. It was on this basis that focus groups and interviews were selected as the methods in the main study.

Focus group composition challenges and 'failed' interviews

Merryweather (2010) notes that, despite the planning that goes into organising focus groups comprised of participants with shared characteristics, in practice, they are often not wholly homogeneous. My experience resonated with such reflections. At the outset, I intended to conduct eight focus groups, each comprised of four to six participants. Securing discrete groups, however, proved challenging. By the end of the fieldwork, I had conducted 16 focus groups. This was partly due to the struggle I encountered recruiting sufficient numbers of participants to each group. Of the 16 focus groups, seven comprised only two or three participants and arguably lacked the group dynamic that characterises the method. In such circumstances, I sought additional participants for further focus groups to build a more coherent sample. Additionally, a number of focus groups did not meet the demographic criteria: two crossed the gender division, two did not meet the volunteer status category and eight did not fall neatly within the age brackets.

These deviations were often a result of the young people who were available at the time of the fieldwork. Due to the largely voluntary nature of attendance at research sites, it was difficult to predict who would be available. Although I did not have a comparative group from a less deprived area, it may be the case that this is a particular challenge with hard-to-reach groups due to a de-prioritisation of the research against other demands on their time (Ellard-Gray et al, 2015). It may also be related to the fact that, as young people, they did not have the same amount of control over their time as adults do. One focus group, conducted during a drop-in session at a youth sports charity, started as a female-only group but ended mixed due to the late arrival of a male volunteer. Similarly, a focus group with males at a school started as a non-volunteer session but became mixed following the late arrival of a volunteer. Generally, these deviations did not appear to prevent participants from contributing; however, on some occasions they did. The late-arriving male volunteer in the group of females, for instance, hardly contributed despite my efforts to involve him. Partly, this may have been because he did not receive the same introduction as the others. Yet, it may also have stemmed from being the only male and not experiencing the same sense of 'safety in numbers'.

While the majority of focus groups were characterised by insightful conversations about volunteering, two were notable for strained silences, awkward laughter and efforts by participants to avoid the topic. Nairn et al (2005) argue for a 'counter-narrative' of a 'failed interview'. They posit that, rather than viewing lack of speech as failure, such encounters offer insight into the practice of qualitative research and knowledge production. The two groups comprised male non-volunteers, a group for whom the threat of informal penalties for volunteering was considered particularly acute, due to its social castigation as 'uncool' (Davies, 2018). The strained silences may, at least in part, have been related to the low status in which volunteering was held. As noted earlier, focus group discussions are moderated by the norms and expectations participants bring. This impacts not only on what is spoken, but also on what is unspoken, that which, in Bourdieu's (1990: 54) terms, is 'unthinkable' by virtue of the social conditions in which participants are positioned. The following extract, during which volunteering was discussed as a way of developing skills, highlights such strained interactions:

Akash:	[Sings Justin Bieber's 'What Do You Mean?' which is playing in the neighbouring room]
James:	How might, I guess why would you describe volunteering in that way?
Akash:	[Continues to sing]
Sahib:	Aye, erm.
	There is a pause. The participants awkwardly look and gesture at each other.
Vic:	Who, me?
James:	Or, just anyone, yeah.
	The participants do not speak. Some make 'pfft' noises.
James:	I'm just curious why you might pick that one?
	Some of the participants laugh.

In their counter-narrative, Nairn et al (2005) contend that 'failed' interviews teach us about interview settings, participant subjectivities and researcher positionality. The focus group took place during a holiday camp at a sports charity. The influence of the setting can be seen in the distracting music from a neighbouring room. Furthermore, the camp was attended by a large number of young people who came to engage in physical activities. The comparative formality of the focus group likely jarred with the participants' expectations of what they would be doing. Moreover, having been asked to take part by one of the coaches, they may have felt compelled, despite my assertion that participation was voluntary. The participants' reactions can be understood as 'act[s] of resistance' towards the subject matter, the interview context and, indeed, the interviewer (Spyrou, 2016: 14).

The insider/outsider researcher

A commonly noted issue in the literature on researcher positionality is the insider/outsider dichotomy, the former occurring when researchers and participants share characteristics or experiences, the latter when they do not (Braun and Clarke, 2013). The distinction, however, is not straightforward. Researchers are positioned in heterogeneous ways and may simultaneously be insiders and outsiders. As noted, one way in which my positionality differed from that of the participants was in our social class backgrounds. This factor, however, did not stand alone but intersected with other characteristics, such as gender, to create varying opportunities and obstacles for the development of rapport throughout the fieldwork.

One obvious difference was my accent, immediately making me as a non-Glaswegian. During a focus group with female non-volunteers, one participant inquired, 'whereabouts are you from? Like I can tell you're no' from here with the accent' (Robyn). I explained I had grown-up in the south-east of England, lived in Liverpool for a few years and moved to Glasgow to study. My assertion that I enjoyed living in Glasgow was met with humorous incredulity – 'really!?' (Taylor) and 'this is the worst place you could go!' (Zoe). Similarly, when meeting young people at another research site, during which my non-Glaswegian identity was noted, I attempted to establish a connection between myself and the area by revealing that my grandmother had grown up in the district. This disclosure, however, prompted laughter from the participants, due to my pronunciation. Yet, in both instances, by presenting something of myself to the participants – where I had lived, where my family came from – and being willing to laugh at myself, my outsider status was put to work to contribute to a more reciprocal exchange.

There were instances where my outsider status created challenges to the research relationship. This primarily occurred when conducting focus groups with male non-volunteers. While these 'difficult' exchanges may have been related to the subject matter itself, they also appeared to relate to the varying ways in which we performed our gender identities. For instance, my lack of knowledge about and interest in football, an activity described by Fraser (2015: 146) as central to the 'social divisions, masculinities and physical prowess' of the Glaswegian identity, appeared to limit my ability to fit in.

James:	Have you ever done any after school clubs?
Sahib:	He still does it.
Vic:	Aye.
James:	What club?
Akash:	Futsal club.
James:	Food science club?
Akash:	*Fut – sal.*

Owen:	Futsal.
Paul:	Indoor football, indoor football.
James:	Oh right, ok. What did you do in that?
Vic:	Futsal, football.
Sahib:	Just play indoor football.

My ignorance about futsal, an indoor ball sport similar to five-a-side football, quickly marked me as lacking knowledge. Fraser (2015) argues that being 'in the know' was an important component of the 'street masculinity' for the young males in his study of youth gangs in a deprived area of Glasgow with comparable demographics to my research sites. The revelation that I was not 'in the know' set the tone for the strained interactions that followed. My clothing choices also appeared to create challenges to the formation of rapport. During the interview, I noticed one participant glance under the table and whisper to another, 'look at his shoes', before both burst into laughter. What I had presumed to be a relatively neutral item of clothing, a pair of black ankle boots, seemingly marked me as ripe for ridicule. Clothing, a central facet to the presentation of self and performance of gender, is an important but often overlooked aspect of researcher positionality (Wilkinson, 2016). In contrast to the participants' trainers and sports attire, my boots, skinny jeans and jumper perhaps embodied a form of masculinity at odds with their group norms.

While the insider/outsider dichotomy impacts on qualitative research in general, it may generate specific challenges in studies of voluntary action, due to the meanings attributed to volunteering. For instance, the wider framing of the volunteer as a 'near-sacred figure' (Eliasoph, 2013: 2), alongside histories of middle-class intervention in working-class life, may have led to my questions being perceived as disapproval for non-participation rather than scholarly inquiry. Volunteering is a complex phenomenon imbued with moralistic notions and, particularly for young people, structural pressures to participate in order to enhance future opportunities. Studies of voluntary action are located within this context and there exists a risk that questions, particularly from outsiders, are caught up in judgemental frameworks.

Conclusion

This chapter has reflected on my experience of qualitatively researching youth volunteering using focus groups and interviews. Overall, these methods provided a fruitful way of gathering information about understandings and experiences of volunteering. By conducting focus groups with specific cohorts, I gained insight into how different groups related to volunteering. The group setting provided a way of exploring how localised norms created varying possibilities for discussion of the topic. Indeed, through this approach, it was possible to analyse how strained interactions were related to the low status of volunteering within a particular cohort. The use of interviews alongside focus groups provided space for greater consideration of individual trajectories and facilitated a more detailed understanding of the personal dimensions of volunteering. They also permitted more in-depth discussions for participants who might otherwise have felt inhibited from speaking in group settings, due to peer norms.

Researchers of voluntary action seeking to innovate may wish to consider organising focus groups with participants from heterogeneous backgrounds. As the hallmark of a focus group is the group dynamic, it may be productive, for example, to mix younger and older volunteers or volunteers and non-volunteers to explore how they compare and contrast their experiences. Furthermore, although the participatory methods I deployed did not result in substantially greater insights during the pilot, this is not to say that they are without value. Using participant-produced drawings about perceptions of what a volunteer looks like as prompts for discussion, for example, could add depth to understandings of volunteering.

Finally, the chapter has emphasised the importance of considering how differing researcher and participant positionalities shape the research process. While such social characteristics cannot be altered, it is important to reflect on the impact they have. For instance, outsider researchers inquiring about the activities of a community project may bring to mind anxieties about external bodies reviewing funding grants to determine their future. The wider framing of volunteering as a social good may present challenges, particularly in the studies of non-volunteering, due to the risk of questions being perceived as judgement for non-participation. Being transparent about the purpose of a study and allowing participants to make inquiries, as well as interacting beforehand, can be key to building effective research relationships. Providing readers with a sense of how interactions in the field shaped the process can enhance understandings of findings and conclusions.

Further reading
- Nairn et al's (2005) reflections on 'failed' interviews provide useful insights into the theory and practice of qualitative research.
- To understand how a researcher's appearance and personality impact the research process, see Wilkinson (2016).
- Merryweather's (2010) discussion of focus groups as a tool for understanding variations in young people's experiences based on their social positions is instructive.

3

Interpretive ethnography: a UK charity shop case study

Triona Fitton

Introduction

Ethnographic research is widely used across social research disciplines examining the voluntary sector, yet the output- and impact-driven culture that directs many research agendas can lead to the value of qualitative modes of inquiry being overlooked. It is helpful therefore for voluntary sector researchers to understand the key uses of ethnography as a qualitative research tool. Drawing on an interpretivist approach, this chapter will outline the utility of ethnography when undertaking a participant observation in two different charity shops. The case study illustrates the importance of immersion within the research setting in terms of recording and analysing 'natural' interactions and behaviours. It also explores the issue of access, the role of researcher reflexivity and how micro-level 'shop floor' studies of voluntary cultures can serve as a critical measure against data-driven assumptions about contemporary charity work.

To begin, this chapter will provide an overview of ethnography and interpretivism as a methodology, before focusing upon how interpretivist participatory research (and its relational and reflexive aspects) and thick description (Geertz, 1973b) are useful tools to better understand the social world. I will illustrate these with evidence from my own ethnographic study into professionalisation in charity retail operations (Fitton, 2013). In the interest of brevity, this chapter will focus predominantly on the contribution of participant observation and fieldnotes as a valuable method for voluntary sector research. However, semi-structured interviews also formed an important part of this project (see Chapter 2 of this volume for a discussion of the utility of semi-structured interviewing) and ought to be of interest to practitioners or academic researchers considering a multimethod ethnographic approach.

Ethnographic research has its basis within the research paradigm of interpretivism, a qualitative methodology that emerged from the field of anthropology (LeCompte and Schensul, 1999). It works on the premise that all knowledge of reality is created and constantly reinterpreted through social constructions such as culture, systems, language, traditions, shared understandings, tools, documents and so on. Placing emphasis on how a reality is created or constructed negates the idea that there are concrete or objectively measurable facts about any aspect of social life – the voluntary sector included – that are not in some way open to interpretation.

Research into the voluntary sector, particularly when it is aimed at aiding practitioners, tends to have a strong focus on enhancing knowledge, practice and efficiency, alongside the ability to measure and demonstrate impact with some degree of replicability. This tendency to privilege measurable, tangible results takes inspiration from the research fields of management and business, which are typically quantitative in nature (Bielefeld, 2006) – in general, the voluntary sector has increasingly taken directive from the for-profit sector in terms of how to improve its operations. In the UK, there has been enhanced scrutiny of the actions and outputs of charitable organisations in recent years, a symptom of the increasing involvement of charities in the delivery of public services (Wilding, 2017) and a number of high-profile mismanagement scandals (for example, the implosion of the charity Kids Company after receiving more than £46 million of public funds [Dean, 2020]). This, alongside a reduction in available funding, has meant that those working in the voluntary sector are most likely to prioritise research that shows demonstrable impact, that can be simply conveyed and that can be used convincingly at a policy level. There is also a misguided assumption that using statistical data is more likely to produce 'neutral' or truthful results – an assumption that has dogged the natural sciences for centuries. Non-profits tend to have a preoccupation with the measurement of outputs and outcomes, with an intention of strengthening accountability towards both donors and beneficiaries (Benjamin, 2012). This, as Wilding (2017) notes, leads to a desire for the voluntary sector to become more data driven, and thus reliant upon quantitative research and findings in order to prove its worth 'objectively'.

It is commonly argued that interpretivism yields a less than objective representation of the world (see Nadel [1951] for a discussion of research objectivity). However, being 'impartial' and 'holistic' is not a prerequisite for good research, and telling the whole story is not always necessary. We do not need to document the minute detail of all interactions, but instead record and consider those situations that we regard as the most important, compelling or concerning. We must act as metaphorical 'pearl divers' (Arendt, in Back, 2007), not by surveying the entirety of an ocean's depths but by sifting through and illuminating the most important and precious elements to be found there.

An obvious question arises: how do we know what is most precious, important, compelling or concerning about the site we intend to research? Prior studies serve to illuminate the aspects of a social setting that have intrigued social scientists previously, and show where a research 'gap' may exist. Reflection upon the present voluntary sector milieu allows subsequent research to aim towards being *transformative* as opposed to generalisable or replicable. This is the primary defence against claims of unrepresentativeness in ethnographic case studies. By building upon or reconstructing existing theories and ideas about how the voluntary sector operates, we achieve 'inclusive generality' (Burawoy, 2009: 43) by offering novel perspectives on hitherto assumed standard practices.

In my particular area of interest (charity shops), academic studies have previously explored everything from small-scale quantitative studies of types of goods sold (Horne and Broadbridge, 1995), shop volunteering (Broadbridge and Horne, 1994) and the 'archetypal' charity shopper (Parsons, 2000), to qualitative studies on aspects such as the shop's role as a 'cultural economy' and second-hand marketplace (Chattoe, 2006; Edwards and Gibson, 2017), and the volunteer's role as a practice of care (Flores, 2014). However, a large body of work on charity retail at the time when this study was undertaken was concerned with a perceived move within the sector from a social to a commercial orientation, with shops operating more like for-profit enterprises (for example, Goodall, 2000; Horne and Maddrell, 2002). This mirrored a general perception of the voluntary sector in the UK as becoming increasingly professionalised and 'business-like' (Dart, 2004). Yet much of the research in this area was from the disciplines of marketing and management, and although some was qualitative in nature – interviews were often used, for example – it would not have collected 'immersive data': experienced, recorded and *lived* by the researchers themselves. This absence of 'lived experience' in prior literature provided the inspiration for my project.

With this in mind, I entered into my ethnographic research study with an aim of understanding charity retail professionalisation *as a shop volunteer would*, and remained open minded about what specific elements within that setting I intended to explore. One of the core tenets of interpretive ethnography is inductive reasoning: aiming not to test a specific research question or hypothesis, but allowing your research interest to develop as you collect, explore and revisit the data. Other components of ethnographic research include non-representative samples (often a small number of cases, with a focus on depth rather than breadth) and naturalistic research fields (non-experimental settings, generally observing behaviours and interactions as they occur in situ) (Payne and Payne, 2005). All of the foregoing were present in the study described in this chapter, explored through participant observation.

Gregson et al (2002) had previously conducted ethnographic charity shop research in a similar way, yielding an insight into professionalisation processes by focusing upon 'talk' within charity shop spaces. This managerial discourse was seen as indicative of how professional authority and volunteer 'goodwill' intersect. Gregson et al highlighted how the 'messiness' of charity shop spaces necessitates a hands-on research approach in order to intensely scrutinise the patterns of interaction, or 'micro-geographies' (Gregson et al, 2002: 1670), that are taking place. They also provided a word of warning, describing the 'seemingly ever-outward-spiralling momentum' of their project as overwhelming (Gregson et al, 2002: 1662). This is a common feature of ethnographic studies, where huge amounts of fieldnote data are amassed, and the research topic intuitively develops throughout. There is always another research avenue to explore, an event that could be described as important, or a series of experiences that warrant further academic attention. In this sense, an ethnographer must be strict with themselves and continually ask the question 'is this relevant to the specific subject I am interested in?' Balance must therefore be struck between achieving your research objectives and not neglecting important findings.

The ethnographic case study

The main purpose of case study research should be to capture cases in their uniqueness. However, charity shops are an amorphous group of shopping spaces, and vary from little more than a glorified permanent jumble sale all the way up to a slick and carefully merchandised retail store. It is wise to select your specific case study through a typological approach: organising the population into categories and then selecting one from each category to study in depth. I used Elizabeth Parsons' (2004) typology of charity shops to select potential case study types, as it defines charity shops on the basis of how much they have professionalised and 'traded up' in business terms. Parsons distinguished between Multiple Charity Retailers (national chains of multiple charity shops operating on behalf of a large parent charity), Hospice Charity Retailers (smaller chains of shops operating within a specific locale, usually on behalf of a local hospice) and Independent Charity Retailers (one-off shops for a local charity). Two charity shops were selected – the former was a Multiple Charity Retailer (MCR) and the latter a combination of both an Independent and a Hospice Charity Retailer (Independent Hospice Retailer, or IHR).

A comparative case study method, contrasting professionalisation processes in two relatively different shop types, developed. This approach aimed to provide clearer evidence of differences when the two cases yielded some basic concrete similarities – for example, both shops were associated with children's charities. Charity shops are a manifestation of fundraising endeavours, but by linking the cause associated with the shop (in this case, children and their welfare) between the case studies, the research hoped to also investigate if there was any difference in impact that this particular cause had within shops that were considered more (or less) professionalised. Children's charities, alongside animal welfare, are also among the most popular in the UK in terms of contributions and favour (Charities Aid Foundation, 2019), and therefore the cause had the potential to be more influential.

It turned out that the shared cause did hold some implications for the fieldwork experience and relational aspects of the ethnography; for example, in the IHR often donations came from bereaved parents, indicating the role the shop played as an emotional arbitrator of the experience of losing a child. Also, the hospice itself was tangible within the IHR shop space: it was located nearby and many hospice workers were closely involved in the day-to-day running of the shop; volunteers often discussed it and promoted hospice events in chitchat with customers; and donations circulated to and from the hospice. This was starkly different to the more professionalised MCR, which, despite being plastered with posters of children and the charity's branding, did not have any concrete physical links to its parent cause. Ethnographic comparative research therefore allows the dynamics of a particular issue that are not self-evident in a single case to be examined in tandem across different cases.

Access and location

Ethnographic studies are also contingent upon access. Some sites can be completely inaccessible, for reasons of insurance, ethics or data protection. A charitable organisation that works with abused children likely will not let you conduct a participant observation of their interventions, for example, although you may be able to gain access for interviews. Securing access is a key consideration when contemplating any form of interpretive ethnography. If you cannot get people to speak to you initially, you will likely experience the same impediments during the research process. Access in this particular study was not hugely problematic, although I did attempt to secure volunteer roles at two other shops before being accepted at the MCR and IHR. I assured the charities they would not be named in the research, which is one consideration to keep in mind in relation to ethics. Charities are sensitive to bad press, much like their public and private sector peers, and any form of investigative research could end up showing them in a bad light (as some of the later examples may have done, were my research not anonymised). Conversely, some organisations will be keen to publicise their involvement, particularly if the research is seeking to build upon or improve sector practices. Because of this, it is wise to decide upon the level of anonymity that you will offer before you attempt to gain access to the field.

Location is key to understanding context within an observational setting. It impacts upon the demographic of those you interact with as well as influencing the physical space. In this study, the shop workers, volunteers, customers, donors and the quality and quantity of potential donations/stock were all dependent upon the location of the charity shop. The shops

I studied were, as the crow flies, located under five miles apart, within a city in the north of England. The larger of the two, the MCR, was situated in a busy thoroughfare near a large railway station, where the area footfall is phenomenally high, while the IHR was on a suburban street in the heart of a local community. It was located on a road near two local schools, in a stretch of shops that encompassed a betting shop, a pound shop, several takeaways and a small supermarket. Locals popped in regularly just to chat to charity shop staff.

The assumption in Elizabeth Parsons' typology is that ICRs have 'a responsibility to their local community to provide low cost goods' over making profits (Parsons, 2004: 37). However, Hospice Charity retailers are also seen as the most profitable in her typology (Parsons, 2004: 37), meaning that the IHR was something of a contradiction. What emerged through the ethnography was how exploration of a specific research setting *interacts with prior theory* and serves to develop upon or counter it. In this case, a hospice retailer that is also small and independent maintained responsiveness to community need, as illustrated by the following fieldnotes.

This area, I don't mean it rudely but it is a poor area. A lot of people are on the social. They haven't got a lot of money. (Derreck, manager, IHR fieldnote)

'Occasionally there are the regular customers who come in, and you know they are tight [short of money] and they've got three or four kids and … circumstances. So, I go "Oh, alright, make it … so and so". Without making a big fuss about it.' (Steve, volunteer, IHR interview)

Staff awareness of the shop's role as a community hub in a low-income area was therefore mediating the professionalising processes that would otherwise be profit orientated. Also revealed in the foregoing is the socio-emotional economy of compassion for less-privileged others, as identified elsewhere in the literature (Flores, 2014). The excerpt demonstrates how participant observation serves to reveal findings relating to the local demographic that participants may have otherwise felt uncomfortable discussing with candour. As I was also a volunteer, Derreck and Steve knew I was familiar with the customers and the shop's position, and as a result offered information that allowed for development upon existing theoretical assumptions about charity shops.

Reflexivity and hidden stories

Social scientists conducting ethnographies are often encouraged to act as 'outsiders' looking in, systematically collecting observational data and maintaining a critical distance from that which they study. In non-participant observation, positivist principles are maintained by not actively involving the researcher in the setting they are studying. However, this method does not heed the fact that even intentionally unobtrusive methods tend to influence findings – they can affect responses, interrupt procedures and impede natural action. The researcher role that developed over time spent in the charity shop setting was that of 'participant as observer', that is, I was a volunteer first and foremost, while also doing research. I opted for this rather than an 'observer as participant' to avoid making the research conspicuous or making other people in the shops uncomfortable.

Fieldnotes were recorded at regular intervals on a notepad during my shifts. Good observation practice was followed at all times, including the recording of exact spoken words where possible and the use of pseudonyms for shop workers and regular customers, and personal feelings were differentiated from observed facts. I used inscription at intervals, when serving a customer or completing a task was necessary. Inscription refers to 'the act of making mental notes prior to writing things down' (LeCompte and Schensul, 1999: 13), perhaps jotting down an indicative word or phrase to elaborate upon later. This was followed by the writing up of ethnographic notes in dated bullet-points using 'thick description' (Geertz, 1973b) to build a narrative of the recorded events. Thick description is a means of qualitative reporting that elaborates descriptions using rich, contextual information. Although my shop floor notes might include direct quotes and a short summary of an event, the writing-up process would include as much detail as possible to conjure up the scene for the reader. As such, thick description not only presents 'what was recorded' but also includes feelings, thoughts, voices, actions and conveyed meanings (Ponterotto, 2006).

Ethnography can serve to capture poignant moments, as the following example attests. During my research, an experience recorded in my fieldnotes from the IHR shop demonstrated how thick description illuminates stories hidden within the voluntary sector that, via other methodologies, would not emerge.

> A man comes in and goes up to Derreck [shop manager], saying he is donating a bike from a family who lost their little boy. 'It was sudden, but it's been a year now and they want it to go here [to the charity shop]', is all he says. Derreck has to sign some kind of form, and takes the boy's bike and a football in a plastic bag from the man. When he comes back in, I ask him what it was about. 'A boy died', is all he says. I ask why the ball is bagged up and he says, 'It's from the police. It's evidence.' (IHR fieldnote)

Fieldnotes such as this serve to reconstruct the way we see charitable donations within the charity shop space, and to likewise bring up broader questions about the interactions and co-dependencies of public sector institutions (such as the police) and voluntary sector organisations. In this sense, ethnography can provide interesting prompts for discussions both inside and outside of a voluntary sector context.

However, it also provides something more: a visceral insight into how human lives intersect, and how individuals respond, within this particular setting. Poignancy can be lost when taking on a more scientific, data-driven or hypothesis-testing approach; as Burawoy (2009) notes, this kind of research can tend to prioritise a social setting, scenario or space (such as a charitable organisation, event or act) over the individuals interacting within them, and the lives they are living.

Through being present and probing this particular interaction with the shop manager (and reflecting on what was actually happening as I wrote up the fieldnotes later), the involvement of the police, and the charity shop's role as an emotional mediator for situations of extreme distress, was revealed. The quiet and monosyllabic response of Derreck belies the combined sense of discomfort and respect that the incident provoked. By contrast, in handling police evidence in the MCR shop:

[The unpaid assistant manager and I] cut into the bags with scissors and pour the stuff onto the [shop] counter. I'm pretty sure Maria [shop manager] wouldn't allow this if she were in charge as it's right in front of a customer. The contents [include] one crusty sock and a really battered, single shoe. (MCR fieldnote)

This fieldnote raises questions around how professional responsibility (that is, having a paid managerial role) interacts with basic humanity in the act of moral redefinition of goods in the shop. Here you can see my own pondering reflection upon how the manager might respond to what we are doing. It is pertinent to discuss here this dialogic relationship between the researcher and that which they are observing. Reflexivity requires the researcher not only to contemplate the observable activities taking place within the research setting, but also to reflect upon *how they are contemplating those activities* (Madison, 2011). Conscious mediation of the researcher's own values within their research is encouraged in ethnography, as a means to demonstrate that partiality is natural and expected, and to 'more confidently resist the slings and arrows of positivism's obsession with evidence' (Madison, 2011: 130). All data collected is usually considered in relation to its temporal, geographical, historical, economic and cultural context, and in relation to the researcher's own background.

In this study, reflexivity throughout the ethnography was essential to ensure I remained aware of the opportunities and limitations my presence in the field allowed. I was a regular shopper in charity shops, and also a prior volunteer, having worked in my local Salvation Army shop in the Midlands. I was also a PhD researcher at a Russell Group university, bringing with me previous customer service experience and other social skills. The data collected during my 340+ hours of participant observation was contingent on the person I was within that setting, including aspects of my gender, race, nationality, age, class background and level of physical ability. For instance, I was trusted to handle cash and price up items, and to work primarily in customer-facing roles, something that other volunteers and community service workers with less educational and social capital were not permitted to do.

An illustration of how reflexivity can feed into the analysis of data is given in the following fieldnote, which depicts a discussion about an elderly male volunteer (Alan) with the MCR shop manager.

> [She] sighs and says, 'He pesters me, he's like "I want to go on the till. Let me go on the till", but he's so slow. He's like, not that useful. So I keep him out the back, but even then he doesn't really do stuff properly. Like this [she holds up a top with a mark on it]. We wouldn't bother to steam and label this and put it out. He's not checking enough.' (MCR fieldnote)

During an occasion when a drunk gentleman is acting suspiciously in the store, my fieldnotes also recorded that 'Alan does not seem to be very effective for surveillance – he doesn't pay attention to the man at all'. In another instance, I described his work on the till alongside me as 'slow' but 'methodical to ensure he doesn't miss anything', and his attitude 'brusque [...] towards customers'. In these fieldnotes, the privilege of the researcher begins to be evidenced, as somebody who is judging their fellow volunteers negatively in relation to their own skill set. Yet, when the notes are reflected upon, it becomes clear that Alan's value as a volunteer is being undermined because of his lack of proficiency in commercial retail techniques, such as offering efficient and friendly customer service. As a fellow volunteer, I was also deferring to the superiority of those qualities, and positioning myself as someone to be congratulated for possessing them. What this reflexive practice revealed was how volunteers unconsciously buy into a pervasive narrative of necessary upskilling in the voluntary sector workforce (Parsons and Broadbridge, 2007), alongside a depiction of blatant ageism.

Thus, the ethnographic encounters that I recorded were not only privileged to a certain level of access but were also inherently biased in terms of my prior experience and the influence that experience had upon those participating in my research. Related to this is the difficulty of maintaining the divide between being a researcher and being a worker/friend to those in the field. This can be particularly difficult if you are a practitioner who feels a professional responsibility towards a cause, an organisation or those working within it. Juggling the conflicting roles you take on during research can be extremely taxing. While a 'participant as observer', I preferred to take fieldnotes when there was no one else around, for fear of being perceived to be slacking off, and also because the note-taking process was recorded as 'seeming to make other workers in the shops feel uncomfortable' (MCR fieldnotes). Maria, the manager of the MCR, at one point said, 'Don't mention me in this book, will you?' Derreck, manager of the IHR, also joked: 'Don't you go reporting back to your other shop about how we do things here!' Both comments prompted a need for a reiteration of ethical consent and reassurance that all the participants would be made entirely anonymous, as would the charity itself.

The wariness of participants was pre-empted in the planning stage, since participatory research is dependent upon being accepted by the research subjects not just as somebody who is objectively studying your actions but also as somebody who is *joining in* with them. Therefore, a moderate amount of participation must be genuinely engaged in. Erving Goffman's (1959) theory of impression management summarises how one must present a positive 'front' applicable to whatever scenario you are confronted with – and in context, that 'front' may not be one of a researcher but of a volunteer, a friendly ear, a confidante and so on. This approach infers some deception, or covert behaviour at least (particularly in Goffman's usage of the term *manipulation*), but in fact it is a requirement in order to fit in and not upset the delicate balance of unspoken trust in interactions by making apparent the dichotomy of roles played. 'Disruptions' to this often result in embarrassment for both the researcher and participants (Goffman, 1959: 212), which was my own experience when caught note taking when I should have been tidying or undertaking other tasks. Therefore, I upheld a combination of both overt and covert roles, despite both charity shops being fully aware of my research imperative.

Conclusion

There are many features of ethnographic research that merit further exploration in its consideration as a useful method for examining voluntary sector practice – particularly in relation to analysis. However, this chapter has predominantly focused upon the practicalities of gaining access and the 'doing' of ethnography. Writing up and using the data gleaned to tell stories is also fundamentally important. This is indicated in the summary of the key benefits of using ethnographic research when exploring the voluntary sector. Some of these were explored in this chapter; for example, the relational aspects of ethnography that result in the formation of bonds of trust between researcher and representatives within an organisation. Relationships with the shop managers and volunteers allowed access to information that would have never been found out via other means – particularly the subtle ways in which the staff negotiate top-down professionalising processes, and community interactions. However, it allowed other nuances to emerge – for example, the way that each charity's mission was important to the managers and workers in various specific ways, through the idle storytelling that went on during a quiet moment sorting bin bags 'out the back', similarly to how storytelling becomes a tool either for fundraising or grant applications. It is also a way to find out otherwise obscured or hidden behaviours, responses and actions. As this case study demonstrates, a core value of ethnography is that it offers a voice to the 'half muted' (Back, 2007) within voluntary organisations, those whose experiences and perspectives may never reach the ears of boardroom decision makers. Many of these actors work unseen and their voices often go unheard. Stories, even those that are difficult or controversial, are more compelling than statistics could ever be in illuminating the human relationships that are critical to voluntary action. How organisations choose to engage with these stories and their impact is a crucial next step.

On a practical level, ethnography also helps to evaluate how well a process is working once it cascades down from senior management. The success of professionalising processes in charity retail tends to be measured in fiduciary terms only. Yet disgruntled volunteers, profit-focused shop managers and haggling customers will all interpret and apply these processes in idiosyncratic ways. Likewise, ethnography also allows for insight into customers as end-users when charities are engaging in the act of selling something. This relationship is often overlooked in favour of the charity–beneficiary or the donor–charity relationship, and certainly more often measured in terms of sales or stock than in terms of the shop-floor experience.

However, the strongest case for interpretive ethnography as a voluntary sector research method lies with the researcher. Their role is to make the familiar unfamiliar, by researching and analysing the voluntary sector as if it were a set of obscure or exotic practices and institutions, rather than a taken-for-granted site of 'doing good'. This role is integral in order to develop more nuanced understandings of how the sector operates.

In the case of this charity shop study, the researcher's role was to dismantle common conceptions and assumptions gathered by viewing these uniquely co-ordinated sites *from the outside in*, by engaging with 'embodied others' within that space. In turn, that engagement influences and changes that space. Both the researcher's participatory role during the collection of data and the subsequent presentation of research findings and potential recommendations have the propensity to fundamentally change and reinvent the phenomena being studied. As Anthony Giddens (1987: 19) argues, social science ideas and theories tend to 'circulate in and out of the social world they are coined to analyse'. Within a dynamic and responsive global voluntary sector (especially in light of the debilitating effects of COVID-19 on all aspects of public life), assumptions based on static and scientifically representative data are, now more than ever, open to reinterpretation.

Finally, ethnography as a method tends to replicate both the positives and negatives of whichever site it is roped in to explain. This particular research study focused upon how market-based criteria are used to systematically measure and rationalise the work of actors within the charity shop space, and how the pursuit of profit is privileged over ideas of charity or care. Yet, as an ethnography, the research violated positivist research norms of replicability and reliability, refuting the idea that such work has to be measurable or rationalisable. Instead, ethnographic analysis allowed the 'bubbles of humanness' (Cova and Remy, 2007: 52) to break through the regimented processes of professionalisation found in the data, in terms both of the unique insights collected and of the subversion of professionalising practices by human actors. Charity shops remain messy and ambiguous spaces that are not easily rationalised by quantitative methods, and therefore are sites well suited to this method of study. As Carey (in Denzin, 1996: 285) succinctly puts it, the ethnography's 'faults and triumphs are pretty much characteristics of the culture as a whole'.

Further reading
- The rich, contextual detail that underpins interactions in ethnographic accounts can be better understood through the work of Geertz (1973) on 'thick description'.
- A useful guide for planning and conducting this kind of research is provided by LeCompte and Schensul's (1999) ethnographer's toolkit.
- For an in-depth multidisciplinary overview of charity shops in the UK and beyond, see Horne and Maddrell (2002).

4

Collaborative philanthropy and doing practically relevant, critical research

Angela M. Eikenberry and Xiaowei Song

Introduction

The purpose of this chapter is to draw on experience doing collaborative philanthropy research, specifically on giving circles or giving collaboratives (GCs), to argue for doing practically relevant and critical research despite the potential challenges, such as philosophical and political tensions.

GCs are collaborative forms of philanthropy in which members pool donations and decide together where these are given. They also frequently include social, educational and engagement opportunities for members, connecting them to their communities and to one another (Eikenberry, 2009). One example of a US-based GC is Washington Womenade, which holds regular volunteer-organised potluck dinners where attendees donate $35 to a fund that provides financial assistance to individuals (primarily women) who need help paying for things like prescriptions, utility bills and rent. In 2002, a *Real Simple* magazine story (Korelitz, 2002) on Washington Womenade led to the creation of dozens of unaffiliated Womenade groups across the country. This article also inspired Marsha Wallace to start Dining for Women, which is now a national network of more than 400 chapters across the US in which women meet for dinner monthly and pool funds they would have spent eating out, to support internationally based grassroots programmes helping women around the world. Another example of a GC in the UK is BeyondMe. It started in 2011 in London, made up of small groups or teams of young professionals affiliated with a particular corporation (for example, Deloitte or PwC) who select a charity or social enterprise with which to partner for the year, providing funding and professional pro bono support. Members of the team give £15 per month, with total funding to the beneficiary organisation amounting to between £3,000 and £5,000, and volunteer support of around 150 hours. Beneficiary organisations supported in the past include those helping jobless young offenders, homeless youth, women who have experienced abuse and sexual exploitation, and street and other marginalised youth, helping them to build businesses.

It is impossible to say how many GCs exist, because of their grassroots nature; however, by many indications they are growing in number around the world. Dean-Olmsted, Benor and Gerstein (2014) estimate that one in eight American donors have participated in a GC. An increasing number of GCs operate in Canada, Japan, South Africa, Australia, India, China, Japan, Romania, Bulgaria, the UK, Ireland and elsewhere. As an emerging phenomenon, GCs provide extensive opportunity to conduct practically relevant and critical research.

There has been consternation in the field of non-profit and philanthropic studies in recent years over the applicability of research for practice, especially in the context of a growing gap between the two as the field strives to be more 'scientific' or 'valid' as a social science (Bushouse and Sowa, 2012; Coule, Dodge and Eikenberry, in press; Fitton, Chapter 3 in this volume), as well as about sometimes narrow practitioner interest in 'usable knowledge for best practices' (Feeney, 2000: 9). For some, however, connecting research to practice is a priority. Frequently, these researchers want to support and learn from practitioners (Taylor, Torugsa and Arundel, 2018), while also considering the context or environment (Feeney, 2000). This is certainly true in the case of most of Eikenberry's GC research, where studying these grassroots-based groups often involves the promise of practically 'useful' data for the GC participants in exchange for access to members, and where research is largely grounded in the lived experiences of participants. GCs also provide a window onto larger phenomena such as the role of philanthropy in democratic governance.

We argue that making research relevant to practice and practice relevant to research, as well as considering the critical social context in which practice takes place, requires a shift in our field as to what typically gets valued as legitimate knowledge, assumptions about the nature of reality and how we acquire knowledge. Some have bemoaned, for example, the difficulty of doing practically relevant research because of the challenge of maintaining the scientific principles of objectivity, rigour and generalisability. This is a problem particular to positivists or post-positivists, who are concerned with maintaining objectivity because they assume knowledge is 'out there' to be discovered deductively. Interpretive and critical scholars understand reality to be socially constructed, so objectivity is not possible and not tied to rigour. Instead, knowledge can be understood inductively and abductively. Beyond these philosophical concerns there are other challenges to doing practically relevant and critical work that are relational and political in nature. We discuss these further later on. We think that doing practically relevant and critical research despite these challenges is essential to building and extending theory and practice in a field that purports to focus on social benefit.

The rest of this chapter is organised as follows: we start by providing a discussion of why doing practically relevant critical research is important for our field and what it looks like in the case of research on collaborative philanthropy. Then, we discuss some of the challenges of doing this type of research and how to potentially overcome these, with more examples of collaborative philanthropy research provided.

Doing practically relevant, critical research

Especially in the field of non-profit and philanthropic studies, where the focus of research and practice is often on improving society in various ways, practically relevant research is valuable and needed. It emphasises gaining understanding to advance both theory and practice (Rynes, Bartunek and Daft, 2001; Docherty and Shani, 2008; Tandon and Farrell, 2008; Antonacopoulou, 2010), which can be achieved through collaborative communities of dialogue, discourse and/or inquiry (Coghlan and Shani, 2008). Hodgkinson, Herriot and Anderson call practically relevant research 'pragmatic science' because it strives to be 'simultaneously academically rigorous and engaged with the concerns of wider stakeholder groups' (cited in Ospina and Dodge, 2005: 410). As Harris and Harris argue, 'when research is driven by genuine organisational problems, it is far more likely that key players who are the subject of the research will engage with it in a meaningful way and derive practical benefit from it, as they have a vested interest in the outcome' (Harris and Harris, 2002: 30).

In addition, critical reflection is pivotal in practically relevant research for the field. Not only does it reveal the incompleteness of research and practice, such as hidden or power dimensions (Tandon and Farrell, 2008), but it also recognises the importance of experimenting and discovering different possibilities for changing research and practice (Antonacopoulou, 2010). Doing practically relevant research through a critical theory lens enables both researchers and practitioners to understand and learn from what is happening, but also to examine and interrogate the meanings of what is happening, which is highly relevant to what people working in non-profit or voluntary organisations face on a daily basis. A key underpinning of any critical perspective, as Harvey Lee (1990) and others describe, is the attempt by critical scholars and practitioners to dig beneath the surface of (often hidden) historically specific, social structures and processes – such as those related to politics, economics, culture, discourse, gender and race – to illuminate how they lead to oppression and then to also reveal ways to change these structures. Thus, a critical perspective does not take social structures, social processes or accepted history for granted; rather, a critical perspective insists on the power of agency – both personal and collective – to transform society. To bring about constructive change, people need to understand oppressive structures and to be able to see the contradictions between what is and what might be. Another key aspect of a critical perspective is that it is based on a belief that knowledge is not simply a reflection of a world 'out there', but is an active social construction by scientists, theorists and others 'who necessarily make certain assumptions about the worlds they study and thus are not strictly value free' (Agger, 1998: 4) and who have the ability to confront and change these assumptions. As Zanetti (1997: 156) defines it, 'critical inquiry must be connected to an attempt to confront injustice within society, either as a whole or within a particular sphere'.

A critical perspective is especially important because non-profit and voluntary organisations are increasingly taking on public administration and governance roles around the world. In a time of perceived austerity across many countries, with growing economic and social inequalities and ethno-nationalisms, perhaps more than ever, research on non-profit and voluntary organisations needs to challenge and change the environment. It sees society as characterised by historicity or susceptibility to change and it is the role of a critical theorist or practitioner to raise consciousness about past and present oppressions and demonstrate the possibility of a qualitatively different future.

Much of Eikenberry's research on GCs strives to be both practically relevant and critical, involving nearly a decade of data collected using various methods, including interviews, surveys, observation and participant observation and document analysis. This research mapped out the landscape of GCs and tried to understand their impact on donors/members (for example, Eikenberry, 2009, 2010; Bearman et al, 2017; Eikenberry and Breeze, 2018; Carboni and Eikenberry, 2021) and funding recipients (for example, Eikenberry, 2017).

The work involved in gathering data took place over many years and in two countries (the US and UK). It involved the tedious work of discovering what was happening, case by case, with GCs in each country, and then more broadly, building relationships and partnerships, especially for access to GC members, and, in some cases, trying to meet multiple goals in the same study – to both help GC leaders or members to evaluate their own impact while also examining broader questions about the impact of GCs. The work also involved examining these groups from various perspectives and directions and across cultures, sometimes drawing on the data to ask new and multiple questions. Some of the work was supported by external funding and much of it was done collaboratively with other researchers and practitioners.

A large segment of this work also questioned assumptions about the degree to which GCs democratise philanthropy, address social problems and bring about improved social outcomes. For example, one of the most often-cited reasons people say they join GCs is to become more engaged in the giving process beyond writing cheques or direct debits – to interact directly with other donors and beneficiaries, to be around like-minded people, to learn and feel empowered. For example, the 'self-help' nature of this allure of GCs was explored in Eikenberry (2010), gathering data through interviews and document analysis. It was found with that data that GCs seem to provide their greatest value as self-help/mutual aid sources for members rather than as mechanisms for supporting non-profit organisations addressing community problems. The article then suggests implications for the broader governance context, pointing out that GCs and philanthropy more generally cannot substitute for collective public and political action. Thus, extending beyond examining affirming aspects of GCs as good for society and good for democracy, this work challenges assumptions about the contributions of GCs and philanthropy and the power of donors, and considers the implications for governance. The work is both practically relevant for those working with or wanting to fundraise from GCs, and also critical in examining assumptions and power dynamics related to these groups.

The research also tried to understand this work from the perspective of who benefits from GCs in comparison to other types of philanthropy (Eikenberry, 2017). It drew on data from interviews, surveys, observations and documentation collected in the US and UK to show that some populations appear to be benefiting more from GCs than is seen in traditional philanthropy, such as women and girls and people from marginalised racial and ethnic groups; however, GCs also may do little to shift the norm that most philanthropy does not go to the poor and needy. GCs also tend to fund certain types of organisations: often small and locally based; new or start-ups or that are reorganising/transitioning; that have a 'business' orientation; and that can engage members or show clearly benefits or outcomes and/or significant impact in relation to the size of the organisation. This has implications for the types of organisations that may be attractive to GCs. Again, the work here is both practically relevant for those working in or wanting to fundraise from GCs, but also critical in examining broader questions about who benefits from philanthropy.

Overcoming challenges of practically relevant, critical research

Doing this sort of research is not without challenges. These relate in part to philosophical considerations as well as relational and political tensions.

Regarding philosophical considerations, from the perspective of the traditional scientific or positivist paradigm, the challenges to doing this kind of work are often expressed as being related to maintaining objectivity and scientific rigour (Ospina and Dodge, 2005). Researchers operating in this paradigm often reject other ways of knowing and believe in the ability of science to solve most problems. However, this paradigm is criticised by interpretive and critical theorists for overstating the possibilities of objectivity, and oversimplifying uncertainty and the complexity of the lived world (Crotty, 1998). More importantly, positivists tend to support the status quo of the lived world and neglect social change and emancipation (Crotty, 1998).

As a result, it can have limited practical impact on addressing complicated social issues.

These challenges may be addressed with a shift in what we value as legitimate knowledge, assumptions about the nature of reality and the logic of inquiry. As with many fields (Foucault, 1977), non-profit and philanthropic studies has increasingly strived to be seen as more 'scientific' or 'legitimate' as a social science. In this framework, practically relevant research can be dismissed as not being 'scientific enough'. Feeney (2000: 7) describes this as a 'sandbox problem', in which academics are seen as smart and authoritative while practitioners are not; where practitioners live in the 'real world' and academics do not; and 'where theory is reified to the exclusion of practice, or practice is reified to the exclusion of theory'. That is, there are seen to be distinctive domains of authority, legitimacy and voice between these two realms. Researchers and practitioners can have

> fundamentally different frames of reference with respect to such things as the types of information believed to constitute valid bases for action, the ways in which information is ordered and arranged for 'sense-making,' the past experiences used to evaluate the validity of knowledge claims, and the metaphors used to symbolically construct the world in meaningful ways. (Shrivastava and Mitroff, 1984, cited in Rynes et al, 2001: 340–341)

Ospina and Dodge (2005: 411) further note that 'the dominant models of scientific knowledge production in the twentieth century are responsible for reinforcing a fixed division of labour, with academics as producers and sometimes disseminators of knowledge and practitioners as consumers and sometimes users of knowledge'.

An interpretive or critical research paradigm challenges these fixed divisions, appreciating the social construction of reality where theory and practice – praxis – occur in relationships. Interpretive and critical research are often assessed against positivist standards or quality criteria that are incommensurate with the logic of critical inquiry and methodologies (Coule, 2013). In interpretive or critical research, 'objectivity' is irrelevant because it is not possible; that is, interpretive and critical research paradigms see bias as inherent in all social situations. Thus, rigour is revised to be about understanding multiple (and hidden) meanings through triangulation and other means to create trustworthiness (Lincoln and Guba, 1986). For example, Ospina and Dodge (2005) argue that narrative inquiry can be treated as a 'rigorous' approach to knowledge production and transformation. Through narrative inquiry, both researchers and practitioners are involved in the research process where practitioners are considered 'as sources of knowledge, as producers of knowledge, and as informed consumers of knowledge' (Ospina and Dodge, 2005: 413), and each research stage is conducted in a collaborative way. The voices of practitioners are particularly valued, since they are assumed to have different perspectives from researchers and their 'sophisticated insider perspectives' (Ospina and Dodge, 2005: 419) can lead to a more rigorous research product. According to Ospina and Dodge (2005), this collaborative research relationship not only allows practitioners to reflect and apply their stories but also enables researchers to have a better understanding of the lived world, which, in turn, provides practitioners with greater utility of knowledge.

It is hard to imagine studying GCs in any meaningful way from a purely positivist or even post-positivist stance, given their collaborative and emergent nature. GCs are made up of groups of people making meaning together and call for perspectives and methodologies that reflect this. GCs are also inherently political and powerful in the sense that members are making decisions about who benefits or receives resources. This calls for critical reflection and interrogation. Studying these groups from a purely positivist perspective would miss examining the political nature and context of these groups. The fact that these groups are growing in number and popular among some groups is interesting, but so what? What do they mean for how we create a good society? Practically relevant, yet critical, research helps us to get at bigger 'so what' questions.

Further, the logic of inquiry in the field of non-profit and philanthropic studies is dominated by scholarship using inductive and deductive reasoning, while practically relevant research often requires abductive reasoning, which 'involves a deliberate and iterative process between actively studying the phenomenon at close range and thoughtful theory development via a frame-breaking mode of thinking whereby the researcher is receptive to divergent ways of understanding' (Taylor et al, 2018: 208). Abduction is essential to the critical theory-informed idea of praxis or putting theory and learning into action to create change. Taylor et al (2018) give an example of the use of abduction in non-profit studies, which also happens to be done by analysing an article using a critical perspective:

An example of the use of abduction in nonprofit research can be seen in a recent study by Dey and Teasdale (2016) of NPOs [non-profit organisations] in the United Kingdom. Initially, the researchers had set out to understand how NPO managers resisted the UK government's increasing push for a socially entrepreneurial nonprofit sector through social enterprise-oriented policies and programs. Unexpectedly, however, the findings from their longitudinal case study of the NPO, Teak, uncovered a surprising behaviour of 'tactical mimicry.' The organization's managers were 'acting as' social entrepreneurs to gain access to important resources. This surprising fact came to light through direct field observations carried out by the researchers over multiple visits to the organization, whereby 'unexpected observations, and an ensuing process of abductive reasoning' (Dey and Teasdale, 2016, p. 489) eventually resulted in their tactical mimicry hypothesis, the testable hypothesis that best explained the surprising fact. Arriving at this 'best guess' is the point at which abduction draws its conclusions. (Kovács and Spens, 2005)

As indicated earlier, Eikenberry's work on GCs has also largely been inspired by this abductive approach. The interest in GCs stemmed from the experience being part of a GC forming in Omaha while simultaneously being in the process of determining a dissertation focus. At that time she had also happened to run across an article in *Fast Company* (Matson, 1996) magazine on a similar group in Chicago. Very interested at the time on Robert Putnam's work on social capital, Eikenberry soon discovered that there were more, similar groups emerging around the US, leading to questions about what was going on, how these groups operated and the implications for fundraising, philanthropy and democratic governance. As these studies continued, other questions emerged through the study of these groups and discussions with the people who are forming, or participating in, or receiving funding from them.

Beyond philosophical concerns there are other challenges to doing this kind of practically relevant and critical work, which are relational and political in nature, particularly related to differing motivations and frames of reference between researchers and people practising the phenomenon (already mentioned earlier, to some degree). Researchers and those in practice can frequently have different motivations for their interest in research (Ospina and Dodge, 2005). For some researchers, their passion in academic reputation might encourage them to write research in highly technical and standardised language that tends to divide communications between researchers and practitioners (Ospina and Dodge, 2005). Some might mix practically relevant research with consulting activities by narrowly looking at certain practical needs and satisfying only practitioners' preferences (Ospina and Dodge, 2005). When it comes to practitioners, they might subjectively consider research as useless or irrelevant to issues concerning their needs and preferences (Ospina and Dodge, 2005). What's more, differences between researchers and practitioners also relate to 'the goals they seek to influence, the social systems in which they operate, the variables they attempt to manipulate, and acceptable time frames for addressing problems' (Rynes et al, 2001: 341). In addition, there are issues of 'trust and respect, equitable distribution of power and control, basic skills and knowledge to participate in the research project, and adequate representation of different functional, hierarchical, and organizational interests in the activity system concerned in the research' (Docherty and Shani, 2008: 176). Finally, the work of using a critical perspective in research can be quite daunting, as it requires bringing people to understand their oppressions and/or how they've oppressed others, and then encouraging them to change the structures that create such oppressions. This may be especially a challenge for people working in the voluntary or philanthropic space, who truly believe what they are doing is good (Dean, 2020). They may not be very pleased to learn that they are oppressed or oppressing others.

These challenges have been experienced in Eikenberry's GC research, which has resulted at times in difficulties with getting access to GC participants and in gaining trust from gatekeepers, and conflicts if the findings do not match up with the expected outcomes of the people in practice or are critical of their work. As groups of people giving away money, GC leaders are sometimes wary of giving researchers access to their members. It is necessary to gain trust in order to obtain this access. In this case, it has required building relationships over time with key people in GC communities and networks who could then make introductions, partnering with other researchers who already had access to these communities and networks, and/or promising access to information useful to those in practice, such as sharing summaries of data particular to a GC (for example, the results of the member impact survey for just their GC). All of this requires investing time to build relationships, to make contacts and sometimes to conduct extra data analysis and reporting. The promise of data for access is complex not only because of the extra work involved in making sure the research meets multiple needs without compromising the integrity of the design, but also because research findings may run counter to what the people in practice expected. In particular, people participating in GCs, and philanthropists in general, frequently see themselves and have been told by others that they are 'doing good'. Findings challenging this belief or that critique seemingly good work are not always taken very well. Building relationships with participants over time can help to minimise this tension.

Conclusion

The purpose of this chapter was to draw on experience doing collaborative philanthropy research, specifically on GCs, to argue for doing practically relevant and critical research despite the potential challenges. Making research relevant to practice, and also considering the critical social context in which practice takes place, requires a shift in what typically gets valued as legitimate knowledge, assumptions about the nature of reality and how we acquire knowledge. Beyond these philosophical concerns there are other challenges to doing practically relevant and critical work that are relational and political in nature, but that can often be overcome through building relationships with those in practice, building research collaborations and spending time in the field and area of focus. Doing practically relevant and critical research is essential to building and extending theory and to changing practice in a field concerned with making the world a better place.

Further reading
- Ben Agger (1998) provides a comprehensive introduction to critical social theories.
- Sonia Ospina and Jennifer Dodge (2005) argue for rethinking the roles that practitioners and academics play in generating knowledge in the field.
- Rachel Taylor, Nuttaneeya (Ann) Torugsa and Anthony Arundel (2018) provide a useful discussion of 'abduction' as a process for non-profit research.

5

Peer research: co-producing research within the context of voluntary and community action

Ellen Bennett

Introduction

Peer research is a method that supports people who have 'lived experience' of the research topic to be involved in the research process (Logie et al, 2012). This chapter introduces peer research as an engaged approach to researching voluntary action. As a voluntary action researcher I have been working within and alongside voluntary agencies for 20 years, both within the voluntary sector and within a university context. This chapter has emerged out of my work on a number of evaluation research projects. As well as providing some practical guidance about how peer research can be designed and put into action, I discuss the potential strengths and challenges of the method, drawing on examples of both good and challenging practice from my work. As part of a research team, I have been on a journey of learning 'on the job', and this learning continues.

Before delving into the 'how to' of peer research, it is useful to understand the context of the approach; co-production within the voluntary sector; and how research communities can learn from and incorporate a co-production ethos. The aim is not to disappear down a theoretical rabbit-hole but, rather, to consider what these broader, underpinning considerations mean for how we approach peer research within a voluntary sector setting without slipping into issues of tokenism, or unsatisfactory research processes and outcomes.

The insights presented within this chapter are born out of several evaluative research programmes that I have been involved in as a researcher within the Centre for Regional Economic and Social Research at Sheffield Hallam University in the UK. As part of a small team of researchers, I have worked with my colleague Nadia Bashir to lead the development of our peer research work on projects alongside voluntary sector partners including a local housing association and a regional learning and skills provider (among others).

The voluntary sector organisations that we have worked with have been keen and supportive partners, eager to embed co-production principles in their work, often beyond the research project that we are involved in. We have reflected on the ways in which the voluntary organisations have worked with us to develop and embed new working practices; how they have been willing to learn through trial and error; and how they have worked with us to reflect on our shared learning in order to improve subsequent cycles of our peer research work. We think that this stems from the approach taken by many voluntary organisations: to engage their members/beneficiaries in their work. The projects that we are drawing upon within this chapter have involved us as 'professional' researchers supporting voluntary organisations, engaging their members/beneficiaries/wider community members (geographical or community of interest) in evaluating, or learning more about, an aspect of their work.

This chapter provides insights into what peer research can offer researchers of voluntary organisations and voluntary action. The chapter also responds to a call for greater clarity on principles, best practice and characteristics of participatory approaches to research so that we can learn from, and build upon, such approaches in different areas (Stanley et al, 2015). I also therefore provide practical guidance for those who want to try incorporating this kind of approach into their work.

A note on terminology

Before embarking on a critical discussion about what peer research is, it is important to spend a little time exploring the terminology used within this chapter. Choosing terminology can be problematic, but it is a necessity. Particular labels have been selected and used within the chapter, but it is done in a conscious way, and in so doing I am not ignoring the problematic nature of language but, rather, sitting with its imperfections.

The term **peer researcher** is used to denote voluntary researchers, deemed to be 'peers' due to their proximity to or experience of a particular place, service or phenomenon.

The term **professional researcher** is used to denote those people who are researchers by profession. They might sit within a voluntary organisation, a local authority, a university, a consultancy, or they might be an independent researcher.

While these labels have been selected, it is important for us to acknowledge that the terms are not value free. The term 'professional' may carry connotations of power and authority, immediately placing this person in a hierarchy above peer researchers; but this is not the aim here. When exploring this as a method, it was important to distinguish between the roles within the research team, but we also do continually challenge the notion of power and authority being in the hands of professionals. Demarcating the two distinct roles is important when exploring the method in detail; however, working towards a position where all individuals are part of the research team is an important emancipatory goal of a peer research process, particularly within the context of voluntary and community sector and voluntary action research.

Researchers within the voluntary sector

Over ten years or more, I have been involved in many programmes of research that have explored aspects of voluntary action. I have learned a great deal, and each time I go into a new research context I draw upon previous experiences. I feel that, as a small team of researchers, we have a degree of understanding and empathy and believe that our research is seasoned, or shaped, by our previous learning, with each encounter laying down a seam of experience that forms part of the lens through which we see the world.

Yet, however much we learn about the voluntary sector, in all its richness and variety, we are always entering the research context as 'outsiders' (see Chapter 2 in this volume). We are not the people who have first-hand experience of running the organisation, volunteering within the organisation or accessing the services/activities/environments that the organisation provides.

If we were to take a positivist standpoint on our research, we would say that this position of being independent to the research context is a strength, and even a necessity, in order to support the quality and integrity of the research. However, as an interpretive researcher, I recognise the challenges posed by my distance from the research context (Harris, 2001). I understand the richness that can be achieved by proximity to the research, by drawing upon not just research 'expertise' but also involvement with the research context. From this philosophical standpoint, being located within the research brings a strength and research integrity. For this reason, embracing peer research, and looking for ways to build it into our programmes of research, has become a guiding principle underpinning how we do our work.

Peer research: what is it and where does it 'sit'?

The term 'peer' is used to denote this closeness to, for example, the topic, place or organisation being researched – for example, someone who has used a particular service, someone who lives within a particular neighbourhood or possibly someone who has certain characteristics (such as someone's age). Sometimes the term 'peer' is replaced by 'community' researcher, but they denote similar approaches of engaging 'non-professional' researchers in the research process.

Peer research is one form of 'community-based participatory research' (CBPR), which encompasses a host of engaged research approaches. Rather than the research process being defined, led, conducted and therefore controlled by professional researchers, the peer research approach attempts to engage wider stakeholders, and 'emphasize the participation, influence and control by non-academic researchers in the process of creating knowledge and change' (Israel et al, 1998: 184). As such, it can be considered a form of research 'co-production', which focuses on involving individuals, groups and communities in the services they use and the activities they access.

Co-production has its genesis in discussions about public services and how engaging people in the design of public services they use might support improved service design and user experience. The idea of co-production has become an important part of the public service ethos, and part of an emerging governance paradigm that centres on the importance of involving people in thinking about the services they use (Brandsen and Honigh, 2016). Co-production has also been used within the context of exploring how voluntary sector organisations can engage in these conversations (Verschuere, Brandsen and Pestoff, 2012).

One of the key arguments for co-production within public services is that engaging people in the process of designing services will lead to a number of associated benefits: greater service innovation, closer relationships with service users and therefore an ability to get 'closer' to the issues affecting people and ultimately more effective service uptake and outcomes (Van Eijk and Steen, 2016). Voluntary organisations are often cited as working in ways that emulate some of these attributes or practices. Although such normative assumptions are problematic, many voluntary organisations are considered to work in ways that enable them to build relationships with 'hard to reach' groups and individuals (Walker, Waterhouse-Bradley and Armour, 2020), as well as being 'fleet of foot' and therefore able to be innovative and responsive.

Co-production runs through the way in which many voluntary organisations are structured and operate, whether from board composition, volunteer programmes or engagement pathways for individuals seeking longer-term involvement. Indeed, voluntary and community organisations often benefit from this engagement (Wellens and Jegers, 2016). Research has illuminated how these co-production practices contribute to the ability of voluntary organisations to adapt, innovate and respond quickly to issues and the associated needs (Dayson et al, 2018). The principles that we consider to be central to co-production within a research context – for example, authentic engagement, commitment to learning and development – are akin to the values underpinning much work within the voluntary sector.

Marrying up engaged, co-produced research with the context of voluntary action enables research practices to cohere with the principles and practices of the organisations and activities being researched. It is useful, therefore, to understand more about peer research as an approach, considering its strengths as well as its potential challenges and limitations.

Core principles of peer research

A useful starting point is to consider the broad principles that underpin this kind of approach to research. These are:

- **authentic engagement**, avoiding tokenism and working to engage people in a meaningful way;
- **working ethically and with respect**, to avoid causing harm;
- **supporting individual learning and development** throughout the process;
- **flexibility**, so that work can be adapted and changed as it progresses;
- **empowerment and emancipation**, recognising that peer research involves ceding power over the research process, with the ultimate goal of empowering both those involved and the wider community.

Understanding these core principles is the starting point; the challenge then becomes how to ensure that people can have meaningful involvement. We need to ask, 'Why do we think it's important to engage community members, service users, volunteers, staff members and other key stakeholders?' The answer is about enabling the research to benefit from the experience of these key individuals – not just learning from them (as data) but enabling them, with their experience and expertise, to help to shape the research we do, devise the questions that we need to be asking and work as part of research teams in order to find the best ways of conducting the research.

Strengths of peer research

In this section I reflect on some of the key strengths that *can* be associated with a peer research approach. It is important to emphasise the 'can'; we cannot treat these strengths as givens. It is possible to undertake peer research without attending to, and thus benefiting from, all the factors considered here. However, if we embark on the research journey with the core principles underpinning our work, then we should be working towards realising some or all of the potential benefits discussed.

A key strength to start with is the way in which peer research can benefit from the richness achieved by the peer researchers and their 'closeness' to the research. Indeed, one of the central strengths of a peer research process is that it provides an opportunity to build on the skills and experience of those who are close to the research topic (issue; organisation; geographical location). Richness that can be achieved by drawing on the experience and perspective of the 'insider' (Warren, 2002), enabling people to use their knowledge and experience to help to shape the research design. Within our research practice, this was particularly important when working with peer researchers within a voluntary sector learning and skills provider. Many in the group had faced barriers to learning in the past, and we learned a great deal from them by listening to their experiences. They encouraged us think about the accessibility of information, appropriateness of research methods and the best way of thinking about dissemination. It was important for us to be flexible, adapting our approach.

A second important strength is the way in which peer research can attend to power imbalance. 'Traditional' research approaches treat researchers as 'experts' and effectively separate researchers and the organisations/ communities they research (Israel et al, 1998), which can impose a hierarchy where the professional researcher has the power to shape what is researched and how. A peer research approach has the potential of ceding some of this power to the community/group/neighbourhood being researched, enabling peer researchers to help to shape the research process, and ultimately therefore have some control over the knowledge being created through an equitable partnership.

The aim of peer research is to bring community members into the research process at each stage. Yet, it is also important to acknowledge what 'professional' researchers bring to this process. It is not about downgrading the contribution professional researchers make but, rather, supporting a collaborative process whereby the contributions of all group members are heard and valued. The peer research process has the potential to embody democratic and transparent research processes that value all contributions (Guishard, 2009). Within this learning exchange it is important to acknowledge that the learning is two way.

An important potential strength of peer research is the way in which it can engender a critical approach. Peer research sits within a critical paradigm, which means that the researcher understands that there are many different factors – social, ethnic, cultural, economic – that impact upon our individual experiences of the world (Israel et al, 1998; Stanley et al, 2015). Prioritising the involvement of peers or community members within the research process demonstrates a degree of understanding about how the researcher and the researched are linked. Those who control and conduct the research also have a degree of control over the knowledge created. It is particularly important, therefore, to consider this with regard to those groups/communities who are often powerless to influence, and those who are denied a voice in influencing processes.

This critical approach can offer a way of challenging these patterns of power in the research process. Our work with the voluntary sector learning and skills provider was a particular case whereby we were working with a group of young people who were often denied a voice within the mainstream, and it was therefore even more important throughout our work to make space for different voices within the group, to demonstrate that we were listening and adapting our work based on what we were being told. The way in which they shaped the research process and influenced key decisions impacted not only on their experience but undoubtedly also on the overarching project outcomes.

Peer research approaches also have the potential to support social action and change beyond the research. As well as conducting a defined piece of research, peer research can empower community members to set the agenda for learning and change. These programmes go beyond the specific objectives of a research programme and engage with issues of power and knowledge to have broader impacts. The term 'ripple effect' has been coined to describe these broader consequences of participatory research approaches (Trickett and Beehler, 2017), highlighting the wider implications and impacts beyond the research itself. From the experience of the individual, right through to community influence and empowerment, the peer research process has the potential to be catalyst for broader change over time.

Although challenging at times, our peer research programmes have enabled us to engender positive research partnerships. To support peer researchers as they develop the skills and experience to undertake research, it is essential that the dynamics between professional researchers and peer researchers is positive. Part of this is thinking about the dynamics across this partnership, particularly as such dynamics are fundamental when thinking about how to keep peer researchers motivated to remain involved in the research endeavour (Vaughn et al, 2018).

We learned early on that it was important to open all aspects of the research process to engagement, recognising that everyone is motivated by, and interested in, different parts of the journey. In one of our first peer research programmes within an older people's project, we were challenged by one researcher who suggested that he didn't feel confident to engage in certain aspects of the work, but had a great interest in working on the final research output. This surprised us, as we had assumed that certain tasks would remain the domain of us as professional researchers. We learned that there are opportunities to attend to issues of power and relationships at each phase of the research.

The final strength to discuss is the way in which this approach supports individuals to develop skills and experience. Individuals involved as peer researchers are supported to develop new knowledge and skills related to the research process and research topic, and also broader skills around communication and working with others. Beyond this, there is also the potential for individuals to develop more awareness of broader systems that their research may be interacting with or working to influence (Trickett and Beehler, 2017). This takes the potential of peer research beyond the individual research programme.

All of the foregoing can be positive for the research process, but also represents important opportunities for the voluntary organisations involved. These benefits can lead to more engaged, empowered and skilled individuals (members, volunteers, community members).

These are just some of the ways in which peer research could enrich and improve voluntary action research, and voluntary organisations themselves as well as wider society. Yet, this kind of engaged and inclusive way of planning, designing and conducting research is not without its challenges and potential drawbacks. It is important to consider these from the outset.

Challenges and limitations of the peer research approach

The following summary of some of the potential limitations or challenges of this research approach are not givens. These challenges may not materialise in your work, or you may find creative ways of mitigating some of them. If this is the case, please find a way of sharing your learning, in order to continue to support positive, innovative research practice.

The issue of control, and therefore power, represents an ongoing challenge when working within peer research programmes. Questions arise about who is setting the terms of engagement, who is making decisions about what is researched, how that research is conducted and with whom (who are our research participants?), how we analyse our findings and how and to whom the findings are communicated (Guta, Flicker and Roche, 2013).

These are very important challenges for a team of researchers to continually revisit, and these discussions form an ongoing part of the process we engage in together. Power is woven into all stages and into the process; addressing this on an ongoing basis can push the research team to continually improve practice, but this can also be challenging.

It is rare that we start a piece of engaged research with a totally blank canvas. We usually have some broad research questions, or at least some objectives that help to broadly frame our research. Unless the research questions come from the community in the first place, to a degree, there is always an existing agenda prior to the programme beginning, and one challenge therefore can be sharing an understanding as to what is possible.

Tensions can sometimes bubble up between the aspirations of the voluntary organisation, who knows what it wants to achieve, the group of peer researchers, who have experience of the research focus, and the professional researchers. We have worked to overcome some of these tensions by starting with an open and honest dialogue, optimistic in tone (looking at what is possible) but tempered by the parameters or limitations. If approached in a transparent and honest way, agreement can usually be brokered.

A key challenge can be recruitment of peer researchers. While ensuring inclusivity, it is also necessary to ensure that someone's involvement in the peer research process is not going to harm them. If someone might be considered too close to a particular research topic, the issue of potential trauma or harm must be discussed (Jones, 2004). This was a particular consideration for us within our work on an employment project working with people who had experienced poor mental health. It was vital that we worked closely with the voluntary sector organisation to ensure that they were recruiting appropriately, but also communicating clearly with all potential peer researchers so that people did not feel excluded from the research.

Research team dynamics can be a further challenge, and it is important to reflect on how to engage organisation/community members in research processes. The dynamics within the research team (between the peer researchers themselves; between peer researchers and the professional researchers) are vital in terms of motivating individuals to get involved and stay involved (Vaughn et al, 2018). In our projects, we work together to establish some ground rules for engagement at the outset, which can help. However, be prepared to revisit these as the group/relationships become more established.

A final challenge that we have often been confronted with is sustaining engagement. Ultimately, people will stay involved if they are interested and enjoying the process. This varies greatly, and, as with patterns in volunteering more generally, we need to understand and accept that people's involvement may fluctuate or wane as you move through the process. You can try to mitigate this by being clear about roles and process from the outset, trying to enable a greater degree of control over the research process. Don't get disheartened if numbers dwindle a little; having a smaller number of very engaged individuals can support the development of strong group dynamics, a real sense of shared ownership over the process, and this is frequently where we see a real shift in the power dynamics.

Box 5.1: Peer research: a step-by-step guide to the process

Here we provide an illustration of how we approach our peer research programmes. Rather than a set of formal processes to follow, the steps outlined are designed to indicate some of the stages that we have found useful or important during our own peer research programmes.

Step 1: Creating a role description

Before embarking on the recruitment of peer researchers, clarity as to what the role entails is important. People need to understand what they are getting involved in and, crucially, what they will be contributing to. What skills will the peer researchers be able to develop and what experiences can they be involved in? What difference will this activity make? How much time commitment will be required?

Step 2: Peer researcher recruitment

Thinking about how and where opportunities are publicised is important; being creative may extend your reach into the communities of focus, thus supporting inclusivity. We have found that it is important to consider the number of peer researchers you are able to work with in a meaningful way. Sometimes we have started with numbers as high as 20, but which have gradually reduced to between 6 and 12, which is an effective number to work with. The group can bond well and feel really engaged in the work.

Step 3: Research training

Thorough research training is important (Vaughn et al, 2018), but existing writing in this area doesn't always provide the detail of how this is undertaken. Within our programmes of peer research, we have found that it is important to be clear about the training content and time-scales from the outset, so that community members understand what they are volunteering to be involved in.

We cover:

- *an introduction to social research and research methods*, starting with interviewing, and then in subsequent phases expanding the focus to include focus groups and participant observation.
- *research ethics*: how we protect those taking part in our research (researchers and participants), and how we distinguish between research and support/advice;
- *health and safety*: thinking about how and where we conduct research, the importance of debriefing after a research encounter, and the usefulness of keeping a research journal to reflect on their own experience;
- *approaches to analysis*: introduced as part of the preliminary training, but covered in more depth when a phase of research has been completed.

Step 4: Designing the research

Working together as a research team during the design phase of the research helps to consolidate a sense of shared ownership over the process. This includes deciding which method/s is/are the most appropriate (if more than one method has been introduced), the scale of the research, how the research will be analysed and what kind of research output will be produced.

Step 5: Research practicalities – health and safety

Ensuring that there are clear health and safety protocols in place for the fieldwork phase is vital. This includes knowing when research is taking place and establishing a 'check-in' system following its completion. The researchers have sometimes found it useful to keep a research diary so that they can write down any key reflections after research encounters, which can then feed into discussions at the debriefing session.

Step 6: Debriefing

A debriefing session, held soon after the research has been completed, enables the research team to share their experiences and feelings about the process. Conducting research can take its toll; we hear difficult stories; we can feel affected by the experiences of others. We can sometimes feel frustrated that we cannot help or act upon the challenges we hear about through the research process. The debriefing session is therefore a vital way of providing a supportive context within which people can listen to and support each other. This session can also help to identify additional points to cover in future training cycles.

Step 7: Analysis

It can be challenging to conduct analysis in an engaging way. However, within the programmes that we have worked on, we find that the researchers are keen to engage in a dynamic process, which involves discussion and interaction. We often start with an open discussion about how the group found the research process, asking what key ideas stand out for them. This can lead to useful, rich discussions, which help the researchers to arrive at a range of key themes.

We remind ourselves of the research questions/objectives that we set out with. Supporting the researchers to discuss the research within the context of the research objectives can help to firm-up the key themes that people feel are important.

Step 8: Reporting the research findings

It is important for the whole research team to contribute to discussions about what they would like to do with the research results. The researchers might want to produce a written report or briefing, or they might want the opportunity to present the research at a meeting or event.

Step 9: Peer research evaluation and improvement

It is worthwhile investing some time in some informal evaluation with peer researchers and reflecting on how well the programme has worked. We have seen our programme evolve a huge amount year on year, and this is in part down to the reflection we have done as an integrated research team.

Future innovations in voluntary action peer research

Voluntary sector scholars have a key role to play in continuing to build co-production into their research processes. However, there are constraining factors that sit beyond individual researcher choice, and therefore it is equally important to work to be part of the conversations that set the frameworks for voluntary action research in the future. Voluntary action researchers need to articulate to research commissioners/funders the impact that co-production can have, which will work to ensure that there is greater understanding about the strengths that this approach can bring to a programme of research. This might change time frames and will impact on budgets. But researchers can be a key part of this conversation.

Being able to clearly articulate the range of benefits that co-produced research can bring to a research programme is an important starting point. Voluntary sector researchers must also continue to innovate, in order to effectively engage a broad range of people in voluntary sector research; bringing research expertise into the organisations and movements that we are researching will support a shift to longer-term engagement and empowerment. Voluntary sector scholars have a key role to play in supporting this positive shift.

Conclusion

Perhaps rather than seeking to aim towards a 'gold standard' or 'ideal type' of peer research within voluntary sector research, it is more useful to consider a set of underpinning principles that should help to guide us and should push us to continually develop and improve our practice. Voluntary action research faces many constraints (such as on time, budget or relationships) and there is a risk that as researchers we feel hamstrung by our awareness of the limitations of our practices. There are numerous pathways into co-production in research, but the fear that we are not achieving a gold standard of engagement can make us fearful of even stepping onto this path and making a start.

A starting point is to ask yourself whether there are particular aspects of the peer research process that you can adapt. Where can you draw on the peer research principles? How can you challenge yourself to pursue greater engagement and, in so doing, cede some of the control over the research process? Seeing this as an ongoing process rather than a destination you can reach (or another requirement you can 'tick off') is a good way of approaching this work.

The point I would like to conclude on is this. It is always worth taking your first, tentative steps down the route of co-produced research. While collaborative approaches to research, such as the peer research outlined in this chapter, are cut through with contradictions and challenge, it is also a hopeful approach to pursue (Janes, 2016), and one that is particularly coherent when researching within and alongside voluntary and community sector organisations, who are often themselves guided by principles of involvement, voice and co-production. A move towards more democratic research practices requires a continual cycle of reflection. Do not be daunted by the limitations, or the fear that more could be done. Recognise that any step you take in this direction will enrich the work and lead to more impactful results in the longer term.

Further reading

- For a good introduction to co-production principles within voluntary sector research see Verschuere, Brandsen and Pestoff's (2012) work.
- A rich and fascinating seam of work on co-production exists within the field of public health, which could be enlightening for voluntary action researchers. A great, critical example would be the paper by Guta, Flicker and Roche (2013) on 'governing through community allegiance'.
- One of the really interesting areas to explore is how we think about power and emancipation within participatory research approaches. For a good starting point with those ideas see Janes' (2016) article on 'epistemic privilege'.

6

Charity advertising: visual methods, images and elicitation

Abhishek Bhati and Jon Dean

Introduction

Visual methods – those methods that utilise photography, video, drawings, art and other similar materials – are underused in research on voluntary action. This is despite such methodological approaches gaining widespread recognition across the social sciences, arts and humanities as important ways of documenting the full gamut of human social experience and being shown to break down boundaries between researchers and participants (including vulnerable or disadvantaged populations). Visual approaches offer 'complex, reflexive and multi-faceted ways of exploring social realities' (Spencer, 2011: 35), and ultimately make statements that cannot be made solely with words (Harper, 1988: 38; Gauntlett, 2007: 106).

In this chapter we discuss two separate studies we have conducted separately with our colleagues Angela Eikenberry and Beth Breeze, which utilised visual methodologies to explore the representation of need in charity fundraising and advertising materials. These studies offer comparative insight into what charity beneficiaries (children in India, and homeless people in the UK) think about their representation, and how they think the services they benefit from should be illustrated.

This chapter first explores the nature of visual methods and examines how and why they have been underutilised in voluntary sector research. The main body of the chapter will then focus on the role visual methods can play in helping us to research and understand charity advertising and fundraising materials, which is important because these visuals are often the way in which most people see, understand and engage with the work of charities to which they are not direct beneficiaries.

Using visual methods

While the study of the voluntary sector is a broad church in terms of disciplinary approaches, it seems strange that such a diverse, creative and representational part of research design has not played a significant part in our academic explorations of philanthropy, volunteering or the work of non-profit organisations. There has been a long history of incorporating the visual into studies of community, work, sport and recreation and everyday life, all fields of research with a deep connection and relevance to voluntary sector researchers. These include Mitchell Duneier's (1999) *Sidewalk*, which reveals the lives of homeless magazine vendors in New York City through ethnography and documentary photography so as better to communicate the realities of lives so different to those of the majority of readers, and White and Green's (2010) map-making project, where the researchers used drawing methods to reveal the perceptual geographies and classed realities of young people's job-market horizons. So, it is important that those seeking to understand, critique and improve the work of the voluntary sector do not overlook the results and findings that could be generated by this form of methodological approach, particularly as visual methods are often seen as more easily communicable than other research methods (Spencer, 2011). Visual approaches can offer alternative ways of understanding the role and successes of, and challenges facing, the voluntary sector.

Both photography and social science, in particular sociology, were born in the mid-19th century (Harper, 1988). This is perhaps ironic, given that the founders of sociology saw the new science as a way to understand how the Western world was changing due to the massive technological advances of the Industrial Revolution and how it was coping with such changes. Yet, despite their developing at the same time, Harper (1988: 54) notes how visual methods were considered 'underdeveloped and largely peripheral to the discipline', where, despite a substantial amount of high-profile journal articles incorporating photographs in the early 20th century, by 1920 the approach had all but died out (Strangleman, 2002). From the 1960s and 1970s, visual methods began to flourish again. Since the late 1990s, especially, visual ethnographic research has moved from an emergent field to an internationally established methodological field of practice (Pink, 2007). Some authors, such as Law and Urry (2004), contend that surveys and interviews may be unsuited to grappling with global complexity; as a solution, Les Back (2009: 213) argues that using 'cosmopolitan' methods like recordings, video and photography 'reworks the relationship between technology, art and critical social science in order to use new media to recalibrate the relationship between observers and observed'.

Further to such arguments, situated as they are in the grander processes of globalisation and sensory complexity, there are also practical and moral reasons why the application of visual methods should grow. Thomson (2008) collates arguments and instances of incorporating the visual into research with children, both for the moral and rights-centred reasons that children have something to say and deserve a voice, and also for the reason that visual and participatory methods provide less formal and more inclusive approaches to getting answers. For example, Young and Barrett (2001) used a variety of visual approaches with street children in Kampala in order to guarantee that the children were an active part of the research process rather than just passive objects within it to be interpreted by Western researchers.

So, what do visual methods entail? In trying to define their possibilities and approaches, Prosser (1998) presents four Rs, which can be utilised by the researcher independently or interchangeably. These are:

- researcher-found visual data (for example, graffiti, cartoons, newspapers, adverts);
- researcher-created visual data (for example, photographs, visual diaries, documentary films);
- respondent-generated visual data (for example, drawings, maps, photographs);
- representation and visual research.

While the first three categories focus on the types and forms of images and imagery that can form part of a visual project, the fourth element focuses on representation, and contains a broader social, political, cultural and historical examination of the three previous categories. It asks questions like 'In what context has this magazine been produced?', 'Why are the images like this?' and 'What does this say about the racial or gender politics of the time?' This is where visual methodology must go beyond merely taking photographs of things, just as interview-based methods seek to go beyond asking people some questions and recording their answers. It is the researcher's job to interpret that data, to contextualise it against other data collected during the research process, with a heightened awareness of the semiotics that regulate and reinforce cultural and social values and practices (Clarke, 1997; Spencer, 2011). On their own, photographs are prone to manipulation, misunderstanding and misappropriation: to be a visual study, images need to be more than a perfunctory add-on; they need to be central to answering the research questions set, with the researcher often acting as both enabler and interpreter.

In participatory terms, researchers increasingly use the visual as a tool to break down the barriers between themselves and the people they are researching. This raises ethical questions, with Pink (2007) suggesting that such visual ethnographies need to be thought of as collaborative projects, with joint ownership of research data and ongoing processes of negotiation and consent with participants. This can go further still, where participants are the key deliverers of data collection, repositioning the participant as 'expert', as seen in research into homelessness utilising auto-photography to 'develop as equitable [a] relationship as possible between the researcher and the participant' (Packard, 2008: 66). At the heart of this method – also referred to as photo-voice, reflexive photography or photo-novella – is the simple idea of providing research participants with (disposable) cameras and asking them to document their own lives, taking photographs of places, situations or events that are important to them. These photographs are often then used in elicitative discussions, where participants are encouraged to explain why they have taken certain photos and why the places documented are important to them, providing a 'pictorial dimension by means of which respondents can tell their story' (Radley et al, 2010: 36). These recorded discussions therefore construct 'shared understandings of the meanings [of participants'] photographed social worlds' (Bukowski and Buetow, 2011: 741). Radley et al (2010) provided homeless research participants with cameras and asked them to document the places that were important to them as they walked around their home towns and cities. The collected images stressed the lack of permanence in the daily routines of homeless people as they continuously moved around the city, walking the streets alongside their also homeless friends being preferable to staying in a hostel (if they had access to a bed) all day and all night. Similarly, Johnsen et al (2008) saw auto-photography as a tool to document the 'hidden spaces' occupied by homeless people and to contrast these geographies with those of the housed public. Bukowski and Buetow (2011) and May et al (2007) have both utilised auto-photography as a feminist research method, specifically seeking out homeless women, who are less likely to be visibly homeless.

Some methodological problems can arise in auto-photography, with the researchers in these studies rightly offering long and detailed explanations of ethical concerns and the practical application of data collection. For researchers looking to utilise such a method to break down the power inequalities in the researcher–participant relationship, at times it can also unexpectedly reinforce existing inequalities. These can be centred on the role of photography as a skill where differentials in cultural capital can become obvious. In Radley et al's (2010) study the homeless photographers often explained that they did not feel that the photos they produced adequately communicated what they wanted to say, that they did not possess the technical capabilities required or they could not access the places they wanted to photograph. Similarly in Packard's (2008) work, wherein one participant really wanted to communicate certain visuals, but his poor ability with a camera (putting his finger over the lens, not being able to frame pictures adequately or not getting close enough to object) was such that he became annoyed, frustrated and embarrassed that he could not communicate what he wanted to get across properly, thereby raising unexpected ethical questions of participant harm.

Exploring fundraising materials and the representation of homelessness

Gauntlett (2007: 93–104, 123–127) discusses several different ways that he has used the visual to explore identity creation, including asking children to participate in documentaries and to draw pictures of celebrities so as to understand how modern media culture may have affected their worldview. Perhaps most innovatively, Gauntlett conducted focus groups with a range of professionals (architects, social care workers, academics and more) and asked them to create models of their identity using Lego™ (Gauntlett, 2007: 128–57), prompted by directions such as 'Create a model of how you feel on Monday morning', and 'Now transform that model to show how you feel on a Friday afternoon'. This method demonstrates an attempt to get research participants to communicate values and knowledges in ways other than talking and provides researchers with qualitative data other than transcripts and sound recordings to analyse, and has been utilised by Dixon (2016) to explore the experiences of hospice volunteers.

In 2012, Beth Breeze and Jon Dean used photo-elicitation to explore what homeless people thought of the way homeless people were represented in fundraising materials for homelessness charities. Photo-elicitation is a simple visual research method, but one that has deep roots in much social research, particularly life history research. At its core is the practice that photographs and other visual media can be used to generate answers, discussions and data within interviews, focus groups and similar suitable qualitative (and potentially quantitative) research, rather than only using verbal and textual questions. These can be photographs of work processes ('Tell me what's going on in this photo') or images that arouse memories of the past ('What was it like growing up in this neighbourhood?'). It is a method of social research that has historically been used to solicit responses from people who respond better to visual rather than lexical prompts (Collier and Collier, 1957; Thomson, 2008), and is useful both for stimulating discussion (Pink, 2007) and for allowing people to express feelings and emotions that words-only research cannot (Harper, 2002). Over five focus groups in homeless shelters and hostels across England, Breeze and Dean (2012) showed groups of service users images used in recent fundraising campaigns for homelessness charities and asked for their opinions on them. Being able to talk about actual adverts, asking service users what they liked about them, which ones they did not like or how they could be changed or what they felt these chosen images said about the issue of homelessness and about homeless people, was a much more visceral experience than an abstract conversation would have been if the focus groups had operated without visual prompts, because the prompts provided common jumping-off points and removed the need for individuals to imagine images others might have been thinking of if the more general approach of 'Do you think adverts for homelessness charities portray homeless people fairly?' has been used. Participants were able to compare, critique and comment in a much more defined way than without core images. Following the previous assertion that visual methods can be particularly useful in researching with individuals who may not feel comfortable expressing themselves verbally, it was felt that this study demonstrated the efficacy of utilising visual methods in certain circumstances and with certain populations.

One of the conclusions Breeze and Dean drew in their study is that charities believe that potential donors have an image of service users in their heads, and that for charities to move away from these images in their marketing materials is an enormous risk. It was felt that this is even more likely for organisations tackling homelessness, because it is a social problem that is quite 'other' for many people, whereas illnesses like cancer and heart disease are more likely to affect individuals personally or close family members. Wishing to test this hypothesis, Dean ran a series of focus groups with university students to understand what they currently thought about homelessness and what they thought homelessness looked like.

Focus groups began with the distribution of pens and paper, and participants were given five to ten minutes to 'draw what homelessness looks like'. No more instructions were given than that, and students were encouraged not to look at each other's drawings or talk about the task. These focus groups were not concerned with an individual's artistic skill, but merely to encourage students to think creatively, and to uncover individuals' initial internal representations of homelessness. After the drawings were finished, students were asked to explain what they had created in quite thorough detail and to explore why they had chosen to address the task in the way they did. The full findings of this research are explored elsewhere (see Dean, 2015a); however, the image drawn by Ashleigh (a pseudonym), a female first-year student, is reproduced in Figure 6.1. This drawing is highly representative of the images produced by students in the project.

The images produced by students show incredible consistency, from the figures produced within them, to the situations and social problems they depict. The vast majority feature bearded men, with unkempt hair, surrounded by a few untidy belongings; alcohol, dishevelment, isolation and begging are commonly recurring themes. Ashleigh's drawing includes passers-by ignoring the homeless person at the drawing's centre. When asked to describe who she had drawn, Ashleigh said 'quite sad' and 'neglected'. Other student participants would talk about an awareness of the 'other world' of homelessness, including shelters, soup runs and voluntary agencies, but often reflected on choosing to draw the most stereotypical image they could, because that is the image that media discourses repeat, with many referencing cult figures like 'hobos' in American films; video games and television programmes were also seen as media forms that centre on one singular image of homelessness.

Following reflective discussions of why students had drawn homelessness in the manner they did, focus group discussion would then turn to more critical discussions of homelessness, its structural and individual causes, its

Figure 6.1: Image drawn by Ashleigh in 'What homelessness looks like' focus group

symptoms, and policies in place to alleviate it. Participants realised that their drawings revealed a lack of subtle knowledge and understanding of the realities of homelessness, and this showed how visual methods can be utilised as a tool of both critical pedagogy and public sociology, encouraging future engagement. Drawings served as a jumping-off point where students could engage in reflection and self-criticism; as such, they offer an opportunity to reveal different forms of knowledge. Voluntary sector researchers could utilise these visual 'making methods' in various ways. White and Green's (2010) mapping exercise, where unemployed young people were asked to draw maps of their local areas, demonstrating their perceived geographies of possible employment (with middle-class young people more likely to see a wider scope of possibilities), could be applied to volunteering, or as mind-mapping exercises with charities seeking funds, to explore where they see the potential for bringing in resources. These would provide an insight into the varied geographical and metaphorical horizons of those working in the voluntary sector.

Beneficiaries' reflections on international aid appeals

Studies suggest that donors are more inclined to donate in response to fundraising advertisements showing images of children, victims of natural disaster, single women with children or cute puppies because they perceive these as innocent and helpless, as they do not have any control over their situation (see Breeze and Dean, 2012; Bhati and Eikenberry, 2016 for examples). Small and Verrochi (2009) found that potential donors were more likely to make donations in response to a fundraising advertisement showing a crying child versus a happy child. Thereby, charities often use simplified or stereotypical images of the beneficiaries, such as crying children or single mothers, to foster guilt and pity among donors so as to solicit donations (see Dogra, 2012). Such representation creates a power difference between donors and beneficiaries, whereby donors appear to have the power to 'transform' the lives of beneficiaries through their contributions when beneficiaries are portrayed as helpless and vulnerable. Therefore, traditional images increase the power differences between beneficiaries and donors, which runs contrary to the humanist view of the equality of all lives. To reduce such a power differential it is important to increase the voices of beneficiaries, which are mostly neglected in the fundraising research.

Bhati and Eikenberry (2016) used similar photo-elicitation techniques to those utilised by Breeze and Dean (2012), to understand how destitute children in India feel about their portrayal in the fundraising material used by non-governmental organisations (NGOs). The study was conducted in the summer of 2014 with four case study NGOs consisting of two small grassroots organisations, a medium-sized and a large international NGO. The locations of the organisation were equally divided between north and south India. A total of four focus groups were conducted with these organisations, with a total of 24 children participating (10 boys and 14 girls, aged between 9 and 17). The participants came from different religious backgrounds and income statuses. One-fourth of the participants were homeless children from Delhi and the rest came from low-income families.

The focus group started with Bhati introducing himself in Hindi and connecting with the participants by stating that he was from Delhi, the national capital of India, and currently researching abroad in the US. This information was considered important, in order for the participants to connect with the researcher as 'one of us' and share their thoughts freely. He also explained the purpose of the study and why participants' perspectives were important so that their voices could be added to the literature in fundraising and non-profit management. After the introduction, Bhati took a minute to go through the ground rules for the smooth functioning of the focus group. The rules included everyone's participation in group discussions and reminding them that they were 'free to say what you think, as there are no right or wrong answers. But be respectful to others at the same time.' Then the researcher asked children to introduce themselves, suggesting that they could use their real or a fictitious name, their age, and their grade if they were attending school. After a brief discussion about the ground rules and purpose of the focus group, the ice was broken with discussions of the latest Indian movies or the children's favourite actors, and some simple games. These discussions and games made the children feel more comfortable with each other and the researcher. Easing into the focus groups and building researcher–participant trust was especially vital in the context of this research, as many young participants had experienced physical and emotional exploitation.

The data-gathering section of the focus groups started by distributing the photographs from a set of seven images. Once the participants had spent a reasonable time looking at a photograph, the researcher prompted the group by asking them to describe it. The discussion was not conducted in any set sequence and any child could begin the discussion; the researcher repeated questions and encouraged other children to share their thoughts about the images. This process continued until all participants had shared their thoughts. After the first question, the researcher prompted 'What do you like or dislike about this image?' and same process was followed. Further questions focused on 'If you were in this image, how would you like to get photographed?', 'Do you understand the purpose of these images? Does it matter to you that these images are used to raise money for the NGOs?', and finally 'Which of the seven images did you like and dislike the most?' Each focus group lasted for an hour and no notes were taken, as the whole session was audio recorded. Whenever 'group think' seemed to emerge, or the children became distracted, the researcher assured the children that there was no wrong or right answer and followed up with a more probing question. To ensure that no child dominated the discussion, the researcher encouraged the quieter or shy children to speak, and stressed that everyone should be given a chance to talk. Generally, children were very actively involved in the discussion and the researcher rarely had to invite participants to contribute by calling on them to share their thoughts. The researcher himself translated the focus groups from Hindi to English and transcribed them into English.

The findings showed that the children liked the photos where they were represented as happy children with clean clothes or neat hair, suggesting that they want to be portrayed in a 'good light'. Ten out of 24 children liked a certain photo. In this image, a girl is wearing a school uniform and happily holds pile of books. The image has the caption 'I want to learn and not earn let me be. #InSchoolNotAtWork.' The children in the focus group repeatedly mentioned that they liked the photo because the child in the image was happy and getting an education, with clean clothes. It is needless to say that this photo is aspirational to a lot of children in developing countries who do not have access to schools, books, clean clothes and kempt hair. In contrast, when the researcher asked which photo participants liked the least, almost half of them (11) chose an image where a new-born baby appeared sick and suffering from a disease. One of the children in the focus group mentioned that the baby was alone because its mother had died and it was an orphan. As most of the children the NGOs were working with were orphans and homeless, this demonstrated one of the key advantages of photo-elicitation, as participants were better able to reflect on their own realities and draw those personal parallels.

Thus, the emergent theme from this study was that children wanted to be seen in a 'good light' but at the same time also stressed that they wanted fundraising images to show the whole story of their everyday struggles, as opposed to simplified, easy-to-process images to foster guilt in donors. The charities oversimplify their fundraising images to get the attention of donors. Using images as a vehicle, children in the focus group expressed that they wanted the world to know that their friends had been pushed into child marriage and child labour, and that they hoped these images would generate enough awareness among people to pressure governments to enforce bans on these ill-practices. This finding resonates with a study of 300 NGOs' campaign advertisements, where Cohen (2001: 179) concludes that images representing poor people are simplistic, stereotypical and negative, thereby 'encouraging dependency and exonerating donors from causal responsibility; ignoring the complex causes of poverty in developing countries and fostering attitudes that remain racist, colonialist and Eurocentric'.

When researching fundraising images, it is important for researchers to look at the images through an historical lens. These images are not produced in a vacuum, and fundraising professionals who are selecting them might be operating under certain biases, creating artificial differences between colonised people of colour and their white colonisers. This 'othering', though not as severe as previous well-documented portrayals of people of colour, reveals NGOs' continuing role in establishing 'us and them' narratives through their fundraising imagery. A more recent study conducted by Bhati (2018) finds that most fundraising images used by NGOs are deliberately positive. However, scrutinising these images more closely using qualitative tools such as semiotics reveals that structural differences between children of developing countries and those developed countries exist.

Conclusion

Reflecting on the conduct and output of these connected research studies, we feel that they show the power of visual methods in producing more power-neutral data that truly speaks to the experiences of charity beneficiaries. In these cases, visual methods allowed the children and the homeless people to whom we spoke to construct their own identities in relation to how they were represented within wider society (and for some students to think about how these wider representations drove – and limited – their understanding). Qualitative research in general *can* challenge top-down, researcher-dominated narratives of what we expect people to say, and doing so with photo-elicitation and creative visual methods doubles this benefit, as accessibility for all populations is generally increased. The methods are flexible and allow for unstructured, non-linear data-gathering processes, and can generate denser data that situates people's opinions and ideas in current narratives about what they are going through. Both studies discussed here also contained an element of emancipatory potential: participants cared about their representation and wanted the/their whole story told, not snapshot images that are both simplifications and reductions of their experiences.

Some years ago, the Sheffield-based freelance photo-journalist Richard Hanson, who had a long career working for charities and NGOs, especially in the field of international development, before his sad death in 2014, explained to Dean why he thought images are so important to voluntary sector organisations. He spoke of one charity that had been actively losing money because their website was not presenting a 'compelling story' of the charity's work and achievements; potential grant funders were actively turned away by the inadequacy of their web presence – in which high-quality visual stimuli should play a significant role. 'People were going "We can't tell what you do, it's not clear". … They were literally losing funding because their storytelling was poor.' Hanson, perhaps unsurprisingly, given his profession, was unequivocal regarding what proper application of 'the visual' can offer to the voluntary sector, particularly those organisations operating with service users who are often thought of as 'other': we are all visual at some level [with some obvious exceptions] but at its best it offers that connection, that point where you go 'I recognise that'. It takes you into somebody's world at its best.

Voluntary organisations have for long understood the importance of the visual as a fundraising tool, as a way to inspire supporters, to lobby and to gain attention. But visual methods are barely used in voluntary action studies. At its best, the work of voluntary sector researchers is diverse, creative, challenging, adds to our understanding of the social world and assists voluntary sector actors in doing their jobs. But, as Strangleman (2002: 189) writes of the lack of visual methods in the sociology of work journal *Work, Employment and Society*, '[t]o not include this long established and growing area is to neglect a whole series of debates – methodological, theoretical and empirical'. To so infrequently bring the full methodological canon into voluntary sector research leads to similar failings.

Further reading
- Doug Harper's (2002) work on photo-elicitation provides an excellent overview of its possibilities for enlarging the realm of empirical data.
- Knowing the lives of homeless people is made much more accessible by providing them with cameras, as Radley and colleagues (2010) did.
- To understand how NGOs have chosen to represent global poverty, and what those choices mean, Nandita Dogra's (2012) work is vital.

7

Using archives and objects in voluntary action research

Georgina Brewis

Introduction

The archives, records and material culture of voluntary organisations are vital assets. They can play an essential role in helping researchers to understand the roles of voluntary organisations in society, as well as remaining important sources of institutional identity, corporate memory and accountability for charities themselves. Archival research enables greater awareness of the significance of voluntary action to society in the UK and elsewhere. We can't fully understand modern societies, and, in the case of this chapter specifically, modern Britain, without acknowledging the ongoing part played by the charities and non-governmental organisations (NGOs) that helped to forge the public health, education and social care systems, form cultural, leisure and sporting lives and shape relations with the wider world. Voluntary organisations' archives are particularly valuable because they often contain the histories of marginalised and vulnerable individuals or communities whose lives may not have been recorded elsewhere or whose voices may go unheard.

The history of voluntary action, humanitarianism and philanthropy is now a flourishing field of scholarship, and there is an encouraging trend for researchers outside the discipline of history to turn to archival evidence when researching voluntary action, including in geography, social policy and sociology, media and cultural studies and international development. Indeed, archives are not solely about 'things already past' but will capture stories 'of the present and the future' (TNA, 2017: 8). The International Council on Archives (2004: 8) describes the preservation of NGO and charity archives as a 'public service designed to meet the known and unknown needs' of people today and in the future. Less scholarly attention has been paid to the source base that underpins this research, although studies have focused on the vulnerability of in-house charity archive services (Newton, 2004; McMurray, 2014); the challenges of records management in charities (Dawson et al, 2004); cataloguing and user engagement (Mills, 2013a); and third-party deposit of archives (Oppenheimer, 2020). This chapter draws on my experience of research using voluntary organisations' records and material culture across several historical and interdisciplinary research projects (see Brewis, 2014; Götz et al, 2020; Brewis et al, 2021a). This includes a study in which my co-authors and I develop the idea of 'co-curation' – the identification, selection, preparation and interpretation of archival materials as negotiated between researchers and owners of records (Brewis et al, 2021b). Such a process can be seen as a form of scholarly 'archival intervention' (DeLyser, 2014) or 'historian-activism' (Oppenheimer, 2020). Indeed, I have actively intervened in this space since overseeing the deposit of the Volunteering England archive at the London School of Economics (LSE) in 2011 (Brewis and Finnegan, 2012). Since 2014 I have directed the British Academy-funded infrastructure project 'Archiving the Mixed Economy of Welfare', raising awareness of the vulnerability of charity archives as well as supporting the preservation of dozens of collections. It brings together archivists, researchers and other users of archives with voluntary organisations who own and care for records. The project has published guidance, case studies and organised events, but its biggest impact has been behind-the-scenes work in shaping an agenda that recognises that while charity archives are an important piece of an increasingly diverse archives sector, they remain uniquely vulnerable and at risk.

Researching voluntary action using archives shares common methodological challenges with other forms of archival research – which are not discussed in detail here – but there remain questions distinct to the sector. Although many thousands of collections have been deposited in other repositories, voluntary organisations' records are mostly held privately. The conditions in which records are stored, the level of preservation, the extent of cataloguing or access for research varies hugely across the sector. Understandably, many organisations prioritise spending on core charitable purposes over administration costs relating to records management, even though record keeping is now recognised as an important aspect of good governance and can work to increase accountability and trust among stakeholders. Only a very small number of charities employ staff with professional knowledge of records management or archiving. Digital record keeping poses additional challenges, while any loss of charity income, staff redundancies, merger or office relocation can threaten physical collections. Other than time-limited financial information there is no statutory requirement in the UK for a charity's records to be preserved, let alone for them to be made available for research. Charity archives therefore lack the long-term legal protection afforded to records produced by government, nor do they benefit from the financial resources and networks that often protect other private collections, such as business archives.

This chapter discusses the ways in which researchers from a range of disciplines can identify, access, analyse and interpret archival sources to inform our knowledge and understanding of voluntary organisations, civil society and public policy more broadly. Key questions addressed are: how do you identify relevant archive collections? How can you negotiate access if collections are retained in-house by organisations? What type of material has been preserved and what voices are missing from the archival record? What are the challenges regarding digital records produced by charities? How do you approach the analysis and interpretation of charity sources? The chapter will address ways of working collaboratively with research partners to identify, analyse and curate archival material.

Identification

Researching voluntary action through archives and objects first requires identification of relevant collections. It is not always the case that a voluntary organisation, charitable trust, campaigning body or pressure group will have retained its own archive or deposited its records elsewhere. Writing the history of voluntary action often involves the piecing together of disparate sources of information, seeking out archival material that might be scattered across multiple repositories. My own first book involved tracking down material relating to student voluntarism and campaigning over a century from 1880 to 1980 that was held in multiple libraries, archives and organisations, including privately held material discovered in forgotten filing cabinets and awkward loft spaces of various charities (Brewis, 2014: 10). Moreover, as with any archival collection, some stories are privileged over others. It may be that material relating to founders and donors, or to property, finance and funded projects, crowds out the voices of individual volunteers, charity beneficiaries or local communities.

In the UK, there is no central archive of voluntary action, despite a failed attempt to establish one in the 1990s. In the US, the Rockefeller Archive Center was established in 1974, initially to preserve the records of the Rockefeller family and their philanthropic foundations. It now holds the archives of more than 50 philanthropic foundations, cultural organisations and research institutions, and has inspired other such repositories around the world, including the much smaller UK Philanthropy Archive at the University of Kent. Models vary around the world. In Australia, for instance, each state preserves its own archives and records, and these may (or may not) include records of philanthropic and charitable bodies. Riksarkivet, the National Archives of Sweden, houses the collections of several national charitable organisations, including Rädda Barnens Riksförbund (Save the Children), Frälsningsarméns Arkiv (Salvation Army) and the Swedish Red Cross.

Geneva is home to an important cluster of archives of international NGOs, including the International Committee of the Red Cross (ICRC), and intragovernmental agencies, including the League of Nations and the United Nations High Commission for Refugees. Belgium has long been an important centre for international conferences and congresses and plays host to many international charitable, campaigning and professional associations (Laqua, 2013). Some of the materials related to such efforts are now held at the Mundaneum in Mons, which has its origin in the work of the Nobel peace laureate Henri La Fontaine (1854–1943) and the bibliographer Paul Otlet (1868–1944), who sought to document and stimulate 'international life'. One of their bodies, the Union of International Associations, still exists as a documentation centre and has recently worked with historians seeking to use its material to consider the relationship between documentation, international organisations and 'global civil society' (Laqua et al, 2019).

Often a starting point for information about any given organisation will be its institutional history. These were – and still are – often written to mark a significant organisational anniversary, usually by an insider with privileged access to records and information not available to other scholars. These studies have tended to elevate the founder(s) of an organisation, and often contain elements of hagiography, such that they can 'obscure as much as they reveal' (Davey and Scriven, 2015: 118). Such celebratory institutional histories have been likened to works of propaganda intent on 'reshaping the past to serve the future' (Porter, 2002: 557). While more recent institutional studies might adopt a more critical approach to organisations, they can be beset by the same challenges of academic independence. Moreover, as Davey and Scriven (2015: 118) note of academic studies of humanitarian organisations: 'Pioneering histories have concentrated on pioneering stories, so that large organisations and high-profile individuals have frequently received the most coverage from academic researchers even though they have greater resources to invest in the preservation of their own pasts.' Other routes into understanding the development of an organisation over time might involve identifying published materials produced by charities in the past. Many printed annual reports, pamphlets, journals or magazines published by charities can be found in copyright libraries, while in the UK the British Library Social Welfare Portal collects born-digital material that is often categorised as 'grey literature'. The personal papers of philanthropists, charity administrators, social workers, politicians and others are also a fruitful source of material.

If you know the name of the organisation you want to research, a good starting point, in the UK at least, is the online catalogue Discovery, maintained by The National Archives, which has descriptions of more than 2,500 archives across the UK. You can search for any organisation and discover if its records are held privately or have been donated to or deposited in a third-party repository such as a local record office or a university library. For example, a search for Oxfam would tell you that the collection is housed at the Bodleian Library in Oxford and a search for the National Trust informs you the records are held privately. However, relatively few charities are likely to have a listing on Discovery, and the information is not always up to date.

The National Archives encourages any organisation to provide information about its collections using the 'Manage your archives' pages on the Discovery website, even if it does not have a formal archive service. Indeed, the National Archives Sector Development Team has a member with charity archives as part of their remit. There are other ways to search for collections, including the DANGO database, which was put together as part of a research project at the University of Birmingham in the mid-2000s. It can help researchers to identify NGOs and access information about the content, location and accessibility of their archival holdings; however, the site is no longer updated and in some cases is very out of date. For example, a search for Oxfam here would (wrongly) tell you that the collection is held privately. It can also be worth checking if there is material relating to the organisation you are researching in the archives of various charitable trusts and foundations that may have funded its work at some point: for instance, the records of the charities linked to the Rowntree family are at the Borthwick Institute in York, and the Barrow Cadbury Trust papers are at Birmingham Archives.

Access

The archives of thousands of voluntary organisations have been donated to or deposited in what are called third-party repositories, such as a local authority record office, a research library at a university or another specialist collection. Usually these are accessible to anyone who wants to access the collections, but you may need to apply for a reader's ticket. A number of university special collections services have made charity, campaigning and activism a collecting priority and have developed considerable expertise in this area. In the UK, this includes the University of Birmingham, the School of Oriental and African Studies (University of London), the LSE and the Bodleian Library, whereas in Australia, Melbourne University acquired the records of the Australian Red Cross as part of the 'Gift to the Nation' project (Oppenheimer, 2020). In Belgium there are some long-established university collections that contain the archives of voluntary associations. For instance, at KU Leuven, KADOC – the Documentation and Research Centre on Religion, Culture and Society – has been operating since 1976, with significant material on a variety of Catholic lay organisations. Outside higher education, there are other specialist institutions. In Denmark, Finland, Norway and Sweden, labour movement archives are significant institutions for research. For example, the Arbetarrörelsens Arkiv och Bibliotek in Stockholm brings together the papers of a number of social movements and labour organisations, including solidarity groups such as the Swedish Anti-Apartheid Movement and the Swedish Support Chile Committee.

The level to which a collection is catalogued varies hugely – you may find every item or set of items is listed individually (item- or file-level cataloguing), or you may have to search through vaguely named boxes to find relevant material. Reading-room hours are likely to be longer than for an in-house archive service, but restrictions will apply. Readers will usually need to make an appointment, review the catalogue and place orders for items ahead of time. Access is usually governed by the rules of the individual repository, and researchers are often asked to sign a reader's undertaking. You are usually allowed to take photographs or scans for research purposes, though you may need to make a list of each document you copy. You will need to request permission to publish images or large sections of text; the copyright holder may be either the original charity or the repository in which the archive is held.

In the UK, around 100 charities have professional archivists or records managers who run an in-house archive service; examples include the British Red Cross, Royal Voluntary Service, the Children's Society, Blind Veterans UK and Barnardo's. Many are members of the Charity Archivists and Records Managers Group, established in 1996. The extent to which these collections are catalogued or available for research varies. Some charities restrict access to, say, people related to past recipients or beneficiaries. In others, opening hours may be limited, due to lack of reading-room space and availability of staff to supervise research. However, many have made digital material and research guides available online. Matthew McMurray's (2014) research on charities with archive services found that many of them operated on a shoestring budget, were vulnerable to internal cutbacks and faced challenges in persuading the charity's senior management of their value. However, the advantage of research using such collections are many. In-house archivists have enormous expertise and intimate knowledge of an organisation and its past and will be able to guide and support researchers. The archivist should be able to help directly with queries regarding copyright, image reproduction or citation.

In many cases, however, the records of an organisation will be held privately, and researchers will need to negotiate access on a case-by-case basis. Archives may be retained in-house by the charity that created them, and they can include inherited collections from predecessor bodies or merged organisations. Records may remain in the personal possession of an organisation's founder, trustee or staff member. Such records may or may not be catalogued or have a simplified catalogue known as a 'box list', and can be in varying states of preservation. Such archives may be held in a charity's offices, in paid-for offsite storage or even in the private lofts and cellars of staff members and volunteers. Although private archives remain the responsibility of the owners, negotiating access for research is possible, and accessing material is exciting and fruitful. Accessing collections 'in the wild' in this way can be enormously rewarding for both the researcher and the organisation, but there are certain ethical considerations that should be borne in mind. Is the owner of the records fully aware of their content? What should you do if you come across potentially problematic material relating to, say, abuse or financial irregularities in the past? How should you reference the material? There are no easy answers to these questions, and I have found that securing access can go either way. Some charities welcome researchers but have not done any due diligence such as checking their records in advance; others prefer to enforce a blanket ban on access, out of lack of confidence or fear of the unknown.

It is worth acknowledging that for organisations, granting researchers access is not without risk, but that the advantages of such openness can outweigh the disadvantages. As head of the ICRC archives Blondel notes, archives 'play an important role in the duty of an organization to be transparent. As part of this duty and in order to benefit from outside perspectives and approaches, the ICRC encourages research and independent critique of its history and the fulfilment of its mandate' (Blondel, cited in Lucard, 2014). Should you be successful in gaining access, it is strongly recommended to draw up a memorandum of understanding between the researcher and the corporate owner of the records – this can protect both sides, particularly if individual staff members with whom you might have a verbal agreement move on. Staff turnover can be high, whereas research projects with lengthy publication processes can last for years. A tried and tested sample memorandum of understanding is shown in Box 7.1, covering key issues such as access to material, making copies, copyright and intellectual property, and researchers should feel free to make use of it for their own archival research projects.

Building a mutually productive relationship with the owner of the collections you want to see is crucial; think about what you as a researcher can offer the organisation in exchange for access. Researchers may wish to invite a representative to join your project's advisory committee, hold a workshop about your project for staff or trustees, write a blog for a website or offer to speak at an annual general meeting about the organisation's history. The process of co-curation that we adopted for our comparative 'Discourses of Voluntary Action' project, focused on the 1940s and 2010s, went a step further than a traditional lone-researcher model. A team of five academics, we engaged with charity partners at all stages of research design, analysis and knowledge exchange (Brewis et al, 2021b). Indeed, securing access to privately held archive material for the 1940s and 2010s was crucial to the viability of the research. The actual memorandum of understanding might be introduced after you have made informal contact and begun to establish trust. Few owners of archives are likely to appreciate a researcher's cold call with a legal document attached! As a researcher accessing an in-house collection, you may be in a position to signpost the organisation to sources of information about good practice in archival preservation or records management. It is worth noting that in 2015 the UK's Independent Inquiry on Child Sexual Abuse issued a notice requesting that records that might fall into their remit should not be destroyed, and this has implications across the voluntary sector. Globally, examples of fruitful collaborations between researchers and the owners of records include the Canadian Network on Humanitarian History, a multidisciplinary group with a strong interest in the archives of humanitarian organisations and NGOs.

Format

Archive material will be preserved in a variety of formats, more or less accessible for research. Most familiar are written documents, which could be in manuscript (handwritten), typescript, print, microfilm or digital formats – examples include letters, minute books, annual reports, telexes, faxes, memos, e-mails, word-processed and PDF documents. Many collections will also contain physical or digital visual material such as artwork, photographs or slides. Audio recordings might be in a range of more-or-less obsolete formats including reel-to-reel, cassette tape, CD, DVD, MP3 and other digital formats. Moving images can be preserved on 8mm or 16mm film, VHS or digitally (including DVD). In some cases, it might be worth digitising this material. Scanning documents using optical character recognition software can turn sources into readable PDFs or editable word-processing documents; this is particularly useful if the intention is to analyse sources using computer-aided qualitative data analysis software like NVivo, but can also facilitate searches for particular words or phrases. Rather than taking photographs of documents, it is possible to scan images using smartphone apps that then allow you to create readable PDFs. Digitising audio-visual material is usually necessary for research purposes.

Alongside the written and audio-visual records produced by voluntary organisations, we must not neglect the material culture of charity and philanthropy. There has been a material turn across several disciplines and fields of study in recent years, with researchers taking inspiration from archaeology and anthropology in recognising the value of studying objects, the social context of their production and their multiple meanings. Girl Guide uniforms, awareness-raising ribbons and poppies crafted by blind ex-servicemen are objects that both serve as sources of inspiration and provide key evidence for research (Proctor, 1998; Moore, 2008; Pollen, 2016). The archives of charities will often contain a range of objects and artefacts. The Oxfam archive at the Bodleian Library, for example, has a fascinating selection of awareness-raising children's games. The Blind Veterans UK archive contains hundreds of examples of adaptive technology such as braille typewriters and watches. Items of uniform, flags and badges will form a significant part of any youth movement's collection, such as the Woodcraft Folk's archive at the University College London Institute of Education.

Objects relevant to the study of voluntary action can be found in museums and galleries of many types, particularly those exploring the history of childhood, education or medicine. In the UK there are several specialist museums devoted to individual voluntary associations or causes, including the Foundling Museum, the Museum of the Order of St John and the Red Cross Museum. In Geneva, the United Nations Museum has staged exhibitions showcasing international organisations. However, entire museums or permanent exhibits on charity or philanthropy are very rare. The Chinese Charity Museum in Nantong City, China, opened in 2016 and has been described as 'probably the only national-level museum in the world to feature a permanent collection of exhibits focused solely on the history and practice of philanthropy' (Jeffreys, 2018: 78). It displays over 2,900 items drawn from 3,000 years of charity history. The Philanthropy Initiative at the National Museum of American History in Washington, DC collects, documents and exhibits materials relating to the history of charity in the US; since 2016 its changing exhibit 'Giving in America' has displayed a range of these objects.

While research using objects often takes place in a museum, gallery or archive setting, the nature of studying voluntary action might well mean identifying a potential object and then searching in second-hand stores or online auction sites to buy it (on using eBay in research see DeLyser et al, 2004). In my own research and teaching, I have purchased a range of charity ephemera from eBay including a 1963 CND badge, First World War paper fundraising flags, items of Boy Scout and Boys' Brigade uniform, a Townswomen's Guild teacup and saucer, youth club membership cards, a papier mâché Barnardo's collecting box and a wooden tray made by blind ex-servicemen for the charity St Dunstan's (now Blind Veterans UK). Many of these items are more everyday than those that might end up in museums and they can help to fill gaps in an organisational archive if, as is common, objects and artefacts have not been preserved with other records. For example, in our research on the National Old People's Welfare Committee in the 1940s (now known as Age UK) we used eBay to purchase some original 1940s reports and a forget-me-knot pin badge designed to be worn by people attending its lunch clubs (Brewis et al, 2021b). Handling the physical objects can also generate research insights. It was only by examining the 1940s badge that we noticed its similarity to the modern forget-me-knot pin promoted by the Alzheimer's Society's campaign 'Dementia Friends'. Similarly, buying individual National Society for the Prevention of Cruelty to Children badges awarded to children who raised money for the charity prompted a realisation that badges from the 1980s – which stylistically were very different to earlier ones – were in fact part of the same lineage of children's charity auxiliaries stretching back to the late 19th century.

Analysis and interpretation

Researching voluntary action through archives requires an awareness of the different rhetorical devices, linguistic conventions and narrative structures used in sources produced by charities. As Kidd (1996) observed, the charity annual reports and publications through which many historians approach the study of voluntary action are 'generic forms with their own conventions and traditions'. So too are minute books, fundraising materials, sets of accounts, as well as audio-visual materials (Götz et al, 2020). Annual reports are concerned to provide indicators of success and progress while at the same time appealing for ever more money, resources or volunteers. Recent studies have begun to 'follow the money' through detailed analysis of charity accounts, starting to write new histories of charities as businesses (Roddy et al, 2019; Götz et al, 2020). Robinson examined how the now ubiquitous charity single was consolidated in the 1980s as a recognisable form in 'cover design, related promotional culture and music video as well as in lyrical and musical structure' (Robinson, 2012: 405).

Scholars have also turned attention to visual analysis of material produced by charities, particularly the affective nature of much fundraising and campaign material (Chouliaraki, 2013) and media coverage (Franks, 2013). Sources produced by charities often relied on metaphor and other tropes to convey meaning that would be understood by the intended audiences, but that today need some unpacking. There were numerous parallels in 'narrative form, chronology and rhetoric' between 19th-century writers on colonial societies and on the metropolitan poor, including the use of shared metaphors of 'degeneration, dirt and blackness' (Marriott, 2003: 222, 127). Preterition, for example, in which attention is drawn to something that the author professes to omit, was commonly used to discuss rape, sexual assault, incest, birth defects and venereal disease, leaving the reader with a vague impression of untold horrors. Delap's (2018) discussion of the euphemistic terminology used to describe child sexual abuse in the archive is useful here. Indeed, researchers need to be aware that within the sources accessed, they may encounter language, prevailing cultural attitudes and moral judgements towards individuals and groups that would not be considered acceptable today, particular on matters of race, ethnicity, disability, gender, LGBTQI status and sexual morality.

The archives of voluntary organisations can form a useful source base for research into voluntary action across different disciplines, and for cross-disciplinary investigation. For example, our aforementioned 'Discourses of Voluntary Action' project drew on methodological approaches from human geography, sociology, social policy and history. In identifying two 'transformational moments' for the welfare state and voluntarism in the 1940s and the 2010s, our research gave equal weight to both historical and contemporary evidence and adopted a common framework of analysis for documentary sources dating to both decades (Brewis et al, 2021a). As such, this study points to fruitful interdisciplinary and collaborative approaches to research using documents.

Conclusion

This chapter has offered an overview of the myriad ways in which archival sources, objects and artefacts relating to charities and voluntary organisations can be used in research. It has argued that such records can form a useful source base for research into voluntary action across different disciplines and for interdisciplinary projects, and has discussed practical details of identification, access, format, analysis and interpretation. Accessing stories in charity archives is one way to amplify the voices of marginalised and vulnerable communities and individuals. Archives and records in the voluntary sector have long gone under the radar of the wider archives sector (Newton, 2004), as well as being undervalued and under-resourced by the voluntary and philanthropic organisations that own them. For charities themselves, opening archives for research can help to build trust and improve accountability to beneficiaries, donors and local communities, as well as informing and supporting current priorities. Like institutions of all kinds in the 21st century, philanthropic and charitable organisations are being encouraged to revisit and confront darker and often problematic aspects of their histories. Sensitive, co-curated research can produce mutually beneficial outcomes for organisations and researchers. Above all, archives and objects can increase our knowledge and understanding of the significance of voluntary organisations to society, past and present.

Box 7.1: Memorandum of understanding between [name of researcher/ research project title] and [name of organisation] [date]

Dear [named contact at organisation]

Thank you for your support for [name of research project] led by [name of researcher] at [researcher's organisation]. [Please find attached a short information sheet about the project].

I should be grateful if you could confirm that you and your organisation are able to provide the level of support we have discussed, and that you are happy with the following specific arrangements.

Access to source material

A key to the success of this research will be in accessing and using documents produced by your organisation [and/or its predecessor organisations]. This would be primarily, but not exclusively, for the time periods covered by our project [insert dates – or other restrictions]. The key material we need access to falls into these main categories:

[insert detail of material here]

[As the material is retained in-house], we will need access to identify, select and copy material or to have access to digital versions/copies. We will work with you to ensure that this takes place with the least inconvenience to you. Unless you are in agreement, all physical material will remain in your care at all times. We will be happy to make available our digital copies for your own use, for example on websites or in publications, as long as there are no third-party copyright or data protection considerations.

We recognise that not all voluntary organisations have records that are well preserved, catalogued or easily accessible. Please do not be concerned if you think your material falls into any of these categories: we have experience of working with organisations whose records and archives are in various states of completeness and organisation.

Ethics

The research will adhere to strict ethical guidelines, and is subject to the approval of [insert university or organisation]. More generally, the research ethics frameworks for [give details of funding body, learned or professional society] will guide the research process.

Data in the form of digital copies of the above material will be securely stored; any hard copies will be kept in locked filing cabinets.

Outputs

Over the course of the project [insert dates], and beyond its formal end, we will be communicating our research findings in a variety of formats including but not limited to: written and oral presentations at conferences and seminars; published articles and books; online blog posts, working papers and social media. We will aim to keep you updated as the project progresses via [insert form of communications].

In line with our commitment to conducting our research to a high ethical standard, we will remain sensitive to your wishes about aspects of your organisation's work that you do not wish to make public. We will give you an opportunity to review every publication in which your organisation is mentioned by name; all that we ask is that you respond with any comments/questions you might have in a timely manner (usually a [two-week] period).

Copyright

Copyright in any document used by [our project team] for research remains with its original owner (which may vary but is likely to be your organisation). However, we ask that you grant us permission to [input material into our data processing software and/or to] use sections of text and/or images in project outputs, including but not limited to: conference presentations, publications, our website and social media. We will always acknowledge that such material is reproduced with the permission of the copyright holder. We are also mindful of third-party copyright (for example, photographs within an annual report provided by an external photographer) and will ensure that this is upheld.

Intellectual property rights

Intellectual property rights generated as a result of the analysis associated with this study will be owned by [research organisation or university].

Knowledge exchange

We expect our project to have an impact on [insert details]. Where relevant, we will work with your organisation to use this knowledge to inform and enhance your work with policy makers and other stakeholders through [insert detail].

If the above is acceptable, I should be grateful if you could arrange for signature and return of an electronic copy this letter to [insert name and e-mail] and we will arrange for countersignature before returning a copy for your records.

Yours sincerely,
[Named researcher]
Signed:
Date:
Signed:
Date:

Acknowledgements

The author would like to thank Nobert Götz, Daniel Laqua, Amanda Moniz, Silke Neunsinger and Melanie Oppenheimer for their insights into collections held outside the UK.

Further reading

- Visit www.voluntarysectorarchives.org.uk for further practical guidance and a set of case studies showcasing different charity archives collections.
- Brewis et al (2021b) present their concept of 'co-curating' voluntary sector archive collections in partnership with the owners of these records.
- Melanie Oppenheimer's (2020) account of her long campaign to secure the preservation of archives of the Australian Red Cross highlights many of the challenges facing this sector.

8

Using Mass Observation as a source of qualitative secondary data for interdisciplinary longitudinal research on voluntary action

Rose Lindsey

Introduction

In 2014, my colleague Sarah Bulloch and I published an open-access paper (Lindsey and Bulloch, 2014a) that looked at some of the challenges we had experienced when designing a longitudinal, mixed-methods study of voluntary action that drew on Mass Observation Project (MOP) writing produced between 1981 and 2012. Seven years on, this chapter revisits some of the themes discussed in the 2014 paper, drawing on subsequent experiences of using MOP writing to undertake longitudinal, cross-sectional and interdisciplinary studies of voluntary action.

The chapter begins with a brief introduction to MOP writing for those unfamiliar with this secondary data source. It then considers two key issues first raised in the 2014 article. Firstly, it discusses the question of representativeness of those contributing to the MOP, asking 'who are the MOP writers?' The chapter draws on recent work to examine whether certain groups are under or over-represented within the MOP writers' panel. Secondly, it examines some of the challenges of sampling from the panel. It outlines the development of different infrastructure, tools and techniques – openly accessible to other researchers – which may help with sampling from large volumes of (longitudinal) MOP writing. The chapter ends with a discussion of more recent work on the importance of context when using the MOP, providing some examples of how context can confirm sampling choices and/or provide insights into writers' lives and identities for researchers researching voluntary action, regardless of disciplinary background.

What is Mass Observation writing?

Mass Observation (MO) writing has its origins in 1937, with the publication of letters in the *New Statesman* inviting volunteers to be involved in a new mass observation science project (Stanley, 1981; Sheridan et al, 2000). This proposed 'anthropology of home' and 'science of ourselves' (Moran, 2007) led to a variety of projects, including the setting up of a national panel of self-selecting volunteer writers who contributed written responses to 'directives' – a list of often unrelated questions on issues such as everyday life, relationships, politics, society, culture, religion and war – that were sent out to writers on a monthly basis. The first iteration of the MO writing project ran from 1937 to the mid-1950s.

When the MO project ended in the late 1950s, the mid-twentieth century writing was stored in a damp basement for a decade. The writing, and other material, was rediscovered, was moved to Sussex, and a curation and archiving process was begun with the setting up of the Mass Observation Archive (MOA) in 1970 (Sheridan et al, 2000; Hinton, 2013). David Pocock, one of the founders of the MOA, and its first director, recruited people to write about the Queen's Jubilee in 1977 (Sheridan et al, 2000: 44). Following on from this initiative, a second iteration of the MOP was launched in 1981. Initially known as the 'Inflation Project', it drew on similar principles to the early MO, recruiting a national panel of self-selected volunteer writers who agreed to respond to questions or 'directives' sent to them by the MOA several times a year. MO writers from both iterations of the project have also produced other forms of writing, such as diaries and reports.

Initially, the structure and form of the directives resembled those of the first iteration of the MO. However, several years into the project, the MOA changed the structure. Padding out the directive questions and providing various prompts, the MOA began asking writers to concentrate on one specific theme at a time. This revised structure has endured to present, with one exception. During the COVID-19 pandemic, existing writers and members of the public were invited by the MOA to record their experiences, thoughts and feelings on the crisis as it evolved. The MOA issued letters/ e-mails/online posts that resembled the shortened directive form employed by the MO during the Second World War.

The MOA sends out directives comprised of two or three separate themes, approximately three times a year. Writers are often asked about contemporary views, experiences or observations; however, questions can also be retrospective, asking writers to look back at past attitudes, events and experiences. Sheridan et al (2000: 48) liken this to writers being both 'investigators' and 'autobiographers'. Writers have also been encouraged to write as much or as little as they like and are not required to answer all questions posed to them. The MOA requests that each time a writer responds to a directive, they provide some basic biographical information at the start of their response. This should include: the anonymous number given to them by the MOA, their age, sex, occupation, marital status and area of residence (although writers sometimes forget to include this information).

The changes to the structure of the directives in the early 1980s influenced the form of many writers' responses (see, for example, Harvell et al, 2012 and Lindsey, 2020), with submissions changing from paragraphs on different subjects to essay-style responses on just one theme that have ranged in size from one page to 20 pages, depending on a writer's enthusiasm or passion for a subject. The archive is seen by many as being a rich source of secondary qualitative data. Both collections can be accessed physically via the MOA at The Keep, in East Sussex, UK. The early collection can be accessed digitally through Mass Observation Online (MOO; www. massobservation.amdigital.co.uk/), to which many university libraries subscribe. The contemporary writing is in the process of being digitised and writing from the 1980s can now be accessed digitally through MOO. This digital service is charged for, but rates vary depending on the financial status of the user/s, and not-for-profit users should contact the host to negotiate access.

The number of writers contributing to the contemporary MOP has varied over time, and there have always been a fluctuating number of writers within the panel, with many contributors joining, leaving or simply taking a break from the MOA across a calendar year. In the early 1980s, the archive hosted as few as 200 volunteer writers. By 1984 this number had grown to almost 1,400 contributors, in part because media interest raised the profile of the project, and because the MOA was accepting 'all unsolicited volunteers ... unconditionally' (Sheridan et al, 2000: 58). Response rates to directives have varied over the years, depending on the size of the panel; however, typically up to half the writers on the panel will respond. Given the large size of the panel in the 1980s, some directives yielded large numbers of written responses; for example, more than 650 people responded to directives sent out in 1987. This can often be too large a number for researchers to analyse in depth, requiring informed sifting and sampling of responses.

In the 1990s the MOA began managing the high volume of writers, gradually reducing the numbers taking part. And, in 1994, under the leadership of Dorothy Sheridan, the new director of the MOA, the archive introduced certain demographic eligibility criteria for potential new writers, so as to address what were perceived as gaps in the demographic make-up of the panel (Sheridan et al, 2000) (discussed later). In 2019, the panel comprised approximately 400 writers. However, during the UK lockdown between March and July 2020, the MOA received more than 500 approaches from people interested in responding to COVID-19 directives and in submitting lockdown/pandemic diaries. These new writers have increased the size of the current panel significantly.

Representativeness and the writers' panel

A key issue identified in our 2014 article was the difficulty experienced by the authors when trying to choose writers to 'follow' for a longitudinal study of voluntary action, which aimed at using responses to 15 directives produced by 38 writers over a period of more than 30 years. Our understanding of the writers' panel was based on Sheridan et al's (2000) inside history of the contemporary MOA, and on lengthy discussions with MOA staff members, Jessica Scantlebury and Kirsty Pattrick. We learned that when the contemporary MOP panel was set up, more than two-thirds of those who volunteered to join were women; there was a great deal of churn in the panel over time (as outlined in the earlier discussion on size); and in the 1980s and early 1990s the typical MOP writer was female, over the age of 50 and lived in London or the South East. However, in 1994, the MOA sought to address the over-representation of older people and women by introducing eligibility criteria for new volunteers. It began rejecting women over the age of 35, and men over 50, giving preference to writers who were young, male and/or living in the north-east of England. While this resulted in the recruitment of greater numbers of writers who were young and male from the mid-1990s, the panel continued to consist of greater numbers of women over the age of 50 – in part, as Sheridan et al (2000) point out, because female writers tended to be long-term contributors and younger men tended to drop out more quickly. This meant that there was less attrition of female writers, and long-term female contributors who joined the panel when aged under 35 have inevitably become older female writers.

Despite its attempts to provide more balance to the panel, the MOA has never sought for the panel to be representative of the broader UK population. Yet, as the 2014 article noted, for some time there had been an ongoing debate between different users and/or detractors of the contemporary collection as to whether the writers' panel should be representative of the UK population (see, for example, Pollen, 2013). These arguments tend to reflect the different disciplinary, epistemological and ontological approaches of the archive's academic users.

When designing our study of voluntary action in 2012, we accepted the lack of representation in the longitudinal panel, because the panel appeared to reflect the demographic make-up of British volunteers, which Mohan and Bulloch (2012) have dubbed the 'civic core' (Lindsey and Mohan, 2018). We felt that the contemporary collection of writing represented a unique source of secondary qualitative data for those interested in researching voluntary behaviours and attitudes towards voluntarism.

Our aim, before making any sampling decisions, was to find out more about the demographic make-up of the panel. We did this by bringing together metadata on the writers that the MOA staff made available to us to create a database of the different writers who had been members of the panel since 1981. As described in the 2014 article, we were able to identify writers' response rates to key directives on voluntary action; their year of birth; their sex (but not necessarily gender identity); their occupations; and their places of residence. These data informed the sampling options open to us, enabling decisions based on writers' response rates, sex, age and occupation (using this as a proxy measure for class). There were no available metadata on writers' race, ethnicity, religion or sexual orientation. While the final selection process was hugely exciting, enabling us to feel like we were going to 'meet' and 'get to know' our writers, the experience of bringing together these metadata was, nevertheless, time and labour intensive. We noted that other researchers whom we talked to had also experienced frustration with the lack of easily accessible biographical data for writers, which made sampling decisions difficult. This has also been acknowledged by the MOA for some time (see Sheridan et al, 2000: 61–62), and the archive had made various attempts, with limited resources, to address this issue.

Composition of the panel

Experiencing these difficulties in understanding the composition of the contemporary MOP panel at different points in time and with being able to gain a picture of the variety of writers that make up the panel led us to design another study: 'Defining Mass Observation' (DMO). This steered the focus away from the representativeness debate, arguing instead that the question first posed in the 2014 article: 'who are the MOP writers?' is a more productive line of inquiry for potential users of the archive.

Working with the MOA, we cleaned and brought together different types of metadata held by the archive that might shed light on the MOP writers. These included: spreadsheets of writers' responses to directives; biographical forms first used in 1991; responses to another biographical questionnaire fielded in 2010; and de-identified postcode data that were used to calculate the levels of deprivation in the area in which writers were/are living. The study used the combined MOP metadata to undertake quantitative analyses of the self-selecting volunteer MOP writers over three time frames: 1981–95; 1996–2005; and 2006–15, drawing on census data from 1991, 2001 and 2011 to compare writers with the broader population of England and Wales. The results are in the process of being prepared for publication by Daiga Kamerāde (University of Salford), an analysis that will include a comparison with the volunteering population of England and Wales. Here we provide a very brief synopsis of Daiga's work on the broad composition of the panel.

When comparing writers with the broader population of England and Wales, the study agreed with the early MOP analyses for the period 1981–95 on writers' gender, age and place of residence. We noted changes after this period, where the panel became somewhat more balanced, presumably influenced by new MOA policies on writer recruitment introduced in 1994. Analysis of the occupational status of writers (as a proxy for class) was frustrated by inconsistencies in the job titles and descriptions recorded by writers when filling out their biographical forms. We made the decision to recode these into Office for National Statistics categories known as Standard Occupational Classifications. We found that, since 1981, higher-level occupations were heavily over-represented within the panel, except for managers and senior officials, who were under-represented. Professionals were the most over-represented group, with between 15 and 21% more professionals than would be expected for their share of the population. This fluctuated over time, dropping between 1996 and 2005, and increasing again after 2005. Associated professionals and technical occupations, as well as administrative and secretarial occupations, were also over-represented, but to a lesser degree than professionals. In contrast, individuals in lower occupational groups were significantly under-represented. This was most pronounced for individuals from skilled trades, process, plant and machine operatives and elementary occupations, and slightly less apparent for sales and customer service workers. From 2006, caring, leisure and service workers were also under-represented. We also noted occupational patterns of responses to directives.

While these metadata provided insights into *some* of the demographic characteristics of the contemporary panel of writers, the study was frustrated to find that the MOA had never collected data on writers' 'protected characteristics' (under the UK Equality Act 2010) in relation to: ethnicity, race, religious identity, disability or sexual orientation. Sheridan, former director of the MOA, and other members of the MOA, have stated anecdotally that the MOA made a formal decision not to collect these types of personal data when the contemporary MOP was founded in 1981. The writing project was set up during a period of extreme social, political and public volatility towards minority groups: Far Right movements were extremely active; the British Nationality Act was passed, reframing notions of British citizenship and belonging; and urban civil disturbances, branded 'race riots', were taking place in multi-ethnic areas of England such as Brixton and Toxteth. The founders of the contemporary MOP writing project had concerns about potential misuse of sensitive data, informed both by the volatility of the time and by the collective memory of data misuse in Nazi Germany and occupied Europe in 1933–45, which underpinned the genocide of certain communities based on their race, religious belief, sexual orientation or disability. Elsewhere (Sheridan et al, 2000: 57), Sheridan has stated that the MOA made attempts to recruit people from 'ethnically diverse backgrounds' and organised a specialised recruitment campaign in 1987, which was unsuccessful in recruiting people from 'Afro-Caribbean and

Asian backgrounds'. This suggests that, while the MOA was not formally measuring the numbers of writers who identified as ethnically or racially diverse, somehow the MOA was keeping an informal eye out for writers with these identities, and noting their absence.

Nevertheless, given the MOA's lack of formal measurement of writers with protected characteristics, it is impossible to know how many writers with these characteristics have contributed to the archive over time. At a time when systemic racism is finally being recognised by the public and politicians through campaigns such as Black Lives Matter, and when there is evidence that hate crime against people with certain protected characteristics is on the increase (see, for example, O'Neill, 2017), this lack of measurement is frustrating. At best, it elides the views, attitudes and experiences of writers with certain protected characteristics, and prevents intersectional understandings of their experiences, views and attitudes. At worst, there may be very little representation of writers whose contributions would be of enormous value to qualitative researchers. The DMO project team recommended to the MOA trustees that the archive's lack of measurement of protected characteristics should be addressed. The MOA is in the process of introducing revised biographical forms that incorporate questions on protected characteristics. All new writers will be asked to complete these, and the form will be sent to existing writers in 2021.

Current sampling tools

As well as looking at the composition of the panel, the DMO study also used combined MOA metadata to create an open access, online database of writers' demographic characteristics and response rates, to enable sampling from the contemporary panel. The database can be used online or downloaded as a Microsoft Excel spreadsheet for analysis on the researcher's own computer. Users of the database can search for information based on responses to one or more directives, or by demographic variables, such as age, gender, occupational status or levels of deprivation in writers' area of residence. They can also make basic comparisons of sets of writers, or the entire panel, with census data for the broader population of England and Wales, in order to compare variables such as age and gender. This should enable researchers to make more informed decisions about which writing and writers to draw on for their research.

The database currently provides the most complete picture of writers and writing available to those seeking to use the archive. However, it is important to note that it also has its limitations. It is reliant on cross-sectional data – snapshots of writers at certain specific points in time – such as the biographical forms filled out by writers in 1991 (or at the time of joining, if they joined after this date) and 2010. For researchers who want to sample writers and writing from the 1980s, data that were relevant for 1991 may/may not reflect an accurate picture of a writer's circumstances in the early 1980s. The online database is therefore a very good tool for sampling, in that it enables a researcher to identify a writer by their age, gender, occupation, marital status, region of residence and length of time writing for the MOP. However, for more detailed work on the context of writers' lives, it is worth checking and cross-referencing this against the biographical material given by a writer in their responses to directives, which will reflect any changes in their circumstances over time. It is also worth looking at writers' responses to certain directives that provide context about writers' lives.

Context, sampling and the MOP

When we undertook our first qualitative analysis of MOP writing, we looked at responses to a single directive commissioned by the Third Sector Research Centre on 'The Big Society' (Lindsey and Bulloch, 2014b) – the UK government's policy agenda to increase citizen action and responsibility between 2010 and 2015. Our next involvement with MOP writing was in 2013, when we began work on the longitudinal study of voluntary action (Lindsey et al, 2015; Lindsey and Mohan, 2018). For this study we were interested not just in writers' volunteering behaviours and attitudes to voluntary action, but also the context and fabric of their lives and identities over time, and how these fitted alongside their voluntary action (or lack of it) and their views on voluntarism. The importance of context in the analysis of secondary qualitative data has been emphasised by researchers in this field for some time (see, for example, Mauthner et al, 1998). Bishop (2007) and Gillies and Edwards (2011) highlight the need for understanding the temporal context of secondary qualitative data, that is, the personal, political and social context at the time at which the data were produced, and the hindsight and meanings that we, as researchers, bring to these secondary qualitative data when analysing them.

MOP writers' responses to directives, particularly when writers have been long-term contributors, offer researchers multiple opportunities to gain context and a sense of the weft and warp of writers' lives. For the voluntary action study, we chose a variety of directives that we felt would provide us with insights on writers' life histories and personalities, as well as their views on voluntary action. For contextual understanding, we chose to analyse directives on the themes Special/Biographical Questionnaire (2010), Belonging (2010), Being Part of Research (2004), Paid Work (1997), Where You Live (1995), Social Divisions (1990), Relatives, Friends, Neighbours (1984) and Work (1983). Some directives, such as those on Belonging, Paid Work, Social Divisions, and Relatives, Friends Neighbours, yielded strong insights into class, life events, personality and writers' sense of community and place, as well as their attitudes towards voluntary action. Using all 15 directives together enabled us to compile educational, work, personal and volunteering life histories of the 38 writers, and to identify shifts, changes, contradictions and elisions in attitudes, views, emotions and identities over the course of 30 years.

We included the Big Society directive as one of the 15 directives to be analysed during this study. Returning to writers' responses to this directive a second time, and reading these alongside their responses to other directives, provided context, nuance and understandings that we had lacked when we undertook our first analyses. This highlighted to us the value of the messages of Bishop (2007) and Gillies and Edwards (2011) on context, and how worthwhile it is to look for this when analysing MOP writing.

We revisited the issue of context when we designed the DMO study. One of the objectives of this project was to complement cross-sectional quantitative analyses of the panel with qualitative analyses of writing that would shed light on writers' identities. This would act as a counterbalance for our own concerns about the loss of the voices and rich insights that can come with quantitative analyses of qualitative material, and that Pollen (2013: 12–13) warns against in her discussion of data 'mining'.

We selected two directives that we felt would provide insights into writers' identities. The first, Social Divisions (1990), which asked writers about their views on difference, enabled us to undertake analyses of writers' experiences of, and views on, class at the cusp of two decades – the end of the 1980s and the start of the 1990s. Our second choice, the Your Life Line directive (2008), which asked writers to map out, or write about, 'key events' in their lives, was informed by Parsons' (2013) work on this directive. We analysed the responses of a large sample of writers, but also returned to the pre-existing smaller sample from the Voluntary Action study, made up of the 38 writers, for whom we had already compiled life histories. Revisiting the lives of those writers who had responded to this directive yielded interesting results, in part because the directive called for a metanarrative of writers' lives.

Writers' responses to the Your Life Line directive did not provide the type of detail found in their responses to the other 15 directives we had analysed previously, so they do not necessarily represent a strong source of direct evidence on voluntary action. However, they did provide a strong sense of the lives people had led, and the events that writers felt were key to their lives at the time of writing. We noted that some events and difficulties that had caused strong emotional reactions (sometimes across directives) some years previously were omitted from these responses. We were not sure whether these events were glossed over, forgotten or just deemed generally less important in 2008. One older female writer noted this phenomenon:

As I think about the key events of my life, I wonder if age has a marked effect on perceptions. I think there are fewer 'key events' I'd list now than perhaps 20 years ago. Things/events that mattered [a] great deal at the time have merged with other things since, to take a less important role in my life line. (M388, aged 77, 2008)

Writing on the MOP as a source of life history, Sheridan's (1996) observation is pertinent to how responses to this directive might be approached or analysed by the researcher:

Just as the reply to one directive may contain many different elements, so the replies over time represent shifts in the life course, and changes in the way people think and feel, and the way they choose to record those changes. It is useful to see the 'chunks' of writing as many-layered life stories, told at different times and from different points of view. (Sheridan, 1996: 13)

The Your Life Line directive represents an excellent starting point when attempting to access the context of individual writers' lives. However, these responses should be read in conjunction with other responses in order to achieve the sense of layering, perspective changes and life-stratigraphy described by Sheridan (1996).

Analytical approaches to the Your Life Line directive

We analysed responses to the Your Life Line directive using similar tools to those described in the 2014 article, when working on the voluntary action study. Although we transcribed all handwritten/drawn scripts, and imported these into a CAQDAS programme for analysis, we read (copies of) the originals alongside the electronic versions so as to retain a sense of the physicality of each script, its form and the way it had been produced.

All directives represent research instruments, in much the way that a set of interview questions does. As with most MO directives that we had encountered, we found that the wording of the directive influenced the form of written responses provided. This enabled a methodical approach to analysis, which focused not just on themes and topics emerging from these responses but on the relationship between themes and the style and form of the responses.

Writers tended to produce metanarratives that started with an opening statement. For example, one writer announced: '1946. Born. This must have been a good event as I feel I've had a very lucky life' (writer A1706, female, aged 62). This was followed by a chronological list of events presented as a life arc or trajectory, and ended with a closing statement, such as: '19: Bought my first car – Silver KA from Slough. 3 trips there – never again. Grandad reveals he has been sleeping with the neighbour for over a year & didn't have the courtesy to tell us' (W3199, male aged 19).

The life trajectory sections of these scripts provided insights into how writers felt their lives have been shaped, and whether they had agency in their own lives (a theme that also featured in our analysis of the Social Divisions directive). Within the CAQDAS programme, we categorised this as: (i) *'Things that happened to me'*, such as: abuse, accidents, evacuation, fostering, adoption, bombing, World War Two, education, relationships, national service, bereavement, awards, divorce, menopause, miscarriage, bullying, child's family buying first television set, redundancy, illness; (ii) *'Things that I made happen'*, such as: affairs, buying something big, marriage, relationships, travel, education, promotion; and (iii) *'Impact of others on me'*, such as: suicide, attempted suicide, others' illnesses.

This approach enabled us to examine how strongly discussion or allusion to mental health and emotional well-being featured in these metanarratives, and to link this with work by Shaw (1994) on MOP writers' mental health and the therapeutic role of writing. It provided insights into how writers had interacted with others, enabling us to examine writers' social networks, and evidence for weak and strong ties (Granovetter, 1983). It revealed the dynamics of writers' life trajectories, providing, for example, evidence of social mobility (upwards, downwards or horizontally). And it enabled us to consider the words, styles and literary tools used by a writer, and what this might tell us about the writer and their motives when writing.

We found that responses to the Your Life Line directive provide demographic data relating to lifecourse that will enable researchers to finalise their sampling choices. However, these responses also represent repositories of rich, multilayered, retrospective, contextual data that will be of interest to those seeking to undertake qualitative research into voluntary action and civic engagement. Musick and Wilson (2008) outline many ways in which research on voluntarism can be approached, looking at issues such as the intersection of voluntary engagement and personality, political views, value systems, accumulation of social and economic capital, different stages of the lifecourse, education, religion and health. While they do not necessarily provide accounts of voluntary action, per se, responses to the Your Life Line directive provide contextual detail that can inform the sampling decisions for studies using a variety of different approaches to explore voluntary action.

Conclusion

Since the publication of our 2014 article, I have been involved in several mixed-method and interdisciplinary studies of voluntary action and civic engagement that have drawn on MOP writing. While the focus of these studies has been on voluntary action, they have also concerned themselves with method, looking at the way in which the MOA collects, measures and records its data, and how metadata on writers and their writing can be accessed by those undertaking research into voluntary action. During this time, some of the flaws of the archive – such as its lack of measurement of writers with protected characteristics – have felt like frustrating barriers to use of the archive. However, the MOA's recent decision to start measuring protected characteristics of writers, the ongoing digitisation of the collection, the introduction of a new database of MOP writers and writing, all mean that the MOP has become a more accessible, relevant resource to those seeking to undertake research into voluntary action.

A final point to note is that research that uses MOP writing always involves the creation of new data. Research Councils UK, which fund much academic work in the UK, require *deposition* of newly created data with key repositories such as the UK Data Service. However, there is a strong case for researchers reusing MOP writing to deposit any newly created digital materials (particularly transcriptions of writing, but also copies of analyses) with the MOA, to enable their reuse by future researchers.

Acknowledgements

Many thanks to: Daiga Kamerāde for quantitative analyses of the contemporary writer's panel and work on the new database; Ian Waldock for work on the new database; Sarah Bulloch for initial work on sampling the panel in 2012; Christina Silver for expertise in CAQDAS and work on the Your Life Line directive; Kirsty Pattrick and Jessica Scantlebury from the MOA for help, support and advice on all funded and unfunded research; MOA volunteers for work on collating data from biographical forms; the trustees of the MOA for their support of our various projects; and the Economic and Social Research Council for funding projects ES/K003550/1 and ES/L013819/1.

Further reading

- Work by Sheridan and colleagues (2000) represents a key source for understanding MOP writers and writing.
- Stanley (1981) is an excellent source for anyone considering using writing from the early MO collection.
- Lindsey and Mohan's (2018) longitudinal mixed-methods study should be a starting point for people using the MOP to research voluntary action.

9

Investigating meanings and messages on volunteering through television media

Kimberly Wiley

Introduction

Pop culture messages, specifically those on television, shape our perceptions of the activities taking place in the real world. We absorb cultural messages each time we engage with media. Television and movies have been used to teach leadership through *Game of Thrones* (Yu and Campbell, 2020), ethical decision making through *The Good Place* and *The Avengers* (Bharath, 2019; Meyer, 2020) and the ins and outs of local government through *Parks and Recreation* (Borry, 2018). Similar to Pautz's analysis of US government portrayed across Academy Award-winning films (2017), I looked broadly across television series to discover how volunteering is portrayed and the messages we absorb. A dataset of 131 television storylines of volunteering was developed for two analyses: one exploring what volunteer managers can learn from television portrayals, and the second capturing the paradox of coercive or mandatory volunteering.

Television messages offer more uniformity and longitudinal consistency than other pop culture messaging, such as social media and film, because they offer space for character development, and characters have a greater number of experiences. Television storylines as data allow us to capture multiple views of a single voluntary act or series of acts from the volunteer, the volunteer supervisor and the beneficiary. We can also observe the volunteers' discussions with friends and family and their inner monologues. These conversations provide us the opportunity to view and interpret the voluntary act itself.

Television provides insight into how society views volunteering and is an interpretive, and even fun, way to study behaviour (McKee, 2003). Television storylines offer multiple avenues to explore the motivations and intentionality in voluntary actions. For instance, characters engaging in coercive volunteering portrayed multidimensional layers of motivations for completing their hours. The motivations moved beyond compulsory to include instrumental, civically oriented and sometimes nefarious impulses. Volunteers are portrayed as driven by complex internal reasoning rather than external incentives and consequences. Of course, these are fictional stories, but the messages reflect societal understandings of volunteering. We mimic and expect what we observe in pop culture messaging in real life (Gerbner et al, 1986; Appel, 2008). To complete an ethnographic study with human subjects at the same scale would require a large amount of time, an enormous research team and hundreds of subjects. Ample participation in such an endeavour is unlikely. Television storylines serve as texts, and textual analysis provides the tools for potential sense-making of viewers' practices (McKee, 2003).

Overall, television portrayals of volunteering emphasise the effect of the act on the volunteer. The volunteer is centre stage so much that the storylines often exclude the beneficiary of the voluntary service and the volunteer coordinator. Coercive volunteering is commonplace on television and is frequently portrayed as burdensome or punishment. If non-profit leaders responsible for managing volunteers better understand the messaging volunteers receive before beginning their service, they may be better able to orient volunteers to the tasks more efficiently and effectively. Volunteer coordinators could better align tasks with the volunteer's perceived needs. In this chapter, I present the methodological approach to a textual analysis of volunteering as portrayed on US television. I also explore the challenges to data collection and how credibility in the dataset and analysis was ensured. I conclude with recommendations for applying this interpretive method to other areas of interest in voluntary sector research.

Interpretive analysis of television portrayals of volunteering

Building a dataset

The unit of analysis was the television storyline. Storylines were labelled as 'cases' in the qualitative analysis software. To be included in this dataset, the terms 'volunteer', 'volunteering', 'community service' or 'service learning' must be stated in the script or episode description. Storylines were excluded from the dataset if the script (presented in closed captioning) or episode description were unclear on whether the workers in the storyline were volunteers. To be included, each case captured a portrayal of volunteering rather than simply mentioning one of the specific terms. The storyline or case may be as short as one scene in an episode (for example, *NCIS*, Season 16, Episode 8) or as long as the plotline for an entire series (for example, *The Guardian*). Some storylines were captured across a season, (for example, *The Wire*, Season 5 and *Good Girls*, Season 1).

I aimed for comparability across cases by setting boundaries around the scope of storylines captured (Yin, 1989). The storylines had to meet five specifications to be included in the dataset:

- aired on US television between 1990 and 2020;
- television rating of TV-PG, TV-PG14 or TV-MA;
- fiction or reality television;
- television series with at least one full season (including productions from streaming services like Netflix);
- portrayal must capture planned and intentional volunteering activities that would likely be overseen by a supervisor, such as a non-profit employee, which excludes heroic acts by superheroes.

Data collection

Nine undergraduate research assistants were recruited to gather storylines. Applicants must have been self-proclaimed 'binge-watchers' via online streaming channels, which ensured that assistants were familiar with accessing television shows online. The recruitment tool is presented in Box 9.1. These assistants worked in small groups to identify storylines in their preferred genre of television. In the second round of data collection, two additional undergraduate students were recruited. The purpose of the second round of data collection was to expand the subset of storylines about court-ordered community service and school-based service learning, two forms of coercive volunteering.

Box 9.1: Assistant researcher recruitment message

Are you looking for a way make use of all those hours of binge watching? Here's your chance! Researcher seeks TV binge-watching undergraduate students to help with research project.

Who may help? Currently enrolled undergraduate students who (1) are avid television viewers via streaming channels such as Netflix, Hulu, Prime Video, and YouTube, and (2) participate in, or at least have an interest in, social justice efforts.

What's in it for you? If selected to participate, you will build qualitative data collection and analysis skills. As a thank you gift for your contribution, you will be provided lunch and $35 Amazon gift card.

What will you do? Student groups of four will work collectively to identify, document, and interpret television episodes. You'll locate television episodes on a specified topic, watch all or part of the identified television episodes, document episode identification information in an electronic survey form, and interpret messaging and behaviour in television episodes. Laptop computers will be available for use or you may use your own.

When and Where? Sessions will take place at [dates and location provided].

To be invited to participate, complete this form [weblink provided]. [The Research Coordinator] will contact you if you are selected. Email any questions you may have to [email address provided].

Assistants were instructed to locate ten episodes in their assigned genre per data-collection session. Six genres were included: action/adventure, animated, comedy, crime, drama and reality television. First, assistants recalled storylines from their personal viewing history. The group setting promoted conversation that helped to trigger memories of storylines they had previously watched. Assistants also contacted friends and family for ideas of storylines or to jog their memory. Once their memory was exhausted, they conducted internet searches, such as, 'Gilmore Girls AND volunteer AND episode' to locate an episode description.

I aimed for a balance in the quantity of shows for each genre. If a show had multiple storylines on volunteering and the coding was similar across the storylines, only one or two storylines were included in the dataset, so as not to skew the results towards the plotline of one television series. Assistants logged 131 episodes of television storylines. After removing duplicates and storylines that did not meet all five specifications, 103 episodes remained for the broad study of television storylines on volunteering. Round two of the data collection identified 15 additional episodes specifically about community service or school-based service learning, bringing the total cases for this subset to 43. Gathering a large quantity of storylines allowed for saturation to occur within genres. For instance, animation shows commonly portrayed volunteering as punishment to be leveraged for monetary gain. Reality shows regularly presented volunteering as an opportunity for the privileged to learn about others in society outside their bubble of wealth.

Once a storyline was identified, assistants watched it on their own devices and recorded show identification information and observations, such as the volunteer's behaviours during the voluntary act. The codebooks presented in Table 9.1 and Table 9.2 provided a standardised method of capturing information across diverse shows and genres. A graduate assistant and I screened contributions to the dataset in real time to correct coding errors or redirect assistants where necessary.

Method of analysis

The breadth of data captured for interpretation makes this analysis similar to conducting an ethnography: the researcher observes behaviour in narrow cultural settings over time to explain structure and cultural meaning

(Geertz, 1973a). The researchers observed hundreds of scripted interactions between individuals in the context of voluntary action. These scripts and directed interactions were interpreted through textual analysis. This form of sense-making allowed the team to analyse 'how the texts tell the story' of volunteering (McKee, 2003).

The analysis took place in three steps. Each step in the coding process required multiple viewers to establish a uniform interpretation of the evidence. Some storylines were viewed up to four times to ensure the storyline was fully captured and appropriate for the study.

Step 1: Locate and document show and volunteer attributes

After locating the show, the researcher collected the Internet Movie Database (IMDb) information to categorise the show in terms of genre and audience. The first round of viewing and coding was primarily for attribute coding and to gather information such as the identity of the volunteer, volunteer supervisor and beneficiary (Saldaña, 2015). Commentary on voluntary action was transcribed as presented in the closed captioning. A structuralist approach to coding was conducted in Step 1 as we identified deep structures that might not be obvious to the viewer (McKee, 2003), such as identifying the actors involved in the voluntary act (volunteer, beneficiary and volunteer coordinator) and defining the context of the service and value to the beneficiary. This stage of coding was collected with an online survey tool presented in Table 9.1.

Step 2: Theoretical interpretation: capturing messages and meanings

Second, the researcher added theoretically driven codes by capturing expressed motivations for volunteering. The coding was captured by research assistants in the online survey tool, which also included space for fieldnotes. Textual analysis was used to interpret evidence of perceptions of the voluntary action in the television scenes, such as quotes and behavioural observations (McKee, 2003; Cushing, 2018). Table 9.2 presents a codebook used for interpreting meaning and messages and reflects a post-structuralist approach as we looked for differences across the texts (McKee, 2003). NVivo qualitative analysis software was engaged for Step 2 of coding and analysis. Heavily coding observations and transcripts allowed for lumping and splitting the codes later (Saldaña, 2015). For instance, additional types of coercive volunteering emerged: parents forcing their children to volunteer, businesses sending their employees to give back to the community during their work hours and religious obligations to be charitable.

The researchers attempted to capture changes in the characters resulting from their volunteering experiences by documenting two points in time and

Table 9.1: Example of storyline attribute codebook

Question	Question type	Answer choices
Coder's name	Open	
TV show title	Open	
Season number	Open	
Episode name	Open	
Episode number	Open	
Air date	Closed	
Show origination (producer)	Closed	Network TV Cable TV Streaming channel
Streaming channel	Closed	Netflix Hulu Amazon Prime video YouTubeTV Disney+ Other
Genre	Open	
Maturity rating	Closed	TV-Y TV-Y7 TV-G TVPG TV-14 MA

labelling perceptions as positive and negative for the volunteer, volunteer supervisor and beneficiary. Not all storylines were this cut and dry, though. When storylines were brief, there was little evidence of change. On the other hand, lengthy storylines demonstrated winding evolutions in perceptions. For instance, *The Guardian* is about a high-powered corporate attorney sentenced to perform community service at a legal aid clinic where he deals with cases of family law. In the pilot, the attorney showed disdain for his mandated community service and was like a fish out of water in the family courts. But by the end of the three-season series he had left his high-paying corporate job and taken over as executive director at the legal aid organisation. The journey evolved with big shifts in character development, but ultimately the lead gained an appreciation for his community service. Throughout the dataset, changes in the character who volunteered were often easy to observe. Changes in the volunteer manager and beneficiary were not as easy to capture, because the storylines typically emphasised the volunteer's experience and perspective. By limiting the analysis to three key components of volunteering (volunteer, intermediary and beneficiary), we limited the number of sense-making positions to three (McKee, 2003).

Table 9.2: Example of codebook for theoretical analysis

Name	Description
Volunteer	Character performing voluntary act or community service
Character building	Does the character change/improve as a result of the service?
Driver	What does the lead character in the storyline express as the main driver or motivation (civic duty, instrumental, to impress someone, nefarious, entertainment)?
Civic duty	Personal obligation to the community or to public service ('it's the right thing to do')
Entertainment	Systemic pursuit of a leisure activity, where individuals can find a non-work career ('serious leisure', volunteer tourism, coaching kids' sports team, organising a cultural event)
Instrumental	Volunteering for personal benefit, but not for monetary gain (experience for building résumé or to learn skills, to meet new people)
Nefarious or malicious	Posing as a volunteer in order to cause harm to a person, animal, group, or the environment
To impress someone	Person volunteers to gain attention from a romantic interest or members of a clique (for example, participating in beach clean-up to gain acceptance of the popular crowd; distributing food at the soup kitchen to demonstrate charity and generosity to a potential date).
Role of volunteer in storyline	Who is the volunteer (main character, supporting character)?
Experience of volunteer	Volunteering is a positive/negative experience for the volunteer. Capture at beginning of volunteer service (Point A) and end of service (Point B).
Intermediary	Person who oversees the volunteer's activities (for example, volunteer coordinator, supervisor)
Job assigner	Who determines how the TV character volunteers (court official, self, employer, volunteer manager, unknown)?
Task manager or supervisor	Who is the intermediary (volunteer manager, church leader, medical provider, school personnel, unknown)?
Experience of intermediary	Volunteering is a positive/negative experience for the intermediary. Capture at beginning of volunteer service (Point A) and end of service (Point B).
Beneficiary	Person, animal, environmental space benefiting from voluntary act
Beneficiary type	Who or what is the primary intended beneficiary of the voluntary action (environment, animals, other people, unknown)?
Presence of beneficiary	Where is the beneficiary (present, absent, unknown)?
Experience of beneficiary	Volunteering is a positive/negative experience for the beneficiary. Capture at beginning of volunteer service (Point A) and end of service (Point B).

Table 9.2: Example of codebook for theoretical analysis (continued)

Name	Description
Service	Voluntary act or acts
Category of service	Who is compelling the character to volunteer (school, work, court, other)?
Completion of service	Does the character embrace the assigned work or avoid the assigned work?
Context of service	How does the job assignor or intermediary portray the service? What is the context of service (charity, punishment, learning or character building)?
Length of commitment	Ongoing, episodic, micro-volunteering
Value of service	Value of service (community contribution, personal development)

Step 3: Ensuring credibility

The storylines were added to qualitative analysis software as unique cases for analysis. Theory checking was conducted as themes emerged (Onwuegbuzie and Leech, 2007). Storylines were watched again to confirm the initial conclusions. Some stories stood out more than others, particularly the nefarious behaviour where the volunteer caused harm to the beneficiary. For example, an episode of *Criminal Minds* (Lucky, Season 3, Episode 6) portrayed a murderer serving as a volunteer who fed chili secretly containing the victim's body to a search party combing the woods for her corpse. Work avoidance was a frequent theme in coerced volunteering and it often resulted in further negative actions such as theft, manipulation and physical abuse. These storylines were quite memorable. But, after looking at the dataset as a whole, it was clear that a majority of the examples of volunteering involved positive interactions. Ensuring credibility in the analysis required *corroboration of interpretations*. The team corroborated interpretations through conversation in data-collection sessions and by comparing fieldnotes and coding. Running matrix and crosstab queries in the qualitative analysis software helped to theory-check the conclusions drawn from the singular powerful stories and avoid *illusory correlation*, or where one powerful storyline leads researchers to identify relationships between variables where none exist (Onwuegbuzie and Leech, 2007).

Demonstration: coding television storylines

In this section, I present three examples of the coding process and data interpretation. These three storylines share a common volunteering context: youth sports coaching. The television genres, motivations for

Table 9.3: Coding TV shows portraying volunteer youth sports coaching

Television show (year aired, genre)	Storyline length	Motivation	Character development	Evidence of perceptions of volunteering
Coach Snoop (2018, Reality TV/ documentary)	Series	Civic duty	Volunteer builds beneficiaries' character	"Music gave me the power to create a football league. But football is taking me to places that music could've never took me to: to be a mentor, a leader, a role model." (Coach Snoop) "I feel like because I touched so many people personally this year, [the league] would be the shining moment of my legacy. Ain't no telling what we could do." (Coach Snoop)
It's Always Sunny in Philadelphia (2006, comedy)	Episode	Coercive volunteering via court-ordered community service	Bad behaviour of volunteers is worsened	"Oh, come on! This isn't fair. You accidently burn down a building and you get 120 hours of community service?" (Mac) "I would rather pay a huge fine than have to give back to the community." (Mac) The coaches curse, insult the players, use racial stereotypes, assault each other, teach how to commit a foul and harm the other team's players, manipulate the players, give the players Red Bull and gamble on the game.
Criminal Minds (2011, crime)	2 brief scenes	Civic duty, guilt	Main character aims to prioritise family over work and volunteers to coach his son's team	The sunny, cheerful tone at the soccer field is in stark contrast to the sombre, dark tone of the rest of the episode. Hotchner and Rossi joyfully coach and cheer from the sideline, giving high fives and encouraging smiles to the team. Upbeat music plays loudly.

volunteering and lengths of the storylines differ across the cases. Table 9.3 presents a side-by-side comparison of the coding of the shows.

Coach Snoop

This documentary-style reality television show portrays the 501(c)3 non-profit organisation Snoop Youth Football League, founded by rapper Snoop Dogg. *Coach Snoop* aired two seasons with a total of 15 episodes on Netflix.

The voluntary action is the core plot of the series: Coach Snoop volunteers to run a sports league for at-risk youth. According to the US Internal Review Services Forms 990, Coach Snoop does not receive payment for his role in the organisation. Through volunteering, he leverages his life experiences and wealth to improve the lives of youths with similar childhood experiences to his own. In the pilot episode, the coaching staff expressed how the main goal was to "keep the boys off the streets" by participating in youth football. The viewer can observe Coach Snoop's demeanour shift from the marijuana-smoking rapper Snoop Dogg to a coach responsible for building the character of his players. He describes the strategies he uses to ensure the youth football players (the beneficiaries) are the focus of the game, not him (the volunteer):

'I like to show up at game time. No need for me to be out there an hour before the game. So when I come off of whatever I'm coming off of, whether it's a show or DJ gig, I'm going out there focused and not turning it into a photo frenzy or a Snoop Dogg concert. I'm here coaching. So when I do get to the game, I'm all about the kids and the time I have with them.' (*Coach Snoop*, Season 1, Episode 1)

The idea of using one's financial wealth to help others was a theme in the reality television genre, but Coach Snoop also invested his social and cultural wealth in his voluntary service, "Music gave me the power to create a football league. But football is taking me to places that music could've never took me to: to be a mentor, a leader, a role model" (*Coach Snoop*, Season 1, Episode 1). By interpreting the discourse between the coaches, players and community members, one can observe how Coach Snoop centralised his voluntary role as mentor to the youths in his programme. Volunteering is portrayed as a meaningful way to give back to the community.

It's Always Sunny in Philadelphia

It's Always Sunny in Philadelphia parodies dysfunctional American life. All characters in the show are considered unethical people for various reasons. In the episode 'The Gang Gives Back' (Season 2, Episode 6), the lead characters are court-ordered to perform community service and are assigned to coach in a youth basketball league in Philadelphia. This assignment provides an opportunity for the show to further demonstrate the characters' poor judgement and unethical behaviour. Over a series of team practices and a game, the volunteers continue to act badly, teaching the players to injure the other team and gambling on the game until they are reassigned by the court to 'interstate sanitation' (otherwise known as highway litter clean-up). Community service is portrayed as something to manipulate or escape, a common theme in comedy shows portraying coerced volunteering: more work is put into avoiding community service than simply completing the assigned task. In the comedy and animation genres, a typical response to coerced volunteering is captured in a quote from Mac in this episode: "I would rather pay a huge fine than have to give back to the community." Charitable acts were portrayed as sound punishment for the volunteer, but often the volunteer passes the punishment on to the volunteer supervisor and the beneficiary. In *It's Always Sunny in Philadelphia*, observing how the youth basketball players (the beneficiaries) become pawns in the game between the lead characters' pranks against each other helped to make sense of how community service is perceived. When the volunteer gains power over the intermediary or beneficiary, they use that power to punish or cause harm.

Criminal Minds

Though the plot of *Criminal Minds* is hunting America's most sadistic criminals, the show does include a few episodes addressing volunteerism. In 'Out of the Light' (Season 6, Episode, 22), the hard-working investigative team's leader, Agent Hotchner, is shamed into coaching his son's soccer team by another team parent. The episode opens with Agent Hotchner cheering during his young son's game and ends with him coaching from the sideline with Agent Rossi. In this case, pure content analysis was not as helpful in capturing perceptions of volunteering in the show. More meaning is communicated non-verbally between Hotchner and Rossi through eye contact and dramatic pauses than in the scripted lines. The opening and closing scenes of Hotchner's son's soccer games were shorter than the two conversations about volunteering that took place in the Federal Bureau of Investigation's (FBI) headquarters and the FBI's jet that returned the agents from their on-site investigation. The location of the scenes emphasised the volunteer, not the beneficiary. This portrayal of volunteering re-emphasised the good nature of the lead characters: Hotchner cared about his son and Rossi cared about his colleague. In this case, volunteering symbolises leadership and good character, though it is motivated through guilt (Nichols et al, 2019).

The same act, coaching youth sports, is portrayed in drastically different ways in these three episodes and required variations in the analysis. Volunteer coaching was centralised and portrayed as mentorship to help build the character of the players in *Coach Snoop*, with discourse analysis being the most useful. *It's Always Sunny in Philadelphia* portrayed volunteer coaching as punishment, with overt mocking of the activity. This storyline benefited from analysis of behaviour and interactions between characters. *Criminal Minds* used volunteer coaching in a sub-plot to further portray a character's leadership abilities. Interpretations of staging and the scene location were most useful to the textual analysis. All three portrayals showed how volunteer coaching could develop the character of the volunteer, each with different outcomes for the coaches and players. Combining these analyses reflects a pseudo-ethnography where we learn through observation and interpretation.

Building a dataset on volunteering with binge-watching students

Strengths

Gathering a wide breadth of storylines across genres, decades, television parental ratings and television channels and streaming services resulted in a nuanced view of perspectives on how volunteering is understood at a societal level. Volunteer managers and beneficiaries were often absent from the storylines, indicating that television presents (and, implicitly, society understands) the value of the voluntary action as belonging to the volunteer. The number of nefarious activities occurring during compulsory community service or service-learning indicated a cynical view of voluntary action and those involved. When making sense of portrayals of volunteering in pop culture, we can identify nuance within types of volunteering and settings.

The project was a playful way to teach qualitative methods to undergraduate students. Students brought with them the basic definitions and concepts associated with qualitative research. They applied their knowledge and built skills in capturing relevant media and engaging in interpretation. The data-gathering sessions began with a brief lesson on qualitative research and voluntary action as well as practice in interpreting three storylines. The project exposed students to a social science lab setting where they gained qualitative analysis skills like translating observations into data and setting boundaries around cases or units of analysis. Because the assistants were not human subjects within the study, institutional review board approval was not required for this study. On the first day, one assistant exclaimed, 'This is fun! I've always wanted to be a part of a research study!' He returned for a second session and helped to coach his peers. Interpreting fictional characters gave the researchers more time with the data and the ability to re-watch interactions as many times as was necessary to capture meaning and messages.

Limitations

Aside from the obvious fictional nature of the data, other limitations are accounted for in the analysis. First, training interdisciplinary teams of undergraduate research assistants in ethnography and textual analysis while ensuring inter-rater reliability came with challenges. Assistants needed to learn qualitative skills and the coding strategy. For instance, the team spent time discussing the logistical differences between Wonder Woman volunteering to save the day versus a student volunteering at the soup kitchen for school credit. First, ensuring credibility in the data required a strong codebook, *intercoder reliability* checks, and an understanding of when saturation had been reached (Onwuegbuzie and Leech, 2007). The data were reviewed for *completeness and accuracy* by the researcher and a graduate assistant in real time as data were collected, ensuring a meaningful dataset but slow data collection.

Second, portrayals of volunteering became repetitive. For instance, the genre of comedy included an abundance of storylines on volunteering, but these were thematically similar in motivations for and behaviour during volunteering, such as the reluctant volunteer who makes themselves the centre of attention through humour. Animated shows parodying American life often portrayed characters as dodging voluntary work. A great deal of effort was devoted to repeatedly viewing similar storylines as the dataset moved closer to saturation. When the data representing a genre of shows resulted in repetitive coding, we moved on to build out another genre. To address this limitation of quick saturation within genres, I grouped assistants based on viewing interests and directed them towards different genres such as crime or reality television (Onwuegbuzie and Leech, 2007).

Conclusion

Clearly, these stories of volunteering are not real. The characters are fictional, and their interactions are carefully crafted by screenwriters and directors. The banter is written to solicit the appropriate reaction from the target audience. Satirical television tells stories of an extreme nature, often disturbing in ways that exude an eyeroll or even dismay. Comedy writers present the humour in each situation. But, in all storylines, a lesson is present. For instance, strong leaders will continue to set a good example when asked to volunteer, as with Agent Hotchner in *Criminal Minds*. People who normally behave badly will continue to behave badly when volunteering, as in *It's Always Sunny in Philadelphia*. As Maya Angelou famously said, 'When someone shows you who they are, believe them the first time.' Like real people, on-screen characters are predictable. Interpreting volunteering on television allows us to see the volunteer behaviour in the context of the characters' lives as presented throughout the other episodes. The long-term existence of the character offers richness to the interpretation of their actions and attitudes and provides depth for employing Geertz's (1973) concept of thick description within popular media.

This playful way to study volunteering could be expanded in a number of ways. First, an important next step in this line of inquiry would be to run experimental studies gauging viewers' actual perceptions of individual scenes or storylines to compare with scholarly interpretations. Second, the dataset could be extended to include television shows from other countries. A comparison between regional portrayals of volunteering would tell us how the voluntary sector is perceived differently. Third, this interpretive method of analysis can be applied to other concepts of the voluntary sector. We came across numerous storylines on monetary or in-kind giving rather than giving of one's time (*Lucifer*, Season 1, Episode 11). Studying portrayals of the voluntary sector broadly would offer insight into how and why individuals engage with voluntary organisations through giving, volunteering or seeking services (*The Wire*, Season 5). Class and symbolism could be captured through portrayals of the wealthy interacting with the working-class and the poor and how the wealthy define 'giving back' (*Keeping up with the Kardashians*, Season 14, Episode 10). Whatever your question about behaviour and motivation in the voluntary sector, television may provide a useful tool for inquiry.

Further reading
- McKee (2003) offers step-by-step instructional tools for textual analysis.
- Using television in the classroom brings variety and depth to online or face-to-face pedagogy (Borry, 2018).
- Alaimo (2016) assesses pop culture depictions of philanthropy across TV and film and presents his findings in a documentary.

Appendix: Television shows
'A Very Kardashian Holiday' (2015) *Keeping up with the Kardashians*, Season 10, Episode 10. Hulu, 26 November.
'Friendly Fire' (2018) *NCIS*, Season 16, Episode 8. CBS, 20 November.
Good Girls (2018) Season 1. Netflix, 26 February.
'Lucky' (2007) *Criminal Minds*, Season 3, Episode 8. Netflix, 14 November.
'Out of the Light' (2011) *Criminal Minds*, Season 6, Episode 22. Netflix, 4 May.
'St. Lucifer' (2016) *Lucifer*, Season 1, Episode 11. Netflix, 11 April.
'The Gang Gives Back' (2006) *It's Always Sunny in Philadelphia*, Season 2, Episode 6. Hulu, 20 July.
The Wire (2008) Season 5. Amazon Prime, 6 January.
'To Live and Die in LA' (2018) *Coach Snoop*, Season 1, Episode 1. Netflix, 2 February.

10

Annual reporting in voluntary organisations: opportunities for content analysis research

Carolyn Cordery and Danielle McConville

Introduction

Across the world, charities and voluntary organisations face increased public expectations of transparency and, perhaps relatedly, increased requirements to file annual reports with regulators. This reporting includes not only financial data, illuminating the financial position and sustainability of these organisations, but also, critically for this sector, a range of (non-financial and narrative) performance information that can help us to evaluate these organisations' progress towards their missions. In many countries this data has also become more accessible: often publicly available at no cost from regulators and/or other intermediaries.

In this chapter we argue that annual reporting data represents a potential goldmine for researchers seeking to understand the fundamentals of voluntary organisations and the sector at large, especially for organisations registered as charities. We reflect on our own 'journey' in researching an article using content analysis of annual reporting data to understand international regulatory approaches. A key aspect of that journey involved building on past research in the area for our research design. In this chapter we use this example and other recent research to highlight opportunities and challenges for further research.

We use the term content analysis loosely to cover a range of analysis types of information that may take a variety of forms, including quantitative and qualitative information. This chapter does not seek to redefine content analysis – the following sections demonstrate that the term is used quite broadly in prior research. Content analysis is widely used in for-profit ('capital market') studies, with researchers often utilising large databases and statistical methods to search for explanations of cause and effect. We show how similar methods have been replicated in the voluntary sector by researchers using mandatory regulatory (often financial) data to answer a range of questions on matters as diverse as performance, governance, regulation and organisational practices. We also show how smaller-sample content analysis has been used to explore what charities report (financial and non-financial), and, when such reporting is voluntary (as is often the case for performance information), why they have reported in this way, and the implications of this. As this book highlights innovations in voluntary sector research, we focus on relevant studies published in accounting and voluntary sector journals in the decade since 2010.

The balance of this chapter provides a definition of annual reporting; a reflection on our own and others' use of content analysis, especially of annual reporting; opportunities and challenges arising; and a short list of further resources. The chapter concludes with a call for further research to help us understand, safeguard and promote voluntary organisations in pursuit of their missions.

What is annual reporting and is it regulated?

Annual reporting takes many forms, including financial and (non-financial/ narrative) performance information. Financial information may be provided in financial statements: these are often akin to commercial financial statements, including a statement of income and expenditure for the year and a statement of assets and liabilities at the year end. Alternatively, financial information may be given via a standardised form or return that is not in financial statement format – an example is the United States (US) Form 990, an annual return focused on financial data that must be completed by organisations seeking non-profit tax exemptions. In either case, the data is ripe for content analysis to search for explanations of cause and effect between different financial variables. Conversely, performance reporting includes reports on operations and performance towards the organisation's mission. These are usually written by the board chair/trustees/senior staff, and employ very different communication methods to financial reporting, including narratives, metrics, photos and case study examples. Performance reporting can be analysed critically for the messages sent (Dhanani and Connolly, 2012) and to enable an assessment of the voluntary organisation's performance in terms of outputs and outcomes (Hyndman and McConville, 2016, 2018; McConville and Cordery, 2018). Finally, some reporting combines financial and performance components, in order to fully inform readers about the voluntary organisation in an 'annual report'. Analysing this fuller annual report data allows, for example, activity and impact to be aligned to size or expenditure (McConville and Cordery, 2018).

Voluntary organisations may be required to undertake annual reporting, or may choose to report voluntarily. Reporting may be mandatory due to legislation (as in the United Kingdom (UK)), accreditation agency requirements (as in the Netherlands) or through tax authorities if the organisation seeks favourable tax treatment (as in the US). Such mandatory requirements have historically focused on financial reporting. Additionally, organisations may choose to report voluntarily, including financial reports (Haski-Leventhal and Foot, 2016) and, increasingly, wider performance-related information (Dhanani and Connolly, 2012; Hyndman and McConville, 2016, 2018). The article we use to reflect on our own 'journey' of using content analysis considered both mandatory (UK) annual reports and voluntarily provided performance reporting from Australia, New Zealand (NZ) and the US, as we now highlight.

Our research

We are both chartered accountants, having worked in practice and undertaken doctoral studies on issues faced by charities. Having completed previous research in the areas of regulation and reporting in the UK and NZ, respectively, we became interested in the attempts being made in various countries to either mandate or encourage charities to report on their performance. With the intention of writing a series of papers, our first paper used entirely desk-based methods: utilising regulatory theories and empirical research, combined with (sometimes substantial) quantities of publicly available information on how a range of countries were developing regulations. We theorised a continuum of possible regulatory approaches. These ranged from a 'command and control' type of approach proposed in Australia, where there is a legislative or regulatory code, the use of audits and sanctions, and that emphasises standard (numerical) measures, to a 'market Regulation' approach in the US, which encourages self-regulation and an information 'market' driven by comparators, and a 'new governance' approach (seen in the UK and NZ), which emphasises partnership in self- or co-regulation and education, sitting somewhere in the middle (McConville and Cordery, 2018). We discussed possible implications of each approach for performance reporting in these countries, and our (at that stage fairly thin) contribution lay in the usefulness of this continuum for charity regulatory policy making.

Maybe unsurprisingly, upon submitting this paper to our preferred journal's conference, reviewers' comments were somewhat mixed, and of these the most substantial is the following: 'What is missing in the paper is examination of reports by charities in these four countries. ... Do their reporting practices differ across the countries? How closely do these reports correspond to the models that are claimed to characterize the reporting in these countries?'

Ah! At first glance, this felt like one of those comments that asks you to improve your paper by writing a different paper, but, once the dust settled, we realised that the continuum, without at least exploratory empirical data to support it, didn't really make much of a contribution. So, we were challenged to include some empirical data to illustrate the theoretical contribution of the continuum, which the reviewer kindly suggested we should do in an exploratory way, through content analysis of a small sample of reports from each country.

As noted, content analysis has been widely used in previous studies of publicly available information of charities and voluntary organisations (although research into charities has historically dominated – as discussed further later on). To give a sense of the types of questions and the data, methods and theories used to answer these, we provide some recent examples of large-scale content analysis, which is mainly undertaken on mandatory data, as well as smaller-scale analysis that often includes information provided voluntarily.

Exploring recent content analysis research

Echoing the cause-and-effect analysis used in for-profit 'capital market' studies, many scholars, especially in the US, have used large-scale, quantitative analysis of mandatory disclosures to answer a range of questions about charities and voluntary organisations. Related to our study, many use such analysis to identify whether certain characteristics are associated with better charity performance, with financial efficiency often being a proxy for performance. Financial efficiency measures used include fundraising expenditure/total funds raised (fundraising ratio), programme expenditure/total expenditure (programme ratio) and/or overhead (or administration) expenditure/total expenditure (overhead/administration ratio). These are based on the argument that donors are interested in their donations being spent 'efficiently' on the cause, and that different entities' 'performance' in this regard can be compared. Despite being a poor proxy of charities' impact and being able to be manipulated (see, for example, Eckerd, 2015), they are readily analysed.

Size is a variable in these studies. Van der Heijden (2013) used data from 1,196 registered fundraising charities from the Dutch Central Bureau for Fundraising for 2005–09, finding that larger charities tend to spend a higher percentage in order to raise €1 than smaller charities do, leaving a smaller percentage of income to deliver programmes. Conversely (and using a much larger US dataset), Ecer et al (2017) identified economies of scale in their content analysis on 97,040 Form 990 returns for 2003. However, they noted that entities earning more than 50% of their income ('social enterprises') managed their overhead and administrative expenses better than those that earned less than 50% of their income ('traditional charities').

Others have also considered the effect of funding source on charities: Lu and Zhao (2019) considered whether efficiency is linked with government funding. Their content analysis of 704 organisations' financial statements filed with the US Agency for International Development (4,884 observations from 1995 to 2014) concluded two relationships from this donor-mandated data. First, that resource-dependence theory explains an increase in administrative costs when voluntary organisations must invest in infrastructure and managerial sophistication, due to the government's funding. Second, as the percentage of government funding increases, interdependence (economies of scale and the accountability control) results in a curvilinear relationship: 'operating efficiency' (low administrative expenses) could therefore occur in voluntary organisations with low or high levels of government funding.

Closely related to these studies, some researchers have charted changes in the reported financial positions of charities, elucidating concerns about the capacity and sustainability of these organisations. Indeed, Lecy and Searing (2015) argue that the publicly proclaimed negative sentiments towards administration and overhead costs have led to a 'nonprofit starvation cycle', where expenditure is cut to meet donor expectations, but that eventually leads to starving 'productive capacity'. Undertaking content analysis of US Form 990 returns (between 6,000 and 16,900 filed from 1985 to 2007), Lecy and Searing (2015) show that reported overheads reduced from 20.9% to 18.3%, noting concern that reductions in overhead expenditure impair the long-term effectiveness of voluntary organisations. Schubert and Boenigk (2019) indicate this is not only a US issue, using German data from the Central Institute for Social Issues, an independent charity-accreditation agency. Their content analysis of ten years of fundraising charitable organisations' financial statements (2,062 from 2006–2015) identified that the greatest decline in overhead expenses was among charities that do not receive government funding; but, dissimilar to Lecy and Searing (2015), they also found falling fundraising expenses and rising staff costs. It is apparent that issues of performance – especially financial performance – and its relationship with different types of funding and spending warrant more research, especially in non-US contexts.

Questions of governance arrangements have also been explored. McAllister and Allen (2017) applied agency theory to their content analysis of US Form 990s from 188 private foundations over five years (2001–05), finding that founders' (and related family members') board involvement ensured efficiency, but that this effect reduces as second- and third-generation family members become involved. In the Netherlands, Perego and Verbeeten (2015) analysed whether recommendations of a voluntary 'good governance' code motivated better reporting in their content analysis of 516 financial reports (of 138 charities from 2005 to 2008). Contrasting agency and stewardship theories, Perego and Verbeeten (2015) show charities moving towards the recommended arrangements of an independent board, increased disclosure of executives' pay and also lowering executive pay levels, when compared to those without independent governance arrangements.

These studies show the potential for large-scale analysis of mandatory financial disclosures to address a wide range of questions of interest to charity and voluntary sector researchers, including the effects of governance and other organisational practices, and environmental factors. Again, research from different national contexts would be useful.

Another significant body of research has explored *what* charities voluntarily report, using a range of theories to explain why, and the implications for charities and voluntary organisations. Haski-Leventhal and Foot (2016) undertook content analysis of 50 Australian voluntary organisations' disclosures in 2011 and 2012. Signalling theory showed no relationship between household donations and voluntary disclosure, but that every 1% of extra marketing spend by these organisations potentially increased their receipts of household donations by 3.24%.

In most countries, reporting on performance is voluntary, and research in this area often involves collecting data from disparate sources and in different formats rather than from large databases of mandatory financial information. Carlson et al (2010) provide a rare glimpse into the impact of US performance reporting. They analysed 46 children and families' programmes funded by government and delivered by voluntary organisations, using contract, quarterly and annual report data, audit reports, correspondence and data from meetings and legislation to ascertain the impact of new public management reforms. Relevant to this chapter, they analysed the impact of the reported performance measures on the state legislature's funding decisions. Carlson et al (2010) found that voluntary organisations performing well and utilising common performance measures received increased funds, while those reporting unique measures lost funding, even though they performed well. Their findings speak to the classic issues with performance measurement.

Dhanani and Connolly (2012) also use smaller-scale content analysis to ascertain *what* charities report. They analysed the 2006 annual reports and associated (voluntary) annual review (a largely qualitative document prepared by the trustees) of 75 of the 104 largest UK charities. While these two publications should have enabled accountability for actions in line with their public benefit objectives (that is, ethical stakeholder theory), instead, Dhanani and Connolly (2012) found that these charities prioritised positive stakeholder theory – that is, they sought to achieve legitimacy through positive messages about their actions. Hyndman and McConville (2016, 2018) reviewed similar data on the top 100 UK charities for the years 2010–11, augmenting this with content analysis of these charities' websites. Their first content analysis focused on the reporting of efficiency, comparatives and links to objectives. They also found that charities' reporting prioritised legitimacy rather than meeting their public benefit aims, and hypothesised that this was related to the voluntary nature of that reporting (Hyndman and McConville, 2016). Their second article (Hyndman and McConville,

2018) expands the analysis to consider measures of effectiveness and reliability, causality and stakeholder involvement. While charities reported more performance information than in the period covered by Dhanani and Connolly (2012), the absence of explanations, comparatives and information to help the reader to judge the reliability of what was reported led Hyndman and McConville (2018) to suggest that transparency levels remained low, indicating legitimacy seeking rather than ethical voluntary reporting.

These studies into *what* is reported suggest a close linkage to *why* it is reported and the potential to combine content analysis with a range of theories to develop better understanding of *why* charities report as they do.

A major benefit of content analysis is its flexibility in the forms of data that can be analysed, but also in its potential to be combined with other methods, including interviews, surveys and case studies. As an example, Cordery et al (2011) examined primary healthcare organisations in NZ where the government funder required these to be 'not-for-profit' but did not mandate public reporting. Cordery et al's (2011) content analysis of the financial statements of 19 of these entities showed that these organisations managed their surpluses to indicate a 'not-for-profit' status. Case study material from other documents, interviews and observations provided granularity to these findings, with the researchers noting that organisations dependent on communities' voluntary contributions were more attuned to community health needs, while others, developed from for-profit entities, struggled to engage their communities in resolving community health issues. At larger scale, Parsons et al (2017) utilised a combination of US Form 990 content analysis and completed surveys from 115 voluntary organisations' executives to confirm that managers manipulate financial ratios, albeit for reasons linked to managerial character rather than resource dependence.

These studies highlight the range of information voluntarily provided by charities in documents variously described as annual reports, annual reviews and other terms, and on their websites. Information that is readily publicly available online, either from regulators' or charities' own websites, has dramatically increased, facilitating further research that provides a more holistic view of charities' performance. Thus, there is significant potential to engage with broader questions on the effect of regulation, governance and organisational practices on such performance.

Reflection on our research

For the research we undertook and on which this chapter includes a reflection, we wanted to understand whether differences in regulatory approaches had an impact on the resulting charity performance reporting. In particular, we sought to understand if there were differences in what was reported, how much was reported and how transparent the reporting was. In designing our content analysis, we needed to address a number of key considerations.

Firstly, our sample: we undertook a substantial piece of work to understand the various requirements and recommendations in four countries. The differences we observed represent a substantial initial barrier in making international comparisons across charities and voluntary organisations: we would expect to see substantial differences in reporting practices where reporting of items was mandatory (UK) versus recommended/voluntary (US), for example. A complication in our research was that both Australian and NZ regulation were still in development at the time of our study, such that reporting was effectively voluntary in both jurisdictions (that is, the command–and–control (Australia) and new governance (NZ) regulation was not yet impacting on reporting practices. A further, larger study in three or four years' time would enable us to observe the impact of new regulation, but for this research we took an exploratory approach using ten organisations per country. While such a small sample couldn't be fully representative, we did consider carefully how we could match our sample cases – aware from previous research that organisational characteristics such as size and mission (Lecy and Searing, 2015; Ecer et al, 2017) significantly impact on reporting levels. Therefore, we chose large voluntary organisations, expecting them to be more capable of producing good reporting (Dhanani and Connolly, 2012; Hyndman and McConville, 2016, 2018). For each country, we selected a sample from the top 100 charities (by donation revenue, thus excluding non-fundraising charities that are subject to different stakeholder pressures) that were primarily involved in overseas aid. While 'overseas aid' is a broad category and includes a wide range of activities, a common factor is donors' inability to observe the impact of donations on geographically distant individuals or societies. In some cases, the same charity operated in each country (for example, Worldvision), in others we matched charities by mission across the four countries (for example, those focussed on child sponsorship, wildlife or religious group-based aid).

Secondly, our data. We utilised the major publicly available communications from these charities: the annual report from the Australian, NZ and UK charities and the annual report augmented by the mandatory Form 990 for the US charities. We accessed this data from either the organisation's or relevant regulator's websites, although some data was more easily accessed than others. For example, in NZ and the UK, a search on the regulator's website returns free, unlimited access to the annual reports and financial statements of any registered charity. By contrast, in Australia, due to the newness of the regulator, financial and performance data was then more readily available from individual charity websites, and in the US we searched both for Form 990 data and the individual charity websites.

Thirdly: analysis. We developed a checklist from previous studies and literature (especially Hyndman and McConville, 2018) to facilitate content analysis. We manually analysed the documents in full to identify the performance-related information, with a deductive, mechanistic content analysis (Beck et al, 2010), identifying which checklist measures were presented (yes/no/quantity), whether these were accompanied by additional information, including explanations and comparisons, and whether stakeholder engagement and 'bad news' were reported. We developed and tested rules of analysis to use during our analysis. Leaning on existing guides on content analysis to maximise reliability of the analysis, we undertook independent coding of measures (such as efficiency/output/outcome measures), then we discussed our positions and agreed coding between ourselves (as recommended by Schreier, 2012). Thus, we developed shared meanings of the checklist items (such as distinguishing between individual and societal outcomes) as per relevant literature (see Krippendorf, 2018); and we revised the checklist during analysis to ensure that rules and definitions were applied rigorously (see Schreier, 2012).

Our analysis highlighted notable differences in reporting across the four countries, even acknowledging the small sample size. Combined with our desk-based research, data analysis supported our broader arguments around the implications of different regulatory approaches for reporting, that is, that new governance approaches are more likely to motivate regulated voluntary organisations to report higher-quality performance information (McConville and Cordery, 2018).

Opportunities and challenges

We have provided an overview of a number of recent articles using content analysis in researching voluntary organisations, as well as brief reflections on our own journey in this space. Now, we turn to the opportunities and challenges of using content analysis.

The strengths of content analysis include that it is well accepted, as is evident by the variety of articles that we have discussed in the preceding sections (noting these are a limited selection). It has supported analyses using a range of theoretical frames: the large financial data content analyses reviewed in this chapter analyse traditional theories, such as agency theory, resource dependence theory and stewardship theory. In addition, these large databases are used to develop new theories that are specific to the voluntary sector, for example Lecy and Searing's (2015) 'nonprofit starvation cycle', which is tested in a different context by Schubert and Boenigk (2019). Smaller-scale studies also draw and build on a range of theories, such as accountability, signalling theory and stakeholder theory.

It is evident that content analysis is suitable for both financial (numerical) and non-financial/narrative performance data and, as such, is a flexible method. Further, although large data analyses typically use mandatory data, smaller-sample content analysis can be undertaken on voluntarily provided information, as well as to develop findings in combination with other data. Indeed, some of the research discussed in this chapter uses content analysis of both mandatory and voluntarily provided information, information that is not generally made public, public information in conjunction with survey analysis, and theoretical analysis of other data (as already noted). It is also an accessible method: in cases where data has been sourced from websites and other databases, content analysis allows for largely unobtrusive analysis that is structured around checklists/research questions (Schreier, 2012; Krippendorf, 2018). Improvements in technologies for analysing qualitative data, greater researcher awareness and acceptance of these, all present opportunities for larger-scale studies of such data. Conversely, manual analysis remains an important tool for specific types of research question, or to deal with particular disparate data where 'keywords' are hard to define.

However, challenges remain. Content analysis can be impaired by the limited availability of material, and this limits the types of questions that can be asked. A particular issue in this sector is that much available information relates to *charities* registered with a national regulator or accreditation agency, and much research focuses on *large* charities that might voluntarily make information publicly available. This excludes smaller charities and voluntary organisations from these analyses, and may pose a significant risk if conclusions from studies on large registered charities are unthinkingly read across to smaller charities and voluntary organisations. A significant opportunity exists for further work on smaller charities and voluntary organisations, facilitated by increasing amounts of publicly available data, to examine the effects of matters such as regulation, governance and organisational practices on these organisations.

As with all data analysis, there could be issues with subjectivity in interpretation, and the validity of the research can be harmed if analysis is not adequately theorised and presents only descriptive reports of the information. In qualitative studies subjectivity or validity issues might relate to categorisations or 'keywords' chosen for analysis, while in quantitative studies the selection of variables or proxies may be an issue. Approaches taken to mitigate this include triangulation, development of methodologies from previous research and team working. Our own experience in McConville and Cordery (2018) is that content analysis is well suited to team investigation, and this is borne out in the relatively small number of articles cited in this chapter that are not team authored.

We also note that the articles in this chapter are mainly from single-case countries, with the exception of our own. Our paper shows that content analysis can be used in cross-country comparisons and international collaborations, although we note that the availability of comparable data, and the need to carefully understand differences in context (for example, regulation) between countries, can be challenging. This is certainly an area for further research.

A final trend that we observe is that research using content analysis typically focuses on questions of and 'how' and 'what' rather than 'why', notwithstanding some attempts to explore this using theoretical framing and triangulation. We suspect that this is explained by a trend to lay the foundations with content analysis (such as our own reflection has shown) and to follow this up with other methods, such as in-depth case studies and interviews. The potential to use content analysis in exploratory or novel work is particularly important for researchers in the charity and voluntary sector, where gaps are regularly seen in available data and previous research.

Conclusion

In this chapter, utilising an example of our own research using content analysis as well as the work of others, we have highlighted a selection of large-scale and small-sample content analysis-based research, typical theoretical frames, areas of study, recent innovations and challenges.

Publicly available annual reporting has the potential to yield insights into voluntary action, and yet its use has been limited beyond a small subset of accounting and finance academics or statisticians. In outlining the benefits of content analysis of annual reporting data, we have aimed to promote this type of research to those in the voluntary action research space who might not be aware of the data available nor how much it can tell us about voluntary action. Thus, we have explained some of the sources for regulatory data that might be useful to others (see also 'Further reading'). In summarising prior work and highlighting gaps for future research, we hope to have expanded the range of researchers beyond those trained in accounting, as we believe that researchers with different backgrounds will bring different questions and ways of analysis and thus improve our understanding of voluntary action. There is particular space for practitioners to challenge researchers to address matters of relevance to them, especially in, for example, comparing and contrasting styles of performance reporting, new regulatory developments and donor reactions to reporting. In highlighting theories used in this area, we also seek to encourage researchers with different backgrounds to bring different theoretical framings to the area, thus to build on the past to improve our understanding of voluntary action.

Naturally, in a short chapter such as this there has not been space to summarise all content analysis of annual reporting in the voluntary sector; nevertheless we have attempted to provide a range of salient, recent references that will whet the appetite for further research. Content analysis can be combined with other analysis, typical theoretical frames can be applied to the analysis and new can be theories developed, and can facilitate more cross-country analysis. In addition, with ready availability of regulatory data, websites to analyse and better performance (rather than just financial) reporting, we suggest there is room for more innovative research, particularly that which minimises challenges, maximises opportunities and answers questions of practical relevance.

Further reading

- Regulatory data on voluntary organisations can be found for Australia at: www.acnc.gov.au/charity; England and Wales: www.gov.uk/find-charity-information; New Zealand: https://register.charities.govt.nz/CharitiesRegister/Search; United States: www.irs.gov/charities-non-profits/tax-exempt-organization-search.
- Krippendorff's (2018) book on content analysis is an excellent and oft-cited introduction to content analysis.
- Schreier's (2012) book provides good practical advice on qualitative content analysis, and we used both this and Krippendorff's work extensively in our research.

11

Researching risk in the voluntary sector: the challenges and opportunities of regulatory data

Diarmuid McDonnell and Alasdair C. Rutherford

Introduction

The behaviour of voluntary organisations, and their willingness to be accountable, is a pressing policy issue around the world. In the UK, for example, legitimacy and public trust are under threat, due to a recent spate of high-profile voluntary sector crises and scandals, including concerns about large-scale and pervasive instances of financial mismanagement, intrusive and potentially harmful fundraising practices and the abuse of vulnerable beneficiaries. Concurrently, charity regulators are in a state of flux, dealing with declining or stagnating budgets and grappling with new strategic priorities to become data-led organisations. Understanding the nature, extent and impact of risk is therefore of considerable importance for the field, sector, public and policy practitioners.

This chapter reflects on the methodological implications and challenges associated with using regulatory data to study risk in the voluntary sector. In particular we describe collecting, operationalising and analysing the large-scale, often complex, administrative data held by regulators that are necessary to study this topic. Drawing on numerous examples from a multi-year programme of research on the UK charity sector, we outline both the promise and the perils for researchers embarking on their own research.

The challenges and opportunities of regulatory data in measuring risk

The nature of risk in the voluntary sector is broad, and derived from the panoply of operational areas and decisions inherent in running organisations: 'Financial, personnel, programme and capital expenditure decisions all entail risk because they involve interactions with changing, complex, volatile or intrinsically stochastic economic, political and social environments' (Young, 2009: 33). In some areas our understanding of risk is good, and backed by strong empirical evidence, in particular organisational failure (Helmig et al, 2014) and financial vulnerability (see Dayson, 2013). There are some areas where there is a burgeoning set of empirical work being conducted, like organisational fraud (Archambeault et al, 2015) and non-financial disclosures. But there remain topics that are under-theorised or lacking in robust or plentiful empirical examination, such as mission completion (Helmig et al, 2014), ethical fundraising practice and safeguarding of vulnerable beneficiaries. What unifies many attempts at examining risk is the use of data held by bodies with responsibility for overseeing voluntary organisations, in particular the various charity regulators.

Data collected, processed and shared by charity regulators are classified as **administrative data**. Administrative data are often referred to as by-product data and are collected routinely by an organisation through discharging its functions: from a research perspective the data are 'found' rather than 'made' (Connolly et al, 2016). This type of data is collected by government departments and other organisations for the purposes of registration, transaction and record keeping, usually during the delivery of a service (Hand, 2018). The repurposing of administrative data for social science research is a long-standing challenge, with numerous large-scale initiatives seeking to support greater use of these data by the research community (for example, Administrative Data Research Network in the UK). From an analytical perspective, administrative data can be used 'to shed light on what has happened, to help to predict what might happen in the future, and to evaluate systems and their performance, i.e. the data can later be subjected to statistical analysis' (Hand, 2018: 556).

It is our strong belief that grasping the 'biography' of administrative data is essential for producing analyses that minimise misunderstandings and mistakes (Foster et al, 2017; Hand, 2018). This applies whether you are a quantitative researcher building predictive models of a rare outcome in the voluntary sector (McDonnell and Rutherford, 2019), or a qualitative researcher using charity regulatory data as a sampling frame (Morgan and Fletcher, 2013). Thus, the focus of the rest of this chapter is on recognising and addressing some of the common issues that arise in the research use of administrative data. We do so by drawing on examples from our own programme of research on the voluntary sector in the UK and other English-speaking nations in the Global North.

Table 11.1 summarises some the main beneficial features of using administrative data for research purposes, as well as offering rejoinders to some of these claims (Smith et al, 2004; Wallgren and Wallgren, 2007; Connolly et al, 2016; Hand, 2018). The rest of this section delves into each of these features and relates them to study of risk in the voluntary sector.

Table 11.1: Key features of administrative regulatory data

Feature	Promise	Peril
Access	Lower cost to obtain compared to other forms of social data collection methods. Unobtrusive to units of analysis, that is, data are already collected.	Lots of effort to attain, clean and analyse; may have to pay for access. Serious concerns about informed consent, that is, data collected for some other non-research purpose.
Coverage	High/complete coverage of units of analysis, time periods and/or variables.	Missing observations for units of analysis are common, as are missing variables.
Quality	Data is often high quality, due to its role in functioning of organisation.	Organisational pressures/lack of expertise can produce low-quality data resources. Data collection process can change over time, overwriting or invalidating previous records or measures.
Capturing reality	Closer to social reality than other data resources/collection methods; records *actual* events, behaviours and characteristics, not those that are *stated* or *claimed*.	Data is often still dependent on self-reporting, for example, self-assessment income tax returns.
Timely	Contemporaneous, continuous updating of fields.	There can be considerable lags between when data is generated, collected, processed and shared. Continuous collection can overwrite previous fields, leading to lost information.
Measurement	Tighter definitions for some measures, for example, defined in law.	Dependent on what is measured by data collector; data is not collected with important social concepts and measures in mind.
Granularity	Data often records information in considerable detail. Captures hard-to-reach samples/rare events/older time periods.	Spurious precision or unnecessary detail may hinder analysis of broader social concepts. Confidentiality concerns can arise with granular records or information.
Linkage	Data often contains unique IDs or sufficient information for each unit of analysis to permit linkage to other sources of data.	Unique IDs not always recorded diligently. Linking multiple, low-quality datasets compounds rather than alleviates issues.

Access

Charity regulators play an important role in public accountability and transparency for the voluntary sector. As a result, data on charities is made publicly available in many jurisdictions. This is a real benefit to researchers, as data can be collected without placing additional burden on participants. Of course, it comes with the constraints of working with any secondary data, that the researcher does not have control over the content and methods used to collect the data. But there is great potential for large amounts of detailed data to be freely accessible.

Box 11.1: Charity data from the Charity Commission for England and Wales

The data collected on charities by the Charity Commission for England and Wales is freely available in an online searchable database (https://register-of-charities.charitycommission.gov.uk/). Details include contact details, finances, activities, trustees, governance policies and more. Many data items are available both contemporaneously and historically. Charities can be found via either their charity registration number or a keyword search. There is also a bulk data download of the current register available, including a selection of the available fields.

However, in many jurisdictions the rationale for making data available is to provide information about individual charities on the register to interested parties, rather than to make data available for research. This means that it can vary widely how straightforward it is to access and download register data at scale. Data may be available in a downloadable file, through an application programming interface (API) or simply on a web page. This can create significant barriers in either the technical knowledge or researcher time required to get access to even publicly available data. Some data may be available on request from the regulator, but even then the researcher may not be able to control the format in which the data is supplied.

Box 11.2: Accessing data on charity dissolution across international jurisdictions

Comparative work requires accessing and analysing data from across charity jurisdictions. While manual approaches suffice for some jurisdictions, it is necessary or more robust to use a suite of different computational methods of access: this is due to the use of differing data formats and web platforms, in particular. In this project we created programming scripts to access and prepare data from eight jurisdictions, and made it available to researchers online: https://github.com/DiarmuidM/charity-dissolution.

Methods of data access are not necessarily stable. Data owners can and do change the mode of access, the layout of information and the content shared – see, for example, the 2020 changes to the England and Wales Register of Charities. This makes it difficult to establish reliable methods of data access, and can jeopardise the building of consistent time series. Documenting and archiving data that is used for analysis is important to support the reproducibility of research.

Source: McDonnell et al (forthcoming)

Coverage

Administrative data is likely to feature good coverage of the population that it encompasses. For example, in Scotland an organisation is by definition a charity only if it appears on the Scottish Charity Register. Working with the data therefore means working with the population of charities, as defined. There are limits to this coverage, however. A register may exclude organisations that meet the regulator's criteria for inclusion (for example, unregistered non-profit organisations in Canada, or very small charities in England and Wales). Or it may include organisations that do not meet the researcher's criteria (for example, public universities, or private schools). So, while coverage of register data is likely to be good, it is not within the researcher's direct control, and one must understand the criteria for an organisation being part of a regulator's register data.

The content of the data collected is driven by the legal context in which the regulator operates. For example, in Scotland the regulator has a focus on public trust in the charitable sector, and detailed data is collected on the governance of charities. In Canada, responsibility for charities sits within the tax authority, and extremely detailed and high-quality financial data is collected.

Box 11.3: Examining charity complaints and regulatory investigations

The Scottish Charity Regulator provides a dataset of complaints about charities and the ensuing regulatory investigations or actions. This dataset has by definition complete coverage: organisations must be on the register to be considered charities, and it includes all complaints and investigations made by the regulator between 2006 and 2014. However, there are some limitations in the information included in these records: researchers are reliant on the categorisation of complaints and investigations made by the regulator, rather than the full circumstances of the complaint. The nature of the data, and the level of detail, changes over time. As a time series it is vulnerable to changes in regulatory practice that might change the meaning of particular terms, or lead to particular data items no longer being recorded.

Source: McDonnell and Rutherford (2018)

Missing data is a perennial challenge for researchers, and administrative data is no exception to this. Organisations are likely to have some sort of legal duty to report to a regulator, but the powers to enforce this and penalties for non-compliance vary widely across jurisdictions. There may also not be an obligation for organisations to complete all the fields in a form. There can be significant delays in data being reported and made available, as there is usually an allowance of several months after a reporting period ends before an organisation must complete a return. Care must be taken when using a time period where not all returns have been submitted, as there could be a systematic pattern in the organisations that report early and those that report late. Regulators vary in their capacity to check information, and so individual data items can be missing, or 'total' fields may not equal the sum of their constituent parts. Researchers need to engage in significant data cleaning and quality checking before conducting analysis on register data.

Data quality

Administrative data are often vital to the effective functioning of an organisation. This is particularly true of charity regulators, who in many cases have a legal duty to maintain an accurate, public register of charities in their jurisdiction. Thus, it seems a reasonable assumption that data collected and shared by charity regulators will be of sufficient quality to permit robust analyses of the voluntary sector. One such example would be the financial information submitted by these organisations to a charity regulator. The legal status of these returns may lead us to expect that the quality of the data is high. But the data is collected for reporting and regulatory purposes, and not primarily for research. As such, care must be taken to understand how questions have been asked each year, and to account for changes in the form of data collection, the definitions of key terms or the intended purpose of the data collection that might influence how and what is reported by organisations to the regulator.

Box 11.4: Changing questions, moving measures

The Scottish Charity Regulator collects data on 'Net Current Assets' and 'Total Funds' to capture the assets held by Scottish charities. In 2011 a small change to question wording in the assets section of the annual return form led a small number of charitable trusts with significant assets to reclassify the reporting of their assets out of the 'Net Current Assets' measure while still including them in the 'Total Funds' measure. The sums of money involved were large enough to move the sector-wide aggregate total of Net Current Assets down without any actual change in the underlying sector's financial position. This highlights the importance of closely checking the annual return forms and being aware of even seemingly minor changes to wording or structure.

Source: Pennerstorfer and Rutherford (2019)

We might expect that financial data is of a high quality, and for larger organisations this is likely true, particularly where accounts have had to undergo an external audit or inspection process. But other data items, such as staff or volunteer numbers, can be of more variable quality, particularly where there are not tight definitions of how to count or record this information. Unlike with primary longitudinal survey data, there is rarely an obligation to maintain consistent question wording or collection methods over time, with returns instead designed to collect the information required to satisfy legal and regulatory requirements at a given time point. So, quality of a data item may vary over time; the definition of a key term may change; or a series of questions may be discontinued or reworded.

Measurement

The use of administrative data provides a degree of measurement validity and accuracy, due to the tight, legal definitions of certain organisational events, statuses and characteristics. For example, researchers interested in examining charity dissolution in England and Wales using regulatory data can do so, confident in the knowledge that the relevant categories in the data – 'ceased to exist' and 'does not operate' – are legally defined under section 34 of the Charities Act 2011. Similarly, the preparation of annual accounts and reports must or should follow a set of standards and rules (known as Statement of Recommended Practice [SORP] in the UK), resulting in a higher degree of reliability and validity across a range of financial metrics (for example, the level of unrestricted reserves held by a charity).

However, even if the data can be considered as high quality (for example, complete coverage of population, well structured, granular or accurate), measurement issues may still bedevil or preclude robust analysis of the data. This is due to a fundamental but understandable reality: administrative data are not collected with important social concepts and measures in mind. Therefore, there can be little overlap between what is measured in the data and the information you need in order to examine the social concept or phenomenon of interest.

The measurement of risk is particularly dependent on high-quality measurement. Despite the reams of information charity regulators collect on the voluntary organisations they oversee, identifying predictive indicators of important risks remains challenging. This can be seen in the reasonably frequent changes that are made to the variety of mandatory and voluntary reporting mechanisms operated by charity regulators. For example, in 2008 the Internal Revenue Service radically redesigned the 990 form to capture information relating to governance and other non-financial domains of US non-profits (Brody, 2012a). This was an attempt to uncover undesirable events and behaviours that previously lay hidden, such as financial relationships or familial relationships between trustees. However, to date there is no strong evidence that capturing information on these domains has led to improved governance in the US non-profit sector (Brody, 2012b).

Box 11.5: Improving charity accountability

The Scottish Charity Regulator previously collected data on a number of 'accountability issues' that the regulator believed were indicative of improper or concerning behaviour by charities. Many of these indicators focused on financial concerns, such as the possible misuse of charitable funds, or the use of unauthorised fundraising methods or third parties. There were 33 of these indicators, which were captured on an annual basis by the regulator. Analysis of these indicators revealed that a majority of Scottish charities included in the study trigger at least one of these accountability concerns and a minority do so persistently; however, no link was found between the indicators and 'more objective' negative organisational outcomes such as being reported to the regulator for alleged poor behaviour, regulatory intervention or charity dissolution.

Source: McDonnell (2017)

Capturing reality

Administrative data is often considered to more closely capture aspects of social reality than data collected by other methods like social surveys or participant observation (Hand, 2018). Such a claim is founded on the 'objective' process by which the information is generated or captured: that is, produced during the operation of some administrative function rather than by a self-reporting mechanism. Consider measuring the risk of fraud in the voluntary sector: it seems self-evident that complaints and case-work data from charity regulators would better capture the nature and prevalence of this phenomenon than a social survey reliant on sufficient participation and honesty from voluntary organisations (see Box 11.3).

However, this paints a misleading picture, as many fields in administrative datasets rely on self-reported information. Regulatory data on voluntary organisations suffers from the same issue, where even key financial information is produced and reported in an inconsistent manner. For example, understanding the level of reserves that a charity possesses – and thus gaining a sense of its resilience in the face of financial shocks – can be reliably measured for only a small subgroup of organisations in the UK (those generating over £500,000 in annual gross income), and even then consistency is not guaranteed, due to differences in the interpretation of financial standards and guidance (Morgan, 2011).

Timely

Charity regulation is a continuous process, and a significant advantage of using administrative data is the potential for the data to be 'real time' rather than requiring lengthy fieldwork. Regulators usually collect annual returns from charities, which often includes their annual financial reporting. However, there are two main threats to having timely access to administrative data. Firstly, there is usually a lag in organisations having to report to the regulator. This could be as much as a year beyond the date of the relevant financial period. Secondly, there can be a delay in the regulator's release of updated data, typically anything between 'real time' and quarterly.

The lag in charity reporting places a constraint on how recent the information available can be. If an organisation is allowed 6 months following their reporting period to submit their return, then the data supplied will concern a 12-month period that runs between 18 and 6 months previously. But organisations may also submit with different delays, some submitting early while others use the whole period, or submit late. This means that care must be taken in analysing data received within this 'submission window', as it will show a partial, and perhaps biased, picture of the sector. Only once the submission deadline has passed can the data be considered complete.

Box 11.6: Capturing the impact of COVID-19 on the voluntary sector

COVID-19 represents an existential threat to many voluntary organisations, while simultaneously spurring new, large-scale forms of voluntary activity. Using comprehensive publicly available data from seven jurisdictions, we examined the impact of COVID-19 on the foundation and dissolution of charitable organisations. We employed an 'excess events' analytical approach, comparing the numbers of foundations and dissolutions in 2020 to what we would expect based on the trends from previous years. What is obvious from collecting and analysing the data is that the 'live' public registers are actually a work in progress: the work of regulators was disrupted by the pandemic (particularly during the first half of 2020), leading to delays in the registration of organisations or their removal from the registers. This considerably hampers efforts to track the 'real time' impact of the public health emergency on the voluntary sector.

Source: McDonnell and Rutherford (2020b)

The delay in a regulator's releasing information reflects their processes for administering the returns data, and their methods of data sharing. It is important to understand this schedule, and the implications it has for the data collected. A regular schedule for a defined period (for example, quarterly) provides clarity for data availability, albeit with some delay. 'Real time' updating reduces the delay, but care must be taken before concluding that a given period's data collection is 'complete'. It is also important to be aware of any of seasonal variations, such as spikes in reporting around financial/ tax year end; or annual 'bulk updates' carried out by the regulator, such as removing dormant organisations.

Finally, 'timely' also reflects the fact that register data is usually a 'live' database. That means that new data may overwrite old data. For example, if a charity changes its areas of activity, these will be updated in the register. The old activities will no longer be listed, and there may not even be a public record that these have been changed. This means that contemporaneous data may differ from an earlier extract, which can create some challenges for replications unless historic data is stored and well documented.

Granularity

The large sample sizes, good coverage and availability of historical data together mean that regulatory data can provide good granularity, and opportunities to study tightly defined subgroups within the voluntary sector.

Researchers are dependent on the level of granularity available to them in the data supplied by a regulator, whether it is made available publicly or confidentially for research purposes. Often details will be categorised for recording, and cases may also be aggregated or anonymised in a way that makes it difficult to explore patterns at the level of the individual organisation.

Box 11.7: Aggregate versus individual-level data: studying notifiable events in UK charities

Charities in the UK are expected to notify their respective regulators of serious incidents that materially affect the charity. While the details of these schemes vary across jurisdictions, they collect similar information about risk voluntarily reported to regulators. In Scotland, we accessed charity-level information about the reporting of notifiable events that allowed us to explore which sorts of charities were most likely to report, and the sorts of concerns that they highlighted. However, for England and Wales, researchers are able to access only aggregate monthly statistics for notifiable events. This allowed us to study patterns across the sector in the level of reporting in response to charity scandals, but not to examine these patterns at the level of the charity itself.

Events that are rare, and so difficult to capture in a random sample, can be filtered to create a sub-sample for analysis with only the organisations of interest. Where historical data is available, these criteria can be applied over long periods in order to increase the size of the relevant group. A threat to this granularity is the potential for rare events to be sensitive and to risk publicly identifying the organisation involved. This would be a concern when working with data on complaints, investigations or serious incidents, and particularly when using regulatory data that is not normally shared publicly.

Source: McDonnell and Rutherford (2019, 2020a)

Box 11.8: Working with data on rare events

The numbers of charities voluntarily reporting serious incidents to the regulator are low in Scotland. Working with this data allows us to explore what sorts of organisations are proactively identifying risks and reporting them to the regulator. We can explore in detail the characteristics of this small group, and the regulator's ensuing actions. However this data is not publicly available, and details of some of the incidents are sensitive. Care had to be taken in analysing and reporting on this data not to disclose the identity of individual organisations, particularly where they had recognisable characteristics.

Source: McDonnell and Rutherford (2019)

Linkage

Administrative data on organisations can provide opportunities to link data to other sources. Data on organisations may be held by other regulators, membership or infrastructure bodies. For example, in the UK many charities are also registered companies and must file returns and accounts with Companies House. Linking these datasets provides a richer picture of the operation of organisations. But a barrier to this linkage is the use of consistent unique organisational identifiers. While regulators often use their own unique identifiers to identify organisations, they do not necessarily hold the corresponding identifier for another regulator on file. In England and Wales, the Charity Commission does also record company numbers, allowing charities to be linked to their corresponding company record. However, in Scotland the regulator does not record these identifiers, meaning that linkage must be done more crudely, based on matches in name and address.

Box 11.9: Linking organisational data to charity register data

Data on third sector organisations who have interacted with their local Third Sector Interface in Scotland was gathered to explore the distribution of organisations across the country. For some organisations a charity number had been recorded. This permits an unambiguous one-to-one linkage between the database record and a Scottish charity. For others, no identifier was collected, and organisation records could be probabilistically matched between the database and the charity register on organisation name and address. For many, however, they were voluntary organisations that are not registered charities, and so no record of them is kept by the charity regulator.

Source: Brook and Rutherford (2017)

Conclusion

We argue that there is great potential to use regulatory data to better understand risk in the voluntary sector. The intersection of several distinct developments – increased data availability, technology to gather and analyse this data and interest in comparative research – has created real opportunities to address a range of important research questions at scale. A desire from many regulators to increase transparency, and a focus on public trust in the voluntary sector, have spurred developments to share more detailed data online. The keen interest of many charity and non-profit regulators in a risk-based approach means that routine data is available to consider risk beyond the financial domain, and across many dimensions.

But we also caution that easy access to data is not a panacea for the analysis of risk. Even when data is 'open' and 'publicly available' there can still be significant technical challenges in accessing and working with it, both through the methods that must be used (for example, programming scripts) and the file formats or data structures in which information is shared (for example, JSON).

While it is easy to focus on the technical challenge of data access, it is just as important that regulatory data be viewed through the lens of critical social science. There is a high bar in the institutional, cultural and contextual knowledge required to make sense of the data that is available, and significant diversity across jurisdictions in the meaning and form of similar phenomena. As social scientists, we still need to consider issues in the measurement, operationalisation and power dynamics of working with regulatory data. Some information is provided by charities as a legal duty, while other items are voluntary reports. Data collected with the intention of evaluating or 'policing' organisations creates a set of incentives for both the regulator and charities in how organisations and their activities are presented.

Our discussion here has primarily considered charity data held in English-speaking Global North countries. Many of the challenges we discuss will also apply to regulatory data in other countries. In many jurisdictions, however, this sort of regulatory data is not collected (for example, Ghana); is collected but not shared (for example, China, Japan); or is publicly available but not in digital machine-readable formats (for example, Singapore, India). This creates additional barriers to accessing data in the first instance, as well as ongoing cultural, linguistic and substantive difficulties in parsing and analysing the data.

But, despite these challenges, regulatory data does provide the opportunity to gain real understanding of risks within the voluntary sector at a scale that would be infeasible with primary data collection. Insights from this data have the potential to support the evaluation of public policies, and help to build public trust in the voluntary sector. Regulators have the opportunity to better target their data collection, and increase the ease of access. Voluntary organisations can benefit from understanding the determinants and predictors of risk across the sector. So, finally, we would like to call for greater collaboration between researchers, regulators and voluntary organisations to collect and share high-quality data that meets all these needs. With suitable consideration of the perils, there is significant promise in the analysis of regulatory data on voluntary organisations globally.

Further reading
- Elizabeth Bloodgood and colleagues' (2014) work on national variation in non-profit regulation provides an excellent account of the political and legal context these organisations operate in globally.
- To understand recent shifts in the resourcing and focus of charity regulators, we highly recommend Oonagh Breen's 2018 overview.
- Brooker's (2020) guide to computational approaches for collecting and processing social data is a useful starting point for researchers interested in developing their programming knowledge and skills.

12

Exploring the benefits of volunteering: combining survey and administrative data in the Nordic 'laboratory'

Hans-Peter Y. Qvist

Introduction

In social science and economics it is a widely held notion that volunteers not only contribute goods and services to others but also benefit themselves. Indeed, it is frequently assumed that people would not contribute goods and services to others unless they somehow benefited or profited from the exchange (Musick and Wilson, 2008; Smith and Wang, 2016). While social scientists typically consider the personal benefits of volunteering as being unintended consequences of action initially guided by other motives, economists frequently assume that the expectation of benefits is an important part of people's motives for volunteering (Andreoni, 1990).

While there is widespread agreement in the literature that volunteers benefit from their actions, there is little agreement on the nature, extent and distribution of these benefits. Some social scientists have suggested that the benefits of volunteering are manifold and diverse, including emotional, social, health and labour market benefits (Musick and Wilson, 2008). Other social scientists have argued that the benefits of volunteering ultimately reduce the 'positive experiences' that people from dominant-status groups enjoy when they act in accordance with socioculturally approved norms (Smith and Wang, 2016: 638). Economists have frequently argued that people can be understood as 'impure altruists', meaning that while they may choose to volunteer in part because they want to do good for others, they simultaneously do so because they want to experience a 'warm-glow', referring to the feeling that people experience in their bodies and minds when they are emotionally satisfied (Andreoni, 1990).

Even though social scientists and economists often theorise about the possible benefits of volunteering, our knowledge about them rests on a remarkably fragile empirical foundation. In this chapter, I suggest that the Nordic countries can be viewed as a valuable yet largely unexploited 'laboratory' for the study of the possible labour market and health benefits of volunteering. The reason for this is that it is possible to merge survey data that includes information about volunteering with high-quality longitudinal administrative register data that includes information about labour market and health outcomes at the individual level. The combination of survey and register data presents researchers with unique opportunities to relate people's volunteering behaviour to changes in their subsequent labour market and health trajectories.

The chapter will proceed as follows. First, I discuss key limitations of survey data in volunteering research. Second, focusing on the Danish case, I briefly introduce how it is possible, without compromising data security and integrity, to merge survey data with administrative register data. Next, I exemplify the power of the combination of survey and administrative register data by drawing on work in the late 2010s that has shed light on the labour market benefits of volunteering. The chapter concludes with a discussion in which I highlight some limitations of the approach and discuss how the combination of survey and register data may nevertheless be exploited further in future research.

The limitations of survey data in the study of the benefits of volunteering

A major challenge in the empirical study of the benefits of volunteering is that it is incredibly challenging to tell to what extent an observed association between two variables reflects a causal relationship in the expected direction. We might, for example, observe a statistically significant positive association between participation in volunteering and wages. However, while this association could reflect that participation in volunteering is helpful in terms of career advancement as indicated by wages, it could also reflect the confounding effect of common causes of volunteering and wage levels, for example education. Luckily, because it is relatively simple to measure educational level, we can use statistical techniques like regression to control for the confounding effect of educational level. However, other possible common causes of volunteering and wage levels, such as innate ability, are less simple or potentially impossible to measure and control for. Moreover, even if we managed to control for all common causes of volunteering and wages, it would remain possible that causality could flow in the opposite direction, meaning that career progression would be a cause rather than a benefit of volunteering.

One possible solution to the mentioned issues is to conduct a randomised experiment. In a randomised experiment we would randomly assign one group of people to 'do volunteer work' and another to act as a control group. If we side-step the practical difficulties that would be involved (for example, that some people in each group would probably not comply with their assigned role) the effect of volunteering on career progression could be estimated simply by taking the difference between the two groups' mean wages at some later point in time. The reason for this is that the random assignment of the 'treatment' (that is, to do volunteer work) would ensure that we would have no reason to believe that the two groups differed systematically before the treatment was introduced (Morgan and Winship, 2015).

Occasionally, experiment designs have been used in studies of the labour market benefits of volunteering. These have included studying the extent to which having volunteering experience on one's résumé increases the likelihood of getting a call back after a job interview, through submitting job applications that differ only in whether or not the résumé includes volunteer work experience, to genuine vacancies (Baert and Vujic, 2018). However, while experiments appear ideal in this context because the expected explanatory mechanism is that volunteer work experience might affect employers' perception of job candidates, they are not ideal when the expected explanatory mechanisms are that volunteers gain human or social resources. The reason is that the notion of a 'randomly assigned volunteer' is oxymoronic in the sense that volunteering, by definition, comprises activities that people themselves freely choose to engage in because they care about a specific cause. Moreover, the possible benefits of volunteering are widely believed to be intrinsically related to its non-compulsory nature. This notion is supported by studies that indicate that volunteering can lose its positive effects, or have negative side effects, if it becomes a compulsory activity, for example, targeted at welfare clients (Baines and Hardill, 2008; de Waele and Hustinx, 2019).

Because experimental designs are generally not feasible, high-quality observational data is vital if we want to learn about how the benefits of volunteering play out in real life. Unfortunately, observational data in volunteering research typically comprises far-from-optimal survey data (Wilson, 2005). Specialist volunteering surveys are typically cross-sectional, providing only a one-time snapshot of a population. Because of the absence of a time dimension in such data, it is impossible to tell whether observed associations between variables reflect causal relationships without strong and untestable assumptions. To elucidate the possible benefits of volunteering, researchers therefore often turn to large-scale longitudinal general-purpose surveys such as the British Household Panel Survey (BHPS) or the German Socioeconomic Panel because they contain information about the same individuals collected at many time points. Longitudinal data generally offers much better opportunities for causal inference than cross-sectional data, because causal interpretations are easier to defend when changes in an explanatory variable can be related to changes in an outcome variable at the individual level. However, unlike specialist volunteering surveys, large-scale longitudinal general-purpose surveys typically contain only a few items about volunteering, which may be worded in very general terms. For example, in the case of the BHPS, information about volunteering is available only through a module about the frequency of 'things people do in their leisure time'. In this module, 'do unpaid voluntary work' is one of ten options. However, by relying on this item, we would know nothing about the organisational context or in what kind of voluntary activities the respondent took part. Moreover, given that no prompts are provided to respondents about what is meant by 'unpaid volunteer work', this judgement is left entirely up to the respondent, seriously questioning which actions are measured by this item.

Surveys of volunteering, like all surveys, are also to a varying degree subject to problems of missing data and measurement error. Missing data problems may arise from different sources, including unit and item non-response. Unit non-response occurs when an eligible sample member completely fails to respond to the survey or does not provide enough information for the response to be deemed usable by the researcher (Cohen, 2008). And it will rarely be the case that it is completely random who fails to respond to the survey: a low survey response rate jeopardises a sample's representativeness and consequently limits the possibility of drawing inferences from sample to population. The problem of unit non-response is a growing concern among researchers because survey response rates have declined markedly in most countries during recent decades (Vehovar and Beullens, 2018). In volunteering research in particular, unit non-response is a pervasive source of bias because evidence suggest that participation in volunteering and in surveys is intrinsically related, meaning that people who engage in prosocial activities such as volunteering are also more likely to respond to surveys (Abraham et al, 2009). To add insult to injury, this problem is often exacerbated in longitudinal surveys because volunteers are not only more likely to respond initially to a longitudinal survey but also less likely to drop out of the survey at later time points. The problem of item non-response can also be inescapable whenever sensitive items are included in the survey, and one such example of a sensitive item is income. Non-response on income items arises either because people are uncertain about their income and therefore refuse to answer questions about it or because they are unwilling to provide information about their income.

Finally, measurement error is another pervasive problem in surveys. Measurement error occurs when there is a discrepancy between the information provided by a respondent and the objective truth (Biemer, 2009). This discrepancy can arise either because the respondent intentionally provided false information or because they misunderstood the question or did not know the true answer to it. Drawing on the example of income, measurement error may occur because respondents intentionally or unintentionally over- or under-report their income. Generally, evidence suggests that over-reporting is most pronounced among individuals who share key characteristics of high-income individuals, suggesting that over-reporting of income is related to social desirability (Hariri and Lassen, 2017).

The combination of survey and register data

In a very helpful piece, Wilson (2005) suggested ways to overcome common problems in survey-based volunteering research by using more advanced survey designs and by adopting more cutting-edge analytical strategies. However, even though Wilson (2005) provides expert advice on how to make better use of surveys, many of their limitations nevertheless remain difficult, if not impossible, to overcome. For example, it is doubtful whether the problems related to missing data and measurement error in income items can be alleviated by rewording survey questions or by using advanced modelling strategies to cope with measurement error. When possible, an alternative and arguably more fruitful way to proceed is to merge survey data with data from more reliable sources, such as administrative registers.

Fortunately, many countries have invested large amounts of resources in improving their social science data infrastructure and to allow for administrative registers to be exploited in social science research (Connelly et al, 2016). Consequently, there is little doubt that the use of administrative registers in social science and economic research will become still more widespread in the coming decades. Since the mid-20th century, the Nordic countries began the process of building a data infrastructure that would allow administrative registers to be effectively used in social science research. Owing to the foresight of early pioneers, the Nordic countries have assumed a role as global forerunners in the use of administrative register data in social science research (Nordbotten, 2008). Moreover, the use of register data in social science research in the Nordic countries has been institutionalised and systematised in a way that makes it exceptionally accessible for social science researchers (Thygesen et al, 2011). In this section, I briefly explain how it is possible to create longitudinal datasets that are suitable for volunteering research based on the combination of survey and administrative register data. I take my point of departure as the Danish case, but readers should note that largely similar set-ups are found in the other Nordic countries.

Since the late 1960s, all individuals in Denmark with a permanent residence have been required to hold a unique personal identification number. This number is used by all government agencies to store person-specific information, which is continuously collected by Statistics Denmark and stored in research registers (Thygesen et al, 2011). These research registers are an incredible source of information for social science research. The research registers, for example, contain information about education, labour market participation, disease incidence, housing, taxation, as well as demographics such as birth, marriage and death (for an overview of the Danish registers, see Thygesen et al [2011]). To create datasets suitable for social science and economic research all this information can be merged at the individual level through the personal identification number. Some information stretches very far back in time. For example, information about causes of death has been collected since 1875 and information about compulsory schooling goes back to 1943. Since the beginning of the 1980s, some variables have been collected continuously at specific time intervals (for example, annually, weekly or daily) or for each service received. This is, for example, the case with education. This means that longitudinal information about education can be compiled retrospectively from 1980 and onwards, allowing for the study of educational trajectories. For other variables, longitudinal information is available from a later time point.

A particularly attractive feature of Danish administrative register data is that it is possible to merge it with data from other sources including surveys (Møberg, 2017). In the context of volunteering research, this feature is essential because administrative registers do not at present contain information about people's participation in volunteering or other activities in civil society. For this reason, research on volunteering, unlike, for example, educational and occupational research, can rarely be conducted entirely based on register data. The role of register data in volunteering research will therefore typically be to enrich rather than to replace information from surveys (Qvist, 2018a).

Fundamentally, the use of administrative register data in social science research can be conceived of as a social institution grounded in trust. The general public must be able to trust that data is used strictly for research purposes and to the benefit of the common good. After all, it is probably not a coincidence that the use of administrative register data in social science and economic research was pioneered in the high-trust and state-friendly Nordic countries. However, data security in the Nordic countries does not solely rely on public trust. In Denmark, a vast amount of legislation that derives from both national and European Union (EU) legislation regulates the use of administrative register data in social science and economic research. It is, however, beyond the scope of this chapter to provide a detailed account of the legislation that guides the processing of administrative register data in Denmark. Instead, drawing on Statistics Denmark's confidentiality policy, which adheres to both national and EU legislation, I will briefly introduce the vital principles that guide the use of register data in social science research in the Danish case. For readers who are interested in more details, Statistics Denmark's confidentiality policy is available in English through Statistics Denmark's website: www.dst.dk/en/OmDS/lovgivning,

In Denmark, a vital principle that guides the use of administrative registers in social science research is that approved researchers are granted access to specific variables only on a 'need-to-know' basis. This means that it is possible for only approved researchers to access certain variables that are essential to conduct a specific research project. To secure this, approved researchers must apply on a case-to-case basis for access to variables that are essential to their project. Given that the research project receives approval from Statistics Denmark and the Danish Data Protection Agency, the researcher is subsequently granted access to variables in the specific registers in anonymised form through a double password-protected remote access. Through the remote access to servers located at Statistics Denmark, the researcher is able to process and analyse the data, but the data itself remains on the servers located at Statistics Denmark at all times. When statistical analyses are complete, researchers are allowed to take home only aggregated results from the analyses, such as means or regression coefficients. The aggregation of results ensures that it is never possible, directly or indirectly, to identify individuals or other units of analysis based on published or unpublished research results.

A challenge when working with administrative register data is that, unlike data that derives from surveys, data from government agencies is produced primarily for administrative purposes and not for research. This means that the data in most cases has to be modified in various ways to make it suitable for research (Nordbotten, 2008). Because of the scope and complexity of register data, this modification process would present the individual researcher with a formidable, if not insurmountable, challenge. However, Statistics Denmark greatly assists researchers in this process by making available a catalogue of pre-coded variables that researchers typically use in social science research. In the context of social science research, a highly attractive feature of Danish administrative register data is that it contains very detailed information about key socioeconomic variables in standard international formats. For example, highly detailed information about education is coded according to the International Standard Classification of Education and occupational status is coded according the International Standard Classification of Occupations. Although occupational status is not measured perfectly in administrative registers and contains some missing data and possible misclassifications, this data is much more detailed than the occupational information that is typically collected in surveys. Another highly attractive feature of Danish register data is that it is possible to link units of analysis. For example, an individual can be linked to their parents, spouse and children (Thygesen et al, 2011). It is also possible to link other units of analysis, for example individuals to schools or workplaces.

Even though Statistics Denmark assists researchers in basic preparatory work, it is paramount that researchers remain aware that the research registers are by-products of existing administrative registers. This means that researchers have to scrutinise the data documentation to learn how the data was generated (Thygesen et al, 2011). Information in research registers, for example, differs in whether it derives from human reporting or is collected automatically by administrative systems. For example, while information about occupations derives from information reported by employers, which is consequently susceptible to non- or misreporting, information about income derives from calculations based on automatically collected information in the tax register. Because information for the private tax register is largely collected automatically from third parties, it greatly limits the possibility for individuals to evade taxes by under-reporting their income (Hariri and Lassen, 2017). This means that values in income variables that derive from the tax register should be very close to true income values. Beside differences in the mode of data collection, researchers also need to be aware that government policy changes from time to time bring about changes in data-collection procedures (Møberg, 2017). If this is not recognised, these changes can greatly distort longitudinal analysis, because researchers may end up comparing apples to oranges if data-collection procedures have been changed during the period under study.

Combining survey and register data in volunteering research

Drawing on examples from published work, this section explains how the combination of survey and administrative register data has been used to break new ground in research on the labour market benefits of volunteering.

One example is a recent study of the link between volunteering and employability (Petrovski et al, 2017). As noted by Petrovski and colleagues, a weakness in existing studies was that employment was typically measured at one time point, and oftentimes simultaneously with volunteering. In longitudinal studies, volunteering would be measured before employment but nevertheless at one time point. This is unproblematic in cases where people's employment status is stable. However, viewed over a period of time, a large proportion of people move in and out of employment. To avoid random fluctuations in people's employment status, Petrovski and colleagues merged the Danish Volunteer Survey (DVS) with information from the Danish labour force register. This allowed them to code the dependent variable such that it captured the average rate of employment measured on a week-to-week basis during a period of two years. Another important feature of the study was that Petrovski and colleagues exploited the longitudinal information about employment to reduce the risk of 'reverse causality' by controlling for employment measured at previous periods (lagged dependent variables). Using instrumental variable regression, the research, unlike many previous studies, found no evidence that volunteers benefit from their actions in terms of increasing their employability (Petrovski et al, 2017).

In my own research, I have together with Martin D. Munk used the combination of survey and administrative register data to examine the extent to which volunteering is helpful in terms of career advancement as indicated by wages (Qvist and Munk, 2018). By merging the DVS with administrative register data, we were able to examine the association between changes in volunteer work experience and changes in the individual's wage in the following year at the individual level during the period 2004–12. A major benefit of using administrative register data was that yearly information about wages could be obtained with minimal missing data and measurement error. Because it is automatically collected based on tax returns, administrative register data information about wage income thus covers 99.9% of the Danish population (Hariri and Lassen, 2017). This means that bias related to lack of coverage and self-reporting of wage income that is pervasive in survey research was almost completely eliminated. Moreover, possible common causes of volunteering and wages, including educational level and years of professional labour market experience, were also measured based on information from administrative register data. Within the Danish research registers, the measure for years of professional labour market experience is approximated based on mandatory pension payments from employers. Using two-way fixed effects regression, we were able to qualify existing research that had so far provided mixed evidence regarding the economic returns from volunteering based on population averages. Our results revealed that the economic returns of volunteering vary significantly across people's working lives. More specifically, we found that the economic returns of an additional year of volunteer work experience were greatest for labour market entrants and during the early stages of working life, but they levelled off as people gained professional labour market experience. After approximately six years of professional labour market experience, the association between an additional year of volunteer work experience and wages was no longer significant. Additional analyses moreover revealed that the results were robust when age was controlled for. On these grounds, we concluded 'that the most important factor to consider when examining the economic returns from volunteer work experience across people's work lives is not age *per se* but the individual's amount of professional labour market experience' (Qvist and Munk, 2018: 3).

Conclusion

In this chapter, I have argued that the Nordic countries can be viewed as a valuable yet largely unexploited 'laboratory' for the study of the possible labour market and health benefits of volunteering. The reason for this is that it is possible to merge survey data that includes information about volunteering with high-quality longitudinal administrative register data at the individual level. The combination of survey and administrative register data presents researchers with unique opportunities to study some of the possible benefits of volunteering because detailed information regarding people's participation in volunteering can be linked to their subsequent labour market and health trajectories. Drawing on examples from research on the labour market benefits of volunteering it was shown how the combination of survey and administrative register data has been used to break new ground.

In the chapter, I highlighted that the combination of survey and register data is particularly useful in research on the possible benefits of volunteering. However, it can also be used in research on the causes of volunteering. For example, because it allows for more accurate measurement of socioeconomic status, I combined the DVS with administrative register data to study religious and secular volunteering among immigrants in Denmark (Qvist, 2018b). Moreover, because it allows for more accurate measurement of key socioeconomic and demographic control variables, I have also, together with colleagues, used the combination of the DVS and administrative register data to examine to what extent the decline in volunteers' contributions of time in Denmark during the period 2004–12 period was explained by 'weakening organizational attachment' (Qvist, Henriksen and Fridberg, 2018). Another possible use administrative register data that was exploited by Hermansen (2018) is to examine patterns of missing data in surveys.

Although the combination of survey and administrative register data is powerful, it is not without limitations. First, it needs to be remembered that while some pieces of information in administrative registers are automatically collected with high precision, other pieces derive from human reporting and are consequently subject to non-response and measurement error. Second, although not a limitation of the data itself, researchers may, if they are not careful, match correct information to the wrong individuals, leading to seriously invalid results. Third, researchers may be swayed to use certain proxy variables that are readily available in administrative registers to capture information of interest. For example, a researcher may rely on annual visits to general practitioners and diagnoses of diseases to proxy health instead of other possible proxy variables like self-rated health that might not be available in the survey data. Fourth, while the combination of survey and administrative register data is advantageous in the study of labour market and health benefits, these advantages disappear in the study of less tangible benefits like emotional rewards, about which administrative registers are uninformative. Fifth, the results that are obtained in a Nordic context in which survey data can readily be merged with administrative register data may not necessarily apply to other contexts. For example, the returns of volunteer work experience appear to depend more strongly on social class in the UK than in the egalitarian Nordic countries (Wilson et al, 2020).

These limitations notwithstanding, I hope that this chapter will inspire researchers to consider whether they might be able to resolve problems in their own research by using a combination of survey and administrative registers. Specifically, I urge researchers to think about whether the powerful combination of survey and administrative register data that is readily available in the Nordic countries might help them to advance our knowledge about the possible benefits of volunteering.

Further reading

- Connelly and colleagues (2016) provide a timely discussion of the role of administrative data in social science research and put its use into perspective by comparing it to other types of big data.
- A detailed introduction to Danish administrative registers on health and social issues is available, thanks to Thygesen and colleagues' (2011) work.
- The empirical work of Qvist and Munk (2018) is an example of how the combination of survey and administrative register data can be fruitfully used to shed light on the labour market benefits of volunteering.

13

Spatial approaches to the voluntary sector

James Bowles

Introduction

How we understand and represent the world through a spatial lens is changing. Spatially referenced data are ubiquitous, and analytical tools such as geographic information systems (GIS) are increasingly accessible and more intuitive than their predecessors. The fruits of the Fourth Industrial Revolution embed novel socio-spatial ontologies into not only our knowledge of the world but our lived experience. Policy initiatives such as the UK's Cabinet Office-led Geospatial Commission see great economic and social value in widening access to spatial data. In the social sciences, proponents of a spatially integrated social science espouse the elucidating power of spatial perspectives and methods for pertinent social challenges.

This chapter shows how this rapidly changing field has been, and can be, applied to study the voluntary sector. It starts by outlining the utility of a spatial orientation for academic and practice-based studies of the voluntary sector, before turning to the benefits and idiosyncratic challenges of regulatory data, grant-making data, spatial indexes and classifications and local government data for exploring the voluntary sector. Relevant data sources having been explored, the tools and approaches to spatial data visualisation are shown and then critically explored in the light of established methodological and ethical concerns. Finally, innovative approaches are encouraged in order to further our spatial understanding of the voluntary sector.

While the chapter draws heavily on the work of academic voluntary sector scholars, it is hoped that it will not only stimulate spatial thinking but also provide practical guidance for practitioners and scholars alike who wish to map and examine the spatial manifestations of the voluntary sector. My primary research interest, the use of spatial data by voluntary sector practitioners, has showed the need for such guidance. To give a broad overview and maintain a focus on the voluntary sector, the chapter only touches on matters of spatial statistics and instead refers readers to in-depth resources.

Understanding the spatial nature of voluntary action

Scholars in this field have utilised a broad range of data sources and methods to present spatially orientated perspectives of the voluntary sector. Studies range in scope from simple analyses of organisational density at varying spatial scales, to understanding the impact of spatially prevalent political ideologies on the aims of voluntary organisations. The question that has received the most attention concerns the spatially equitable distribution of voluntary effort in response to social need. In the UK, there are approximately 166,000 general charities, giving an average ratio of 2.5 organisations per 1,000 people. Analysis at the local authority level shows great variance in charity distribution; Blackpool, Hull and others have a ratio of less than half the national average, while Suffolk, Oxfordshire and others have a ratio of over 50% above the national average (Mohan, 2015).

A more nuanced picture is developed by concentrating on organisations that operate at the local or neighbourhood level. Using data drawn from a nationally representative survey of English voluntary sector organisations (including Community Interest Companies and cooperatives), Clifford (2012) demonstrates that more deprived areas have fewer voluntary sector organisations per head operating in their area than less deprived areas (however, the very most deprived areas do see a slight uptick in organisations per head). The negative relationship between organisation density and deprivation at the local level holds when Charity Commission data on organisations that operate 'locally' is used (Clifford, 2018; McDonnell et al, 2020). Spatio-temporal analysis reveals that rates of charity dissolution also differ significantly by deprivation; 'after 25 years, 34% of organisations remain operating in the most deprived neighbourhoods, compared to 56% in the least deprived' (Clifford, 2018: 1580). Similarly, McDonnell and colleagues (2020) demonstrate enduring differences in charity density as measured against deprivation, although a slight change over time towards a U-shaped distribution (where more deprived areas experience a growth in the density of charities) could be explained by targeted policy efforts, or in national and international charities registering their headquarters in large urban areas, which are typically more deprived.

Looking internationally, Song and Fu's (2018) study of the distribution of charitable foundations in China finds significant spatial concentration and clustering in wealthier, more economically developed cities in the east, such as in and around Beijing, Shanghai and Guangdong. Therefore, Song and Fu (2018) position the work of many charitable foundations as being inconsistent with their mission of delivering resources to the people most in need. McDonnell et al (2020) comment that studies that explore the distribution of charities over a small spatial area or within a specific subsector find a positive correlation between charity location and need;

Peck's (2008) well-known study of antipoverty non-profit organisations in Phoenix, US shows that antipoverty non-profits are *more* likely to locate themselves in areas of high social need than in areas with low social need. Similarly, Fyfe and Milligan (2003) assess the distribution of social welfare voluntary organisations against need in Glasgow, UK and report a strong representation of voluntary organisations in deprived areas of the city, which exist largely because of concentrated state funding programmes.

Beyond exploring the spatial distribution of organisations alongside need, scholars have spatially examined a range of other facets of the voluntary sector. Using data from the UK's Home Office Citizenship Survey, we know that levels of social capital and volunteering in England are positively associated at the regional scale, but that both are determined by deprivation (McCulloch et al, 2012). At the local authority level, the presence of voluntary sector organisations that operate locally has a positive impact on volunteering rates, whereas there is no association between the presence of organisations that operate at the regional and national levels and rates of volunteering (Mohan and Bennett, 2019). In the US, Lecy and colleagues (2019) find that more liberal (Democratic) communities are twice as likely as Republican communities to host organisations that target vulnerable populations and are more reliant on donations versus grants or earned revenue.

A wide range of spatial data is used by the sector itself; the National Council for Voluntary Organisations' (NCVO) Civil Society Almanac provides yearly updates on the composition of 'general charities' registered with the UK's Charity Commission. Insights provided include the high concentration of voluntary sector assets in London, a city in which only 19% of organisations are registered but that holds almost half (48%) of all income for the sector (NCVO, 2020). Data provided by 360Giving, a voluntary organisation that provides open access to published grants data, has been used to explore the spatial distribution of grants to organisations that are not registered with the Charity Commission (Hornung et al, 2020). It reveals that while only 5% of grants go to organisations in Wales, 19% of grants in Wales go to 'below-the-radar' organisations (compared to 13% in the north-west of England and 5% in London). Social Enterprise UK, the national body for social enterprise, undertook a large-scale survey in 2019, the results from which offer useful spatial insights, such as the highly uneven distribution of senior leaders from Black, Asian and minority ethnic (BAME) backgrounds; in London, 69% of social enterprises have at least one member of the leadership team from a BAME background, compared with 22% of organisations across the rest of the south of England (Mansfield and Gregory, 2019).

While quantitative studies of the voluntary sector that make use of administrative and secondary data sources provide great insight, concern from critical cartography scholars in the 1990s of power imbalances between researchers and the researched led to an agenda that prioritised co-produced and participatory spatial studies of the sector. University–voluntary sector partnerships have enabled community groups to use GIS to engage in urban planning discussions (Elwood, 2006) and gain access to otherwise inaccessible datasets and spatial analysis tools (Robinson et al, 2017). The later methodological discussion in this chapter aims to provide the foundation and inspiration for further use of GIS as a participatory research tool.

Voluntary sector data sources

This section explores the advantages and limitations of using data on the voluntary sector that is spatially orientated. If data are abstracted representations of reality, then spatial data are representations of our reality that say something about a location or movement through space. We can refer to it as *geo*spatial data when that location or movement maps onto the Earth's surface. Geospatial data are not much different to many other forms of data, except that they have attached (as attributes) something that gives 'where' to the data, such as a pair of coordinates, or postcode or administrative codes that denote a particular area. This will be demonstrated later in the chapter. First, key sources of data in the UK are discussed.

Regulatory data

Previous chapters in this volume give some detail on the regulatory landscape and accompanying datasets. Here, particular attention is paid to the spatial aspects of regulatory data, and while the discussion primarily concerns regulatory data in England and Wales, many points are equally salient for other regulatory environments.

In England and Wales, a charitable organisation must register with the Charity Commission if it has an income of at least £5,000 per year or wants to take on the legal status of a charitable incorporated organisation. Registration provides the Commission with data on: income and expenditures (more detail on financial matters is available for organisations with an annual income over £500,000); charitable sector (arts, education and so on); beneficiaries (the elderly, other charities and so on); charitable function (provides services, grants and so on); and location. The full register of charities (including inactive organisations) can be downloaded from https://register-of-charities. charitycommission.gov.uk/. The files are intended to be queried using SQL and are provided in .bcp format alongside the necessary SQL scripts to link the separate files. To convert the files from .bcp to a more useable .csv format, see NCVO's guide on compiling a database for Charity Commission data.

Once downloaded, the register of charities contains three spatial attributes. The first is the postcode of the organisation (and any subsidiary charities). There are some postcodes that will require cleaning (numbers in place of letters, incorrect spacing and so on) before they can be used. Once cleaned, the availability of a distinct postcode field is useful for individual mapping, or converting/aggregating data to other geographic units. However, there is a significant methodological caveat that must be acknowledged when using charity postcode data: the headquarters (HQ) effect. The postcode given denotes where the charity is registered and is not necessarily an accurate representation of where funds are spent and missions are delivered. The HQ effect becomes particularly problematic when charities are aggregated at scale, such as at the local authority or regional level, as expenditure and charitable activity will be overestimated in areas that possess a large number of charity headquarters. The City of London, in particular, has a charity ratio of 115.8 charities per 1,000 people, compared to a national average of 2.5 charities per 1,000 people (without the City of London), due to its high density of solicitors' offices through which many charities are registered. For this reason, the City of London is often excluded from studies. In addition, attributing sizeable expenditures to the location of a national HQ can be misleading; the Royal National Lifeboat Institution has an annual income exceeding £190 million and is registered in the mid-size town of Poole, Dorset. Given its national reach, it would be nonsensical to apportion the entire £190 million to an analysis of Poole, or even Dorset. Over 60% of charities with annual incomes of greater than £1 million have a head office with branches in other regions (Mohan and Breeze, 2016), bringing limitations to simplistic spatial studies of resource distribution. Even advanced studies must account for the HQ effect; McDonnell et al (2020) postulate that while the sector overall is more densely populated in less deprived areas, charities that are national or overseas in operation are more densely populated in more deprived areas, possibly because of HQs being in large, urban conurbations that are typically more deprived than smaller, rural areas.

The second spatial attribute provides us with a slightly clearer picture of where the charity *actually* operates. Charities have the option of providing the Commission with details of their 'area of benefit', either as they see it or as it is described in their governing documents. Around half of registered charities do not define their area of benefit. Those that do give us some idea of the spatial extent of their operation. However, area of operations can vary in scale so as to be near meaningless (for example, 'the UK'), or, as the section is free-text and not standardised, entries can include 'The catchment area covered by X school', making large-scale comparisons and mapping exercises difficult. An artefact of the UK's long history of charitable activity is organisations with governing documents that define an area of benefit in relation to an administrative region that existed when the charity was founded, but no longer exists. Mohan and Breeze (2016) estimate that there are around 20,000 charities that define their area of benefit as obsolete administrative units.

For example, Harborne Parish Lands charity is one such organisation, a housing association and grant-making charity with an annual income of £1.5 million and founded from a bequest made in 1576. The area of benefit, as listed in the governing documents, is the Ancient Parish of Harborne, Birmingham, an area obsolete since the abolition of ancient parishes in 1851 that now crosses two local authorities and several local wards. The charity's beneficiaries must come from within the boundaries of the ancient parish (larger, lighter shaded area of the map in Figure 13.1), yet the contemporary ward of Harborne, and the area that people would know as Harborne, is found within the smaller, darker shaded area of the same map. While the historic and contemporary boundaries overlap, a significant spatial mismatch exists.

The third spatial attribute is the most promising, given that the HQ effect limits the utility of postcodes, and stated areas of benefit can suffer from both imprecision and obsolescence (Mohan and Breeze, 2016). The charity commission collects data on an organisation's 'area of operation'. Charities can specify the areas in which they work from a choice of standardised responses. Charities can state between one and ten local authorities/London boroughs in which they work. Listing over ten requires them to state that they work 'throughout England and/or Wales'. Analysing the area of operation alongside financial information and area of activity gives a good picture of

Figure 13.1: Harborne Parish Lands Charity's area of benefit and the ward of Harborne today

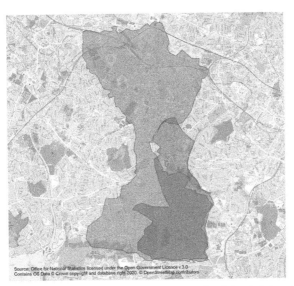

Note: The larger, lighter shaded area is Harborne Ancient Parish. The smaller, darker shaded area is Harborne Ward.

the composition of the registered charity sector in England and Wales: the organisations that work within one local authority make up 62.2% of the registered sector, but they are fairly small, with a median annual expenditure of less than £10,000 (Mohan and Breeze, 2016). Disaggregating by area of operation and focusing on 'local' charities that operate at the local authority level can partially negate the HQ effect and cast an accurate picture of the spatial distribution of local charitable activity in England and Wales. However, it excludes the organisations that operate at a national level and possess the majority of the sector's assets (NCVO, 2020). Therefore, disaggregation by area of operation presents a tale of two sectors, and spatial studies should seek to account for this.

Beyond England and Wales, regulatory regimes and availability of regulatory data differ significantly between jurisdictions (Cordery and Deguchi, 2018; Kane, 2018). The format and extent of available spatial data also differ between regulatory bodies. The Scottish Charity Regulator provides separate fields for the registered address of each organisation, postcode and geographic scope of operation (standardised descriptive options). The Australian Charities and Not-For-Profits Commission, and New Zealand Charities Services both provide separate fields for each part of the registered address and standardised named geographic areas of operation. The Charity Commission for Northern Ireland, the Irish Charities Regulator, and the Commissioner of Charities for Singapore all provide one field that contains the full registered address. The US Internal Revenue Service (IRS) and the Canada Revenue Agency both provide separate fields for each section of the registered address. The IRS Form 990 (which non-profit organisations are required to file) is particularly complex, and there are known issues with the accuracy of the data (McDougle, 2015). The Republic of South Africa's Department of Social Development gives few details, but gives the province in which an organisation is located.

Local voluntary sector listings

Regulatory data, and its inclusion of spatially descriptive variables, provides researchers with a useful resource, but it does not provide a comprehensive picture of voluntary action. To better understand voluntary action at the local scale in the UK, data on grassroots organisations, volunteering statistics and grant-making activities can be sought from voluntary sector infrastructure bodies. Infrastructure bodies serve many functions in supporting their local voluntary sector, such as providing training and capacity-building opportunities, advocating more widely for organisations, coordinating demand and supply of volunteers and distributing grant funding. Organisations such as Macc, the infrastructure body for voluntary and community organisations in Manchester (UK), openly publish aggregated data on the organisations in their local directory, including the areas in which they work (in this case at ward level), and spatially referenced data on the recruitment of volunteers. In many cases, requests will need to be made to infrastructure bodies individually for access to more granular data.

Data held by infrastructure bodies can shed light on work undertaken by grassroots organisations that fall 'below the radar' of regulatory purview. Estimates suggest that there could be between 200,000 and 300,000 such groups in the UK (Mohan, 2012a), and infrastructure-body listings capture part of that population. Following an analysis of 30 local infrastructure-body directories, Mohan (2012b) found that 24% could be cross-referenced with regulatory datasets, meaning that up to two-thirds of listings could comprise 'below the radar' groups. Similarly, Rutherford and Brook's (2016) analysis of data held by the Scottish Council for Voluntary Organisations presents a more comprehensive account of organisations working in rural and deprived areas than regulatory data alone can do. Infrastructure-body listings often capture multiple areas of operation for organisations, aiding in negating the HQ effect discussed earlier. Data on volunteering and grant making held by infrastructure bodies offer researchers a source of granular and timely data with which to undertake local and hyper-local spatial analysis. However, data from infrastructure bodies are supplied to differing standards, making comparisons between localities difficult (Mohan, 2012b). In addition, data may be only captured on groups that benefit from interaction with infrastructure bodies and may exclude the work of 'club-like' groups that do not interact with the wider voluntary sector ecosystem. In the US, data on local voluntary sector listings may be held by organisations such as a local association of non-profits.

Grant-making data

Researchers are fortunate to have access to open and comparable datasets on grant making and international aid, thanks to data standards that have been adopted by the sector. Launched in 2008, the International Aid Transparency Initiative (IATI) has pioneered an open data standard that has reached a point of critical mass where many of the world's leading non-governmental organisations and foundations publish their overseas grant-making activities to the same standard. The IATI data standard schema encourages publishers to include a range of spatial data, from standardised codes indicating the spatial scale of activity, to the exact coordinates of the recipient organisation. In the UK, 360Giving has achieved similar success, as data on over 400,000 grants from 152 funders is openly published with a schema that encourages funders to submit information on the location of grant beneficiaries. The 360Giving dataset is useful for spatial analysis, as it features geocoded grant-making data from both locally focused organisations, such as community foundations, and the UK's largest grant makers, such as the National Lottery Community Fund and the Wellcome Trust.

Local government data

Local governments around the world have been spurred on by the wider open data agenda to publish government-held and produced data in open data 'portals' or 'hubs' (Davies et al, 2019). The English Local Government Transparency Code 2015 requires details of expenditures over £25,000 by central government, and £500 by local government, to be published as open data. This data will often be grouped by sector, giving an insight into local voluntary sector activity. Spatial data that feeds into wider decision-making processes and public health strategy, such as Joint Strategic Needs Assessment data is frequently made available for use. Spatially orientated datasets that may prove useful to researchers include local population and demographic statistics, health and well-being data, crime and antisocial behaviour, and economic data such as job density and unemployment. However, while such data 'portals' or 'hubs' often contain granular and locality-specific data, efforts to publish data, and the formats and spatial scales at which they are provided, vary significantly by local authority. In addition, topics of interest to social researchers and the voluntary sector can be hard to define and measure, and therefore limited data is available. Homelessness statistics are one such example, where accurate and uniform measurement is difficult, and statistics are often provided at a spatial scale that obscures significant variation.

Mapping voluntary sector data

How can our data be turned from tabular data into a compelling visualisation? This section outlines the composition of spatial data and a few key tools and forms of visualisation. Digitally, geographic data is represented in raster and vector forms. Raster representations are a collection of pixels, which are scaled and shaded to represent geographic features. Satellite imagery and aerial photography are forms of raster representations. Vector representations are a collection of points, which are either captured individually or joined up to form lines and polygons. Vector representations are more commonly used in social, economic and administrative mapping exercises, as they are easily adjustable to fit custom spatial representations and are lightweight. Both raster and vector representations are used in a GIS. A GIS compiles spatially referenced layers (Figure 13.2) of data to reveal novel insights.

A plethora of tools exist for spatial visualisation and analysis: ESRI's ArcGIS and ArcGIS Online, QGIS, Mapbox and CartoDB are all designed with spatial data in mind, while general data analysis tools such as Tableau and

Figure 13.2: Illustration of GIS layers

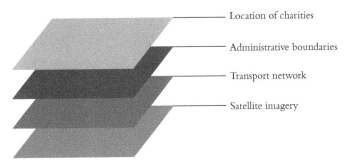

Location of charities

Administrative boundaries

Transport network

Satellite imagery

Microsoft's Power BI have some spatial functionality. Here, I demonstrate some basic building blocks of visualisation and analysis in QGIS and R, as they are both free, open-source and likely to withstand the passage of time. The latest version of QGIS can be downloaded from www.qgis.org, and instructions for getting started with R and RStudio (the integrated development environment commonly used for R) can be found at www.rstudio.com.

There are two primary options when mapping data: use coordinates to locate an object of interest on Earth or join data to a vector layer that represents an area or administrative boundary. To directly locate data on Earth, most packages will require coordinates (latitude/longitude, or easting/northing) for each data point. If you have an attribute with postcode/ZIP code data in, then the centre (centroid) of the postcode area can be added as coordinates by using a free, online tool (such as www.doogal.co.uk for postcodes), via the MMQGIS package in QGIS, or using the 'geocode' function in the R package 'ggmap'. This would be useful for mapping the location of individual voluntary organisations.

More often, we want to group individual data points by geography. To do so, we need to perform a table join where the postcode/ZIP code or another variable is joined to a look-up table that contains the codes for various geographies. In the UK, the Office for National Statistics' (ONS) Open Geography Portal hosts a wide variety of files required for joining data to statistical geographies and then mapping it. The National Statistics Postcode Lookup contains the centroid coordinates and a wide range of statistical geography codes for each postcode area. Table joins can be undertaken in QGIS, by adding both files as 'delimited text files' and joining the layers within 'properties', based on a common attribute. There is more flexibility in R, as the 'join' functions in the 'dplyr' package provide us with several types of join (which also apply for joining datasets discussed in Chapters 11 and 12 in this volume). If you are not comfortable with QGIS, or R, then there may be alternative tools that add the fields based on a unique identifier

Table 13.1: Example merger of datasets based upon postcode

Org_ID	Charity name	Classification	Postcode	Latitude	Longitude	LSOA_Code	LSOA_Name
12345678	The GIS demonstration organisation	Education	SW1A 1AA	51.501009	-0.141588	E01004736	Westminster 018C

or common attribute without the need for much user interaction. One example is David Kane's Find That Charity/Postcode tool, which adds geographic fields based on charity registration number or postcode. Using the postcode as a common attribute, data on a charity (Org_ID, Charity Name and Classification) can be merged with spatial attributes (Table 13.1).

Having added spatial attributes to our data, we can now visualise it. To do so, we need to perform a spatial join, where a vector that displays the boundaries of the area we are interested in is joined to our tabular data (such as Table 13.1) using a common attribute, such as the LSOA (Lower Super Output Area) code in Table 13.1. The ONS's Open Geography Portal holds a wide variety of boundaries in multiple formats and is a highly useful resource. Step-by-step instructions on performing a spatial join are provided in the further reading section at the end of this chapter. Finally, spatial data can be visualised in multiple ways. For example, the distribution of charities by local authority in England looks different when mapped as a choropleth (Figure 13.3) or in a hexbin format (Figure 13.4). Dot-density maps can also give a visual overview of distribution, such as the distribution of social service charities in England that operate at the local or national level.

It is beyond this chapter to delve into the field of spatial statistics, and readers are directed to Comber and Brunsdon (2021) for a comprehensive overview of undertaking statistical analysis of spatial data in R. However, there are a few statistical concepts that readers should know. The first is Kernel Density Estimation, a technique used on nonparametric data to estimate density based on observed points or lines. It works by smoothing data points across a continuous space to present kernels of density (picture a histogram that spreads out over space). The second is Geographically Weighted Regression, a spatial extension of ordinary least squares regression that allows for an assessment of the spatial heterogeneity in the estimated relationships between the independent and dependent variables. The third is Moran's I, a measure of spatial autocorrelation, that is, how similar one object is to others around it. Readers should also be aware of the Modifiable Areal Unit Problem (MAUP), a statistical bias that occurs when different statistical results are observed due to (a) the grouping data of the same data at different spatial scales, or (b) spatial data being aggregated in different spatial patterns. Various mitigating measures can be taken to address the MAUP, but anyone undertaking spatial analysis should be cognisant of it.

Figure 13.3: Choropleth map of charities per 1,000 people in England by local authority in 2015 (excluding City of London)

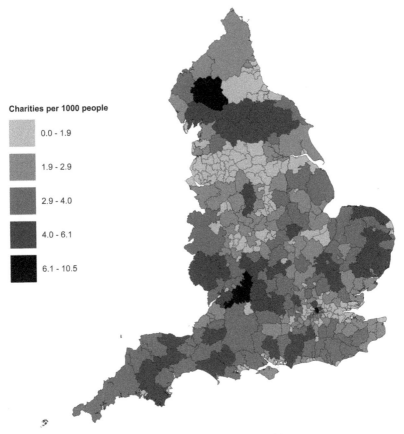

Charities per 1000 people

0.0 - 1.9

1.9 - 2.9

2.9 - 4.0

4.0 - 6.1

6.1 - 10.5

Source: Office for National Statistics licensed under the Open Government Licence v.3.0
Contains OS Data © Crown copyright and database right 2020.

Finally, there are ethical and normative considerations to attend to when taking a spatial approach to the voluntary sector. The discipline of critical cartography, and the work of various critical voluntary sector scholars, draws attention to mapping as a politically engaged practice in which power and authority are exercised. Spatial analysis and map-making necessarily must draw a boundary within the sector, therefore privileging groups or parts of the sector at the expense of others (Appe, 2013). While mapping the voluntary sector can raise the profile of grassroots groups and strengthen wider policy processes through enhanced knowledge, it also classifies the work of groups in ways that can be co-opted for unwelcome agendas, such as state policy delivery (Nickel and Eikenberry, 2016). In addition, when studying a sector that is by definition voluntarily organised, to what extent

Figure 13.4: Hexbin map of charities per 1,000 people in England by local authority in 2015 (excluding City of London)

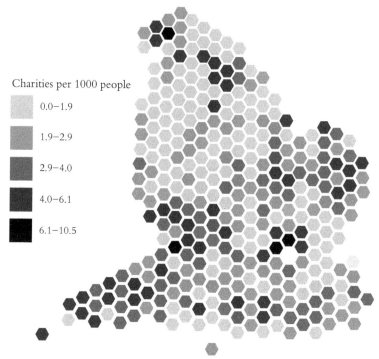

Source: Hexagon Cartogram boundary by Ben Flanagan, reproduced under a Creative Commons Attributions 4.0 International Licence, no changes made.

can or should researchers dispense prescriptive advice on the most efficient or optimal location of the voluntary sector and its resources (Mohan and Breeze, 2016)?

Conclusion

This chapter has presented readers with an overview of the utility of a spatial approach to the voluntary sector for academia and the sector itself. The socially just distribution of voluntary sector resources is a concern that is well suited to a spatial approach and has been investigated across time periods and spatial scales. Knowledge and understanding of spatially observable facets of the voluntary sector such as grant making and volunteering is enhanced through a spatial approach, as their allocation, density and proximity to each other are measured. While we are fortunate to have access to many spatially orientated voluntary sector data sources, the spatial scales, format and availability vary by source. Caveats such as the HQ effect and MAUP present particular challenges for undertaking spatial analysis.

Innovation in this field could emerge from two sources, with the first being the gathering of data on the spatial manifestation of both traditional and emerging spaces of voluntary action. Traditional aspects of the voluntary sector leave digital traces on platforms that often contain spatial attributes and constitute a new resource for voluntary sector resources. These include adverts for volunteers, tweets about events and online fundraising pages. New spaces of digital volunteering and community action such as the growth in digitally organised mutual aid groups during the COVID-19 outbreak all happen *somewhere*, both virtually and physically. They are not aspatial and will leave digital traces or ultimately lead to action in physical space. Understanding the location of digital volunteers, and the dynamic interaction between digital spaces for organising and physical voluntary sector spaces could be fruitful areas of research. Second, advances in geoparsing (the extraction of free-text descriptions of places) and natural language processing offer researchers the ability to better understand the allocation of resources as described textually in funding bids and reports, the areas of benefit described by organisations and real-time spatial trends in digital and physical community and voluntary action through social media posts and content on digital platforms.

Further reading
- David Abernathy (2017) gives a practical guide to capturing and visualising spatial data using a range of tools, including QGIS and R.
- Mohan and Breeze (2016) theoretically, normatively and empirically explore the UK's charity sector through a spatial lens.
- Work from leading geographers and social policy scholars is brought together by Adam Whitworth (2019) to show the utility of a spatial approach in the social sciences.

14

Restudies, surveys and what counts as volunteering

Jon Dean and Diarmuid Verrier

Introduction

In 1996, *Nonprofit and Voluntary Sector Quarterly* published an article by Ram Cnaan, Femida Handy and Margaret Wadsworth entitled 'Defining who is a volunteer: Conceptual and empirical considerations' (Cnaan et al, 1996; henceforth CHW). At the time of writing it has been cited nearly 1,000 times, according to Google Scholar, and is widely known by those researching volunteering as an influential article on how we think about 'what counts' as volunteering. Musick and Wilson (2008: 14) rightly refer to CHW's work as 'remarkable', arguing that it cements the idea that volunteering is one of very few activities that will take place even if costs exceed rewards, and the more this balance is breached (that is, more cost to the individual in completing the activity), the more the public are likely to classify an activity as volunteering. CHW's work has been extensively built on by its authors in international collaboration to examine volunteering definitions in a cross-cultural context (for example, Handy et al, 2000; Meijs et al, 2003; Liu et al, 2017), showing both that the original instrument has internal reliability, and also how this innovative and malleable piece of work can be applied temporally across cultures.

In the light of the 25th anniversary of this important article's publication, this chapter will first reflect on the significance of CHW's original methodological and knowledge contribution; second, report on an attempt by the authors to replicate and update CHW's work using a revised version of the original survey, exploring the ways in which a new generation conceptualise and define volunteering outside of the US; and third, reflect on the methodological issues at stake. The use of adapted restudies in this field is significant because of the changing nature of (youth) volunteering, particularly in relation to more interventionist government policy in the field and increased necessity for students to volunteer so as to gain experience and derisk the transition from education to work (Dean, 2014) as part of a neoliberal economic and social order. We do not seek to comment on 'appropriate' motivations or to understand the rewards sought by volunteers, nor do we argue that motivations should be considered when *defining* an activity as volunteering or not, but the chapter's findings demonstrate that people *do* take motivation into account in their personal judgement of 'what counts' as volunteering (but that notions of 'free will' are prioritised in judgements). As such, this chapter will serve as a methodological note to try to explain the gap that exists between the practitioner/researcher/legal definition and the public's everyday approach to the concept of volunteering.

The original study

CHW is a comprehensive and systematic study of two closely related issues: how volunteering has been defined by a range of organisations and academics, and whether the general public views certain activities as volunteering or not. The first element of CHW is an examination of 11 definitions of volunteering from the 1980s and early 1990s, drawn from organisations and academic work. The sample definitions were frequently cited, or came from a variety of arenas and disciplines, or covered definitions used by practitioners and scholars, or, more subjectively, ranged from 'broad' definitions of volunteering to 'pure' ones. By this means, CHW sought to identify how stringent were the 'rules' for being 'counted' as a volunteer: whether the definition provided room for everyone who works without full financial compensation to class as a volunteer, or whether 'only those who give extensively of their time and effort without recompense are volunteers' (p 366).

Using a Guttman scale, the authors identified four dimensions common to definitions of volunteering – free choice, remuneration, structure, intended beneficiaries – within each of which exists a spectrum from pure to broad categorisations (that is, within free choice we move from 'free will' to 'relatively uncoerced' to 'obligation to volunteer'; within intended beneficiaries we move from 'helping strangers' to 'helping friends or relatives' to 'helping oneself'). They reasoned that individuals who would generally take a broader view of volunteering would accept purist definitions within these (although perhaps feeling that these were too constrictive), but that those with a purist view would not feel that broader conceptualisations counted as volunteering.

So, for example, within remuneration, the purest conceptualisations of volunteering state that no money must change hands for an activity to count as volunteering; yet as we move down the list we see this grip loosen, with first there being no expectation of any financial deal between parties, to the (common) payment of expenses such as public transport fares, or money to cover fuel costs or lunch. Finally, we have perhaps the least common, that of a weekly stipend or very low pay, such as in schemes where volunteers take full-time positions fulfilling roles such as care work and not only have larger expenses such as housing costs covered but are given a weekly allowance to cover essentials.

The second element to CHW, and perhaps its larger contribution to scholarly studies of volunteering, is the principle that public perception of what counts as volunteering is related to the net cost of undertaking an activity to the individual: ultimately the more inconvenience (cost) there is to the volunteer, the more likely their work is to be considered by others as volunteering. This has been tested across several different countries and societies (Handy et al, 2000; Meijs et al, 2003), with some variation, but a general feeling that some remuneration and obligation or pressure to participate consistently leads individuals to be less likely to define an activity as volunteering.

CHW tested this theory using a survey (n=514) completed by members of the general public in Pennsylvania, drawn from patrons of local libraries, local volunteers and volunteer training workshop attendees, employees from a manufacturing company and university students. The sample is discussed at length in CHW (p 375), with the authors pointing out that it was largely a sample of convenience. Two-thirds were female, over half were married and three-quarters were active volunteers. Key for our adapted restudy, 90% were aged 25 or over. Building on McCurley and Vesuvio's (1985) 'Who is a volunteer?' inventory, the CHW survey asked participants to respond to 21 examples using a five-point Likert scale. A score of 1 indicated that the respondent thought the individual was *definitely* a volunteer; a score of 5 that the respondent thought the individual was *definitely not* a volunteer. CHW (p 376) used the mean result for each item as a way to rank the activities in terms of whether respondents thought the fictional actors were volunteering or not, and the standard deviation to indicate how much discrepancy or disagreement there was about each one. The final rankings allowed the authors to conclude that their hypothesis was supported and that 'an individual who incurs a high net cost ... is likely to be viewed as more of a volunteer than someone who incurs a low net cost' (p 378–379).

The restudy

Teaching a final-year undergraduate module on voluntary sector issues, Dean always asks his students to read CHW. They rarely enjoy it: most find it repetitive, dully obsessed with minor and abstract differences, achingly technical at times, and see the survey as relatively simple compared with much other quantitative work they study. However, when they unpick the survey, and discuss whether the items are in the right order, an argument generally ensues. Ranking volunteering is something students and the public want to engage with, but of more interest to the younger generation is the issue of motivation, why the volunteers are doing these tasks, not just in terms of obligation but also in terms of self-aggrandisement (Dean, 2020). One of the criticisms Musick and Wilson (2008: 15) make of the CHW study is that psychological benefits are absent, meaning that cannot examine whether respondents would judge an activity as 'impure' volunteering if the personal benefit were non-material.

In this spirit, we devised a more contemporary and youth-focused take on CHW. Undergraduate students at Sheffield Hallam University in England (n=356) were given a new survey based on the one initially developed by McCurley and Vesuvio (1985) and CHW, but with the examples radically changed to explore psychic benefits and motivations. The main reason was to create scenarios that were much more youth focused, to understand specifically what an undergraduate student sample would feel about activities and behaviours that they themselves were more likely to participate in or see among their peer group. Volunteer motivations were a key part of this, a well-studied aspect of volunteering, being that they are at the heart of recruitment. That CHW use the word 'purist' in some of their discussion about volunteering is, in hindsight, a really interesting way to think about participation in voluntary activities, especially at a time when many authors (for example, Hustinx and Meijs, 2011; Dean, 2015b) have written about the role of individualisation and instrumentality when it comes to volunteering. Neoliberalism, the extension of market forces to non-market activities, has led to young people being much more guided into volunteering, not through explicit obligation, but through a need for a competitive edge in the jobs market and in university applications. These forces mean that young people's ability to think about volunteering in purely altruistic terms are diminished.

The sample for the restudy was centred on convenience. Every participant was a social science undergraduate student and the mean age was 20 years. The sample was 56.2% female to 43.8% male; 46% of students said that they currently volunteered or had done so recently. There were no significant differences for any of the items based on gender, volunteer status or age.

As can be seen in Table 14.1, where a lower mean indicates that an item is perceived more as volunteering, motivations matter when judging 'what counts' as volunteering. The first three ranked statements are all variations on a theme, from the direct 'A teenager who assists unpaid for five hours a week in a homelessness hostel', to the motivationally specific 'A lonely teenager who assists a charity without pay for five hours a week in order to make new friends' and 'A teenager who assists unpaid for five hours a week in a homelessness hostel solely in order to develop their CV'. In these cases, the mean score rises from 1.06, to 1.79, to 2.05. We see how motivations matter, that being motivated by something instrumental and personal, as opposed to 'pure' giving, means that your act of altruism is less likely to be seen as volunteering even if it is still altruistic. However, not all instrumental motivations are the same. Volunteering to make new friends

Table 14.1: Student perceptions of volunteers, by rank order, with factor loadings

Rank	Variable	Mean	SD	F1	F2	F3
1	A teenager who assists unpaid for five hours a week in a homelessness hostel	1.06	0.29			
2	A lonely teenager who assists a charity without pay for five hours a week in order to make new friends	1.79	0.98	.78		
3	A teenager who assists unpaid for five hours a week in a homelessness hostel solely in order to develop their CV	2.05	1.02	.74		
4	A teenager who mows their elderly neighbour's lawn every month	2.57	1.24		.54	
5	A student who assists in organising a collection for a food bank, who does so solely because they are attracted to an existing student helper at the food bank	2.63	1.24	.75		
6	The worker who after 15 years continues to sit on the board of a charity for no pay, but no longer cares about the charity's work	2.87	1.28	.64		
7	A recent graduate who assists a severely disabled university student full time, and who receives money for their food, rent and a small weekly stipend	2.93	1.29		.31	
8	A student who organises a protest against government budget cuts	3.01	1.30		.84	
9	The worker who, by their own choice, works overtime without pay	3.06	1.36		.39	
10	A student who is doing a community service project as an enforced part of their educational qualifications	3.40	1.29			.63
11	A student who participates in a protest against government budget cuts	3.61	1.16		.87	
12	The person who has been unemployed for six months and is required to work at a supermarket without pay in order to continue receiving Jobseeker's Allowance	4.26	1.08			.69
13	A step-parent who looks after their spouse's children from a previous marriage	4.27	1.04			.40
14	The convicted fraudster who chooses to complete 200 hours of community service instead of serving a prison sentence	4.44	0.94			.67
Mean of factors				2.32	3.05	4.13

(1.79) and doing so to develop one's CV (2.05) are noticeably lower scores than that of 'A student who assists in organising a collection for a food bank, who does so solely because they are attracted to an existing student helper at the food bank' (2.63). While the activity is slightly different, and volunteering for a food bank may be considered less charitable than helping at a homeless shelter, it is interesting to see that volunteering due to a teenage crush is viewed in a harsher light by young survey respondents. This may be because the discourse of CV-building and making friends is one commonly articulated by both government and non-profit sector-led volunteer recruitment campaigns; or it may be that in a culture that is far more aware of stalking and 'creepy' behaviour such a motivation is considered unreasonable and hugely diminishes the volunteering activity, irrespective of its efficacy. Equally, if respondents view volunteering due to attraction (that is, implying less of a cost) as likely to be short term, this could be understood through CHW's net cost theory.

'A student who *organises* a protest against government budget cuts' (3.01) is seen as slightly more of a volunteer than 'A student who *participates* in a protest against government budget cuts' (3.61), indicating that the amount of commitment given to a task does have some bearing on an activity's likelihood of being judged as volunteering. (This suggests that micro-volunteering, signing petitions or sharing a social media post to spread awareness, is not likely to be seen as a good example of volunteering.) Further, participants felt that neither activity really counted as volunteering (that is, scores for both were at the mid-point of the scale or higher). This finding suggests that political activism is not a field that young people associate with volunteering, yet we know that political parties' local operations and campaigns would crumble without volunteers. The boundary between political action and voluntary labour is one that is under-explored in the academic research literature and could be a fertile ground for volunteering researchers, especially those looking to understand motivations rooted in passion and partisanship. Similarly, volunteering boundaries are worth discussing in relation to the teenager mowing their neighbour's lawn, who is not judged as much of a volunteer as a young person assisting in a hostel. While this is likely due to the inferred time commitment required, as per net cost theory, it may also be to do with the formal/informal split in volunteering, and the greater respect given to volunteering formally for an organisation rather than informally on an ad hoc basis for a friend or neighbour: just considered part of ordinary community life, rather than going 'above and beyond'.

Finally, one intuitive way to split the data would be to suggest that any item that scores 1.00–2.33 (the lowest third of possible scores) is counted as volunteering by this sample, any item that scores 3.67–5.00 (the highest third) is not counted as volunteering, and all the measures in between are, in the public's mind, up for debate. Therefore, only 3 of these 14 items classify 'as volunteering', according to respondents. We could suggest that this sample, and perhaps the wider public, takes a more puritanical approach to titling an activity as 'volunteering' than scholars and professionals would: that, in CHWs terms, purity is easily lost.

Factor analysis

One development that we were able to bring into our data analysis was the use of factor analysis. The volunteering examples that the participants were asked to rate each contained a volunteering activity, but typically also implied a reason for why the person was engaging in that activity. With these data, it is possible to investigate whether there are different factors underlying what people consider volunteering to be. For example, it could be the case that *only* people's motivations for their activity matter. In this case, all items would relate to a single 'motivation' factor and people's responses to items would be primarily influenced by their subjective view of the person's motivations. Alternatively, there could be an additional factor alongside a 'motivation' factor, such as one relating to the kind of activity being done. Factor analysis is a statistical procedure that reduces many variables into a smaller number of factors, and helps us to assess these questions. These factors underlie how people respond to items on a scale. While the questionnaire was not designed with factor analysis in mind, the data were found to be appropriate (KMO > .7; Bartlett's test < .05). Specifically, we used principal components analysis (PCA; technically different from a factor analysis, but essentially identical in outcome for a dataset of this nature), using oblique rotation (a method of clarifying factor structure that allows factors to correlate with one another).

PCA is an exploratory technique that does not set up an a priori model for how many factors there should be or which items should load onto which factor. Thus, it is necessary to make a decision as to which of several possible factor solutions is best for the dataset. An initial PCA produced a scree plot, which shows the relative explanatory strength of every possible factor. Those factors that explain markedly more variance than others should be considered worthwhile and retained. In this case, there were three factors that met this criterion. An additional technique for determining the number of factors to retain is called parallel analysis. This compares the strength of the factors observed in the current dataset with those from a random dataset (where strength refers to the amount of variance in the data explained by the factors). Those factors that are stronger than the comparable factors from a random dataset should be retained. For the current dataset, three factors were stronger than would be expected based on comparison with factors from random data. As such, parallel analysis suggested that three factors were appropriate. This decision being made, the PCA was carried out again, with the constraint that items had to load onto one of those three factors.

By and large, the distribution of items across the three factors made good conceptual sense (see Table 14.1). The first factor (F1) represents items where the underlying motivation for volunteering is instrumental in some respect, for example, in order to make friends, develop a CV or to pursue a romantic relationship, and where the context is a traditional charitable endeavour. The second factor (F2) represents items that include idealistic or selfless motivations for volunteering, such as protesting against government cuts or mowing an elderly neighbour's lawn, but that do not refer to traditional 'charity' contexts. And the third factor (F3) includes items wherein people are constrained or forced to volunteer, such as to receive Jobseeker's Allowance, or as part of their qualifications, or instead of serving a prison sentence. In other words, this factor represents external motivation.

This demarcation fits within a major theory of motivation from within the psychology literature. Self-determination theory (SDT) (Ryan and Deci, 2000) posits that motivation for behaviour ranges along a continuum from fully intrinsic (entirely self-determined behaviour) to fully extrinsic. Formally, this continuum is characterised in terms of six types of behavioural regulation (from most to least self-determined): intrinsic motivation, integrated regulation, identified regulation, introjected regulation, external regulation and amotivation (where there are neither intrinsic nor extrinsic reasons for taking part in an activity). At the extremes of the continuum, intrinsic motivation is associated with activities that are carried out in the absence of any external impetus, due solely to one's own interests and the inherent satisfaction that they bring. Extrinsic motivation occurs when one takes part in an activity because one feels forced to do so, or for external reward (for example, money). The second factor maps well onto intrinsic motivation, while the third maps well onto external regulation. The first factor relates most strongly to a combination of integrated, identified and introjected regulation. These, collectively, reflect internally generated reasons for taking part in an activity that go beyond a pure interest. For example, to maintain one's self-concept, to develop oneself, or out of a sense of guilt. The fact that these factors mapped onto SDT so coherently is particularly impressive, given that the measure was not constructed with this theory of motivation in mind.

What is also revealed by the factor analysis is that there are clear hierarchies within groupings driven by participants' responses to certain stimuli within the items. Factor 1 (mean 2.32) contains a group of items that all mention an explicit charitable context ('assisting a charity', 'collection for a food bank', 'sit on the board of a charity') and no indication of a lack of free will; Factor 2 (mean 3.05) contains more complex activities not traditionally associated with charity (protests, mowing a lawn) but that also do not display any lack of free will; whereas within Factor 3 (mean 4.13) the items all either directly mention or imply a level of enforced participation ('required to work', 'enforced part of their educational qualifications'). Therefore this shows a hierarchy of what counts as volunteering, where free will is established as the primary driver of whether respondents view an activity as volunteering or not – the items in Factors 1 and 2 both demonstrate free will and therefore score lower then Factor 3.

Within Factor 2, while there is little to no stated personal benefit within the items, the intended beneficiaries are less clear as well. There are many more potential critiques that one could make of these activities as volunteering than in Factor 1, where the only critique one can reasonably make is that the individual is benefiting themselves at the same time as benefiting others. Within the items that make up Factor 1, intended beneficiaries are clear, with a charitable purpose or outcome of the activity listed, alongside an obvious client group (such as charity service users, the homeless or food bank users). But within Factor 1 there exists another hierarchy, where respondents are less likely to view an activity as volunteering if instrumental personal motivation is mentioned as well as an external (charity focused) intended beneficiary.

Therefore the methodological innovation within this adapted restudy allows us to build on the initial work of CHW by demonstrating to some extent how the young public in this case rank the importance of CHW's four dimensions: free will appears most important to respondents when assessing the nature of volunteering activity. More work needs to be done to examine the ranking of the four dimensions: researchers could design similar surveys that have activities explicitly linked to the four dimensions and the categories within them, and then use a factor analysis to demonstrate how the four dimensions inform the general public's opinion, and whether our young sample's views correspond with those of older adults.

Conclusion

Non-profit studies is, like the sector it seeks to understand, a 'loose and baggy monster' (Kendall and Knapp, 1995). In part this is because voluntary activity happens both in public and in private, and not just in the non-profit sector, as public services are increasingly outsourced to non-profit providers and corporate social responsibility projects mean that private sector is increasingly engaged in 'giving back' through altruistic activity. What we are left with is an activity (the giving of one's time) that can exist in any social scenario, in any field, anywhere. That is why CHW is so valuable and deserves some specific recognition a generation on. It is a research project that has helped us to plant a flag in the ground in terms of codifying a number of definitions of volunteering; it was a key contribution in the net cost approach to volunteering; and it popularised and established a role for attitudinal surveys in scoping volunteering.

This modified replication of the classic study had two key procedural amendments. First, we updated the examples used in the original study so that they are more relevant to young people today. Second, while in CHW only 7.4% of respondents were aged 18–24, we wanted to collect data from an undergraduate population (mean age = 20), for whom volunteering is a significant issue. We recognise, however, that the specific nature of this sample limits the degree to which our conclusions can be generalised to non-students. Future work in this area should consider including examples relating to micro-volunteering. While micro-volunteering acts involve an extremely low investment of time and effort, there are still factors that might influence the degree to which people see particular acts as being better or worse examples of volunteering, such as sharing a charity appeal on social media for selfless reasons versus sharing the same appeal as a method of signalling virtue. Applying a more rigorous methodology would also be useful. Both this study and the original did not perfectly isolate the factors that might be relevant to deciding the degree to which an act counts as volunteering (for example, employment status, time, cost, motivation, context), making it difficult to ascertain whether the decision was due to one factor or another. Using an experimental vignette approach (Atzmüller and Steiner, 2010) would avoid this problem, and assist in fulfilling the factor analysis-centred research agenda previously outlined.

Restudies are an underutilised possibility in social science research, even though learning through looking at already existing data forms a key part of most budding social scientists' training. Looking again at others' data can be a rewarding experience, as it fosters the critical examination of both others' and one's own research practice (Wilson, 2014), challenging the notion that we should be guarded in our research practice and the anti-historical idea that interpretation and analysis can be carried out only by the original research team. Several authors (see Charles and Crow, 2012) demonstrate how restudies have (re)emerged, due to the increased availability of archives (see Chapter 7) and the comparable richness and breadth of previous studies when compared to the specialised narrowing of modern social inquiry, driven by the pressures of the neoliberal academy. Looking at old data afresh, using new methodological techniques (see Chapter 8), drawing on new histories of the period or applying theoretical ideas or learning from social change can be insightful rather than repetitive.

For those teaching non-profit studies and other similar courses, creating, distributing and collectively analysing responses with students is not a difficult task; samples of 500 or 300 are not required. As a small-scale classroom activity, using CHW as a jumping-off point for discussions of what counts as altruism, and to what extent motivations matter in the volunteer workforce, are key debates for future non-profit leaders to be having. Asking respondents why some causes are more worthwhile than others, and how non-profits working in those less popular areas can adapt, or if they should, are debates stimulated by the CHW model and will be of interest to sector practitioners. Students frequently undertake restudies and surveys of student populations. By combining these here, and adapting the survey in the light of recent research findings and theoretical ideas, and by incorporating an extra data analysis tool from a different discipline (here psychology), hopefully we have demonstrated the possibilities of bricolage in research, how small innovations and changes can reveal big changes. Research findings are not set in stone, fundamental findings need constant testing, and by doing so, even on a small scale, contributions to the sum of what is known can be made.

Further reading
- Cnaan et al's (1996) original study is a foundational text for thinking about what counts as volunteering.
- To see the original survey restudied in a different cultural context, Lui and colleagues (2017) sample students in Hong Kong.
- For a critical engagement with how people benefit from volunteering, see Dean (2020).

15

Conclusion

Jon Dean and Eddy Hogg

As we outlined in the Introduction, this volume is an effort to encourage scholars in the field to focus on methodology rather more than at present. Our hope is that it will start a conversation about how we can best research and understand the myriad different forms of voluntary action across the world. Given the numerous books, journals, articles and reports devoted to exploring new facets of giving, charity and voluntary organisations, it seemed strange to us that methodological debates appear to take place mostly in disciplines rather than the field itself. This book has presented a rich compendium of methodological innovations, and the challenges that different researchers face in gathering, using and explaining their data, in different approaches. By taking the case study approach, we have shone a light on new and modified approaches that leading and emerging scholars are taking in applying different methods to our field. The study and practice of methods is, in our view, very much a lived discipline, as it is much easier to understand and grapple with the use of a methodological approach in practice as opposed to seeing it described as a dry process. Hopefully, the cases presented here will offer inspiration for your work, which in turn abets replication and validity to a new approach, as the twin projects of Dean and Bhati have done.

We have seen calls in the last 10 years, from policy makers and organisations in the voluntary and community sector alike, for particular types of measurement when it comes to the impact of voluntary action. Often this is framed around calls to quantify 'impact' in terms of contributions to gross domestic product or savings delivered for the state. The contributions to this volume have shown that this kind of dogmatic emphasis on a certain type of highly positivist method does not serve the best interests of those who want to understand the contribution that voluntary action makes to individuals, communities and societies. Demonstrating impact does not need to mean only spelling it out in hard currency. By embracing a range of methods and using those that are suited to understanding the different facets of voluntary action, we can gain the richest possible understanding, one that is celebratory, critical, nuanced, precise and so much more.

While the book is broken up into chapters that focus on a specific method or data type in order that readers can have direct advice, we hope that people will read across chapters – to see how our understanding of volunteering, for example, can be grown by conversations between researchers who sit and conduct focus groups with young non-volunteers and those who study data that covers every citizen in a given country. While the scale of these approaches could not be further apart, they are united by the overarching goal of both researchers to better understand the phenomenon of volunteering. What therefore emerges from contributors is a strong argument for epistemological pluralism – there is more than one way to skin the research cat, and research hierarchies and methodological rigidity do not serve any of our ambitions to better understand the social world. Eikenberry and Song's (Chapter 4) call for greater respect for interpretivist approaches and their role in effecting social change speaks to a still divided methods landscape where some approaches are still valued more highly than others (a valuing that is context dependent), and to a long-established hierarchy of knowledge (Harding, 1991: 15). This is not to decry any methodological tradition, but to see that 'methodology can move beyond data collection and interpretation, toward becoming an active process enabling change' (Kingston et al, 2021), especially when it foregrounds the beneficiaries and service users of charities, their experiences and the realities of 'doing' voluntary action.

There is a balance to be struck in a book such as this. Methods are boundaryless, in that one can learn to be a good researcher in one field from material, stories and knowledge from another. People can learn to be ethnographers through Van Maanen's police ethnography or Annette Lareau's work in schools, even if they are not exploring criminal justice or education. Those developing their statistical skills won't always get to practise and play with datasets in their own field. So, there is no reason why the methodological insights offered here cannot be applied to other spheres of action. Charity shops are shops. Charity annual reports are annual reports. There are lessons in Fitton's (Chapter 3) ethnographic account of the difficulties of working in retail that span sectors, profit-making and non-profit, just as it is also a story of class and community, useful to scholars working in those more abstract arenas. Cordery and McConville's call in Chapter 10 for us to pay more attention to annual reports is good advice not just for those of us who concentrate our time on the voluntary sector but, rather, for all who want to better understand how organisations operate and how they think about and present themselves. Scholars of a wide range of topics can make use of archives to better understand the past and the present, not just those studying the charity archives that Brewis documents in Chapter 7.

But it is also true that charity shops are not shops, or at least they have radically different institutional logics to most shops. Archives are archives, but there are differences in accessing charity archives as compared to business or government archives. Brewis sets out how to continue the work of accessing and making use of voluntary sector organisation archives, and some of her processual lessons and insight will be useful for those looking into non-voluntary organisations, and some won't. It sounds trite, but some things are the same and some things are not the same. As such, the book is useful in both a very specific and a far broad sense. Lindsey's Chapter 8 will be hugely useful for anyone thinking of working with data from the Mass Observation Project but will also have wider use for any scholars planning to undertake archival or diary research. And it offers a different way to think about methods than is offered by the standard textbooks such as those by Bryman or Babbie. The chapters here discuss grounded examples of research projects that the authors themselves have undertaken, rather than general commentary on a range of different approaches. They tell the reader both something about using a particular method to better understand a particular facet of voluntary action and something about the wider strengths, weaknesses, opportunities and challenges with that research method. It is not just a 'how to', it is a 'how I did' and 'how you could do better'.

What isn't here, and writing during a pandemic

We do not claim, and indeed, it would not be possible, for this volume to contain reflection on every method or methodological issue. The book has been generally organised around methods (a chapter on participatory methods, for example, a chapter on visual methods, a chapter on content analysis) in order to try to help others researching voluntary using a specific method or mix of methods. Authors have articulated in varying ways how the doing of 'their method' or approach is suitable for investigating an element of voluntary action, and the specific challenges they faced in doing so, or how they see innovation and change occurring in data-collection approaches in the future. Some touch on issues of ontology and epistemology, and how these philosophical framings within research come to bear on the nature of data analysis, with such debates emerging organically through chapters, including focus on data quality and how we know what we know.

The issue of research ethics is also one that emerges only occasionally. Conducting ethical data collection is of course paramount, and has become a central topic of research practice in recent years, following rather more laissez-faire attitudes a generation ago. Social research has witnessed a shift from the 'do no harm' approach to one of social justice (Kara, 2018: 9), exemplified here in Bennett's Chapter 5, with a greater amplification of issues like processual consent (where participants are continually asked for consent and reminded that they are in a study), greater cultural sensitivity by researchers and improved representation. What some see as over-cautiousness in the social sciences is perhaps due to overzealousness in the natural sciences that leads to unethical practices (see Saini, 2019). The importance of and how we operationalise concepts as diverse as anonymity, data security, General Data Protection Regulations, emancipation, egalitarianism and the moral aim to conduct 'research with' rather than 'research on' participants cannot be overstated. The fact that ethical considerations appear infrequently in this book is not to disavow our belief in their significance. Rather, given research ethics' importance, while devoting one chapter to ethnography or restudies feels appropriate, doing the same for 'ethics in research on voluntary action' would be both an almost impossible job for an author, and unbecoming of the issues at hand. We invite scholars to consider this point, and think that if the focus on methods of research into voluntary action has increased, the next stage should be the ethics of voluntary action research. Some work in this regard (for example, Third Sector Research Forum, 2021) is underway, and academic researchers have a dual role to play, both in helping charities to understand good ethical practice and the current expectations of data gathering, and also in listening to those charities and their beneficiaries of what are realistic and expected ethical rules for research. A key element of chapters in this book has been challenging the notion of 'ivory tower' academic research, and instead working in a form that fits with research participants, objects and the wider world, rather than making these fit rigid academic expectations.

There are moves within social research towards decolonising curricula and thinking (see Bhambra et al, 2014, among many others), and moving towards more ethical and indigenous methods (Kara, 2018; Smith, 2013). Similarly, the voluntary sector is engaged in debates about representation and equality, particularly related to the lack of people of colour in positions of leadership across the sector (see, for example, Lingayah et al, 2020) and within voluntary sector research. It would be remiss of us as editors to not point out that it is to the book's detriment that its contents almost entirely take as the focus issues within voluntary action in the Global North, with researchers based in Europe and North America. While methodological issues, more than most other elements of research practice, cross both national and cultural boundaries (as compared to policies, perhaps, or theories and concepts), we do recognise our role in failing to help change the ways in which research on voluntary action is organised. We can't change the iniquitous and unfair ways in which the academic world is structured, but we can and do acknowledge that the contents of this volume and its authors are representative of how research into voluntary action is, rather than how many calls for change are arguing that it should be. Diversity and equality in participation and leadership entail a commitment to diversity in epistemological approach and sources of theoretical knowledge, such as understanding that indigenous communities often possess different ontological and epistemological mindsets, where, for example, spiritual or experiential knowledges are prioritised (Kara, 2018).

It would also be remiss not the mention the strange and sad noise against which this book was put together. At the time of writing, the coronavirus pandemic has taken four million lives around the world, caused endless heartache and loss and made work more difficult. For academic researchers, the pandemic often meant a shift to remote working, teaching and researching from home, all the while balancing childcare, family responsibilities and the general ensuing ennui of being locked away from loved ones and normal life during a crisis that engulfed the world and laid bare our continuing inequalities and injustices. The move to online research and data collection is not covered in the book, although this is a necessarily growing field (Adams-Hutcheson and Longhurst, 2017; Fielding et al, 2017), including texts specifically on researching during COVID-19 (Kara and Khoo, 2020). Growing too is the field of research into the pandemic and its aftermath, including the huge outpouring of voluntary effort, both channelled through existing voluntary organisations and that which led to the formation of a massive number of formal and informal mutual support groups (see, for example, Bynner et al, 2021; Thiery et al, 2021). If voluntary action is to play a key part in the recovery – and it surely is – then understanding it is more important than ever. Researchers will continue to innovate, to adapt to the 'new normal' and to question which methodological approaches will best illuminate the social phenomena they wish to better understand.

In an ever-changing world, the final point to make about the content of the book is that there are many, many more methodological approaches that could have been covered here. Experimental approaches, social media analysis and more arts-based approaches are topics especially that we would have liked to incorporate. Unfortunately, some of these topics were lost to the pandemic, with authors' schedules and home and personal lives hugely disrupted, alongside the vagaries of the long publishing process. Any issue's lack of attention here does not mean we and our colleagues who have contributed chapters do not think it worthy of attention: the volume is not meant to be the last word on researching voluntary action, but merely one of the first.

Final thoughts

The recent growth in the study of voluntary action around the world, during the two decades since the turn of the century especially, has meant an increase in the number of researchers and research centres undertaking the study of voluntary action in all its diverse forms. Researchers have undertaken these studies because they believe that voluntary action matters and that we therefore need to understand it as best we can. And, as researchers, our methods are the crucial link between what we want to understand better and how we gain that understanding. Voluntary action matters in part *because* of its difference. It is not driven by compulsion. It occurs in public but is undertaken by private individuals. This book has explored how researchers have grappled with how best to study and understand this field of activities, what their experience has shown to work well and what it has shown the challenges to be.

We believe that the reflections and analyses of the new and established researchers whose work is presented in this volume will have been of value to everyone in the field: early-career, returning and experienced academic researchers of voluntary action; students at undergraduate and postgraduate level taking the burgeoning range of modules and programmes on voluntary action and those who have chosen the field as the focus for their dissertation; and researchers working in the voluntary, non-profit and community sectors, who are seeking to evaluate their work and impact. Theoretical, philosophical and methodological rigidity within silos produces more limited work than that influenced by a variety of perspectives. Hopefully, this volume has introduced readers to some new ideas, and avenues they hadn't considered before in their research.

References

Abernathy, D. (2017) *Using geodata and geolocation in the social sciences: Mapping our connected world*. London: SAGE.

Abraham, K.G., Helms, S. and Presser, S. (2009) 'How social processes distort measurement: The impact of survey nonresponse on estimates of volunteer work in the United States', *American Journal of Sociology*, 114(4): 1129–1165.

Adams-Hutcheson, G. and Longhurst, R. (2017) '"At least in person there would have been a cup of tea": interviewing via Skype', *Area*, 49(2): 148–155.

Agger, B. (1998) *Critical social theories: An introduction*. Boulder: Westview Press.

Ainsworth, D. (2009) 'Third sector should be called "first sector", Cameron says'. *Third Sector*. www.thirdsector.co.uk/third-sector-called-first-sector-cameron-says/policy-and-politics/article/917732.

Allen, A. and McAllister, B. (2018) 'CEO compensation and performance in US private foundations', *Financial Accountability and Management*, 34(2): 117–132.

Andreoni, J. (1990) 'Impure altruism and donations to public goods: A theory of warm-glow giving', *The Economic Journal*, 100(401): 464–477.

Antonacopoulou, E. (2010) 'Beyond co-production: Practice-relevant scholarship as a foundation for delivering impact through powerful ideas', *Public Money & Management*, 30(4): 219–226.

Appe, S. (2013) 'Deconstructing civil society "maps": The case of Ecuador', *Administrative Theory and Praxis*, 35(1): 63–80.

Appel, M. (2008) 'Fictional narratives cultivate just-world beliefs', *Journal of Communication*, 58(1): 62–83.

Archambeault, D.S., Webber, S. and Greenlee, J. (2015) 'Fraud and corruption in U.S. nonprofit entities: A summary of press reports 2008–2011', *Nonprofit and Voluntary Sector Quarterly*, 44(6): 1194–1224.

Atzmüller, C. and Steiner, P.M. (2010) 'Experimental vignette studies in survey research', *Methodology: European Journal of Research Methods for the Behavioural and Social Sciences*, 6: 128–138.

Back, L. (2007) *The art of listening*. London: Berg.

Back, L. (2009) 'Researching community and its moral projects', *Twenty-First Century Society*, 4(2): 201–214.

Baert, S. and Vujic, S. (2018) 'Does it pay to care? Volunteering and employment opportunities', *Journal of Population Economics*, 31: 819–836.

Baines, S. and Hardill, I. (2008) '"At least I can do something": The work of volunteering in a community beset by worklessness', *Social Policy and Society*, 7(3): 307–317.

Bearman, J., Carboni, J., Eikenberry, A. and Franklin, J. (2017) *The landscape of giving circles/collective giving groups in the U.S., 2016*, https://scholarworks.iupui.edu/bitstream/handle/1805/14527/giving-circles2017-2.pdf?sequence=4&isAllowed=y.

Beck, A.C., Campbell, D. and Shrives, P.J. (2010) 'Content analysis in environmental reporting research: Enrichment and rehearsal of the method in a British–German context', *British Accounting Review*, 42(3): 207–222.

Bekkers, R. and Wiepking, P. (2006) 'To give or not to give, that is the question: how methodology is destiny in Dutch giving data', *Nonprofit and Voluntary Sector Quarterly*, 35(3): 533–540.

Bell, A., Hartman, T., Piekut, A., Rae, A. and Taylor, M. (2020) *Making sense of data in the media*. London: SAGE.

Benjamin, L.M. (2012) 'The potential of outcome of measurement for strengthening nonprofits accountability to beneficiaries', *Nonprofit and Voluntary Sector Quarterly*, 42(6): 1224–1244.

Bhambra, G.K., Shilliam, R. and Orrells, D. (2014) 'Contesting imperial epistemologies: Introduction', *Journal of Historical Sociology*, 27(3): 293–301.

Bharath, D.M. (2019) 'Ethical decision making and the Avengers: Lessons from the screen to the classroom', *Public Integrity*, 22(4): 1–4.

Bhati, A. (2018) 'Market, gender, and race: Representations of poor people in fundraising materials used by International Nongovernmental Organizations (INGOs)'. Doctoral dissertation, University of Nebraska, Omaha. https://www.proquest.com/docview/2089465041.

Bhati, A. and Eikenberry, A.M. (2016) 'Faces of the needy: The portrayal of destitute children in the fundraising campaigns of NGOs in India', *International Journal of Nonprofit and Voluntary Sector Marketing*, 21(1): 31–42.

Bielefeld, W. (2006) 'Quantitative research for nonprofit management', *Nonprofit Management and Leadership*, 16(4): 395–409.

Biemer, P. (2009) 'Measurement errors in sample survey', in D. Pfeffermann and C.R. Rao (eds), *Handbook of statistics, vol. 29A, Sample surveys: design, methods and applications*. Amsterdam: North-Holland, pp 281–315.

Bishop, L. (2007) 'A reflexive account of reusing qualitative data: Beyond primary/secondary dualism', *Sociological Research Online*, 12(3): 43–56.

Bloodgood, E.A., Tremblay-Boire, J. and Prakash, A. (2014) 'National styles of NGO regulation', *Nonprofit and Voluntary Sector Quarterly*, 43(4): 716–736.

Borry, E.L. (2018) 'Linking theory to television: Public administration in parks and recreation', *Journal of Public Affairs Education*, 24(2): 234–254.

Bourdieu, P. (1990) *The logic of practice*. Cambridge: Polity Press.

Brandsen, T. and Honingh, M. (2016) 'Distinguishing different types of coproduction: A conceptual analysis based on the classical definitions', *Public Administration Review*, 76(3): 427–435.

Braun, V. and Clarke, V. (2013) *Successful qualitative research: A practical guide for beginners*. London: SAGE.

Breen, O. (2018) 'Redefining the measure of success: a historical and comparative look at charity regulation', in M. Harding (ed), *Research handbook on not-for-profit law*. Cheltenham: Edward Elgar Publishing Limited, pp 549–569.

Breeze, B. and Dean, J. (2012) 'Pictures of me: User views on their representation in homelessness fundraising appeals', *International Journal of Non-profit and Voluntary Sector Marketing*, 17(2): 132–143.

Brewis, G. (2014) *A social history of student volunteering: Britain and beyond, 1880–1980*. New York: Palgrave Macmillan.

Brewis, G. and Finnegan, A. (2012) 'Volunteering England', *Contemporary British History*, 26(1): 119–128.

Brewis, G., Ellis Paine, A., Hardill, I., Lindsey, R. and Macmillan, R. (2021a) *Transformational moments in social welfare: What role for voluntary action?* Bristol: Policy Press.

Brewis, G., Ellis Paine, A., Hardill, I., Lindsey, R. and Macmillan, R. (2021b) 'Co-curation: Archival interventions and voluntary sector archives', *AREA*, https://doi.org/10.1111/area.12768.

Broadbridge, A. and Horne, S. (1994) 'Who volunteers for charity retailing and why?' *The Service Industries Journal*, 14(4): 421–437.

Brody, E. (2012a) 'U.S. nonprofit law reform: The role of private organizations', *Nonprofit and Voluntary Sector Quarterly*, 41(4): 535–559.

Brody, E. (2012b) 'Sunshine and shadows on charity governance: Public disclosure as a regulatory tool', *Florida Tax Review*, 12(4): 183–234.

Brook, O. and Rutherford, A.C. (2017) 'Using administrative data to understand civil society organisations in Scotland'. Working Paper.

Brooker, P. (2020) *Programming with Python for social scientists*. London: SAGE.

Bukowski, K. and Buetow, S. (2011) 'Making the invisible visible: A photovoice exploration of homeless women's health and lives in central Auckland', *Social Science & Medicine*, 72: 739–746.

Burawoy, M. (2009) *The extended case method: Four countries, four decades, four great transformations, and one theoretical tradition*. Berkeley, CA: University of California Press.

Bushouse, B. and Sowa, J. (2012) 'Producing knowledge for practice: Assessing NVSQ 2000–2010', *Nonprofit and Voluntary Sector Quarterly*, 41(3): 497–513.

Bynner, C., McBride, M. and Weakley, S. (2021) 'The COVID-19 pandemic: the essential role of the voluntary sector in emergency response and resilience planning', *Voluntary Sector Review*, https://doi.org/10.1332/204080521X16220328777643.

Carboni, J. and Eikenberry, A.M. (2021) 'Do giving circles democratize philanthropy? Donor identity and giving to historically marginalized groups', *Voluntas*, 32(2), 247–256.

Carlson, J., Kelley, A.S. and Smith, K. (2010) 'Government performance reforms and nonprofit human services: 20 years in Oregon', *Nonprofit and Voluntary Sector Quarterly*, 39(4): 630–652.

Charities Aid Foundation (2019) *CAF UK Giving 2019*. www.cafonline.org/docs/default-source/about-us-publications/caf-uk-giving-2019-report-an-overview-of-charitable-giving-in-the-uk.pdf?sfvrsn=c4a29a40_4

Charles, N. and Crow, G. (2012) Community re-studies and social change, *The Sociological Review*, 60(3): 399–404.

Chattoe, E. (2006) 'Charity shops as second hand markets', *International Journal of Nonprofit and Voluntary Sector Marketing*, 5(2): 153–160.

Chouliaraki, L. (2013) *The ironic spectator: Solidarity in the age of post-humanitarianism*. Cambridge: Polity.

Clarke, G. (1997) *The photograph*. Oxford: Oxford University Press.

Clifford, D. (2012) 'Voluntary sector organisations working at the neighbourhood level in England: Patterns by local area deprivation', *Environment and Planning A*, 44(5): 1148–1164.

Clifford, D. (2018) 'Neighborhood context and enduring differences in the density of charitable organizations: reinforcing dynamics of foundation and dissolution', *American Journal of Sociology*, 123(6): 1535–1600.

Cnaan, R.A., Handy, F. and Wadsworth, M. (1996) 'Defining who is a volunteer: Conceptual and empirical considerations', *Nonprofit and Voluntary Sector Quarterly*, 25: 364–383.

Coghlan, D. and Shani, A. (2008) 'Collaborative management research through communities of inquiry', in A. Shani, S. Mohrman, W. Pasmore, B. Stymne and N. Adler (eds), *Handbook of collaborative management research*. Thousand Oaks, CA: SAGE, pp 601–614.

Cohen, M.P. (2008) 'Unit nonresponse', in P.J. Lavrakas (ed), *Encyclopedia of survey research methods* (2nd edn). Thousand Oaks, CA: SAGE, pp 927–928.

Cohen, S. (2001) *States of denial: Knowing about atrocities and suffering*. Malden, MA: Polity Press.

Collier, J. and Collier, M. (1957) 'An experiment in applied anthropology', *Scientific American*, 59: 37–49.

Collins, S., Grace, R. and Llewellyn, G. (2016) 'Negotiating with gatekeepers in research with disadvantaged children: A case study of children of mothers with intellectual disability', *Children & Society*, 30(6): 409–509.

Comber, L. and Brunsdon, C. (2021) *Geographical data science and spatial data analysis: An introduction in R*. London: SAGE.

Connolly, R., Playford, C.J., Gayle, V. and Dibben, C. (2016) 'The role of administrative data in the big data revolution in social science research', *Social Science Research*, 59: 1–12.

Cordery, C. and Deguchi, M. (2018) 'Charity registration and reporting: a cross-jurisdictional and theoretical analysis of regulatory impact', *Public Management Review*, 20(9), 1332–1352.

Cordery, C.J., Baskerville, R. and Porter, B. (2011) 'Not reporting a profit: Constructing a non-profit organisation', *Financial Accountability & Management*, 27(4): 363–384.

Coule, T. (2013) 'Theories of knowledge and focus groups in organization and management research', *Qualitative Research in Organizations and Management*, 8(2): 148–162.

Coule, T., Dodge, J. and Eikenberry, A.M. (forthcoming) 'Towards a typology of critical nonprofit studies: A literature review', *Nonprofit and Voluntary Sector Quarterly*.

Cova, V. and Rémy, E. (2007) 'I feel good – who needs the market? Struggling and having fun with consumer-driven experiences', in A. Caru and B. Cova (eds), *Consuming experience*. New York: Routledge, pp 51–64.

Crotty, M. (1998) *The foundations of social research: Meaning and perspective in the research process*. Thousand Oaks, CA: SAGE.

Cushing, I. (2018) *Text analysis and representation*. Cambridge: Cambridge University Press.

Damm, C., Chan, O. and Kane, D. (2021) 'Classifying the charity register', *Voluntary Sector Studies Network*. www.vssn.org.uk/2021/01/11/classifying-the-charity-register.

Darbyshire, P., MacDougall, C. and Schiller, W. (2005) 'Multiple methods in qualitative research with children: More insight or just more?', *Qualitative Research*, 5(4): 417–436.

Dart, R. (2004) 'Being business-like in a nonprofit organization: A grounded and inductive typology', *Nonprofit and Voluntary Sector Quarterly*, 33(2): 290–310.

Davey, E. and Scriven, K. (2015) 'Humanitarian aid in the archives: Introduction', *Disasters*, 39(2): 113–128.

Davies, J. (2018) '"We'd get slagged and bullied": Understanding barriers to volunteering among young people in deprived urban areas', *Voluntary Sector Review*, 9(3): 255–272.

Davies, R. (2015) *Public good by private means: How philanthropy shapes Britain*. London: Alliance Publishing Trust.

Davies, T., Walker, S., Rubinstein, M. and Perini, F. (eds) (2019) *The state of open data: Histories and horizons*. Cape Town and Ottawa: African Minds and International Development Research Centre.

Dawson, E., Dodd, R., Roberts, J. and Wakeling, C. (2004) 'Issues and challenges for records management in the charity and voluntary sector', *Records Management Journal*, 14(3): 111–115.

Dayson, C. (2013) 'Understanding financial vulnerability in UK third sector organisations: Methodological considerations and applications for policy, practice and research', *Voluntary Sector Review*, 4(1): 19–38.

Dayson, C., Baker, L., Rees, J., Batty, E., Bennett, E., Damm, C., Coule, T., Patmore, B., Garforth, H., Hennessy, C., Turner, K., Kacklin-Jarvis, C. and Terry, V. (2018) *The value of small: In-depth research into the distinctive contribution, value and experiences of small and medium-sized charities in England and Wales,* Project Report. Sheffield: Sheffield Hallam University.

de Waele, E. and Hustinx L. (2019) 'Governing through volunteering: The discursive field of government-initiated volunteering in the form of workfare volunteering', *Nonprofit and Voluntary Sector Quarterly*, 48(2): 72S–102S.

Dean, J. (2014) 'How structural factors promote instrumental motivations within youth volunteering: A qualitative analysis of volunteer brokerage', *Voluntary Sector Review*, 5(2): 231–247.

Dean, J. (2015a) 'Drawing what homelessness looks like: Using creative visual methods as a tool of critical pedagogy', *Sociological Research Online*, 20(1): 2.

Dean, J. (2015b) 'Volunteering, the market, and neoliberalism', *People, Place and Policy*, 9(2): 139–148.

Dean, J. (2017) *Doing reflexivity: An introduction.* Bristol: Policy Press.

Dean, J. (2020) *The good glow: Charity and the symbolic power of doing good.* Bristol: Policy Press.

Dean-Olmsted, E., Bunin Benor, S. and Gerstein, J. (2014) *Connected to give: Community circles.* Los Angeles, CA: Jumpstart.

Delap, L. (2018) ' "Disgusting details which are best forgotten": Disclosures of child sexual abuse in twentieth-century Britain', *Journal of British Studies*, 57(1): 79–107.

DeLyser, D. (2014) 'Towards a participatory historical geography: Archival interventions, volunteer service, and public outreach in research on early women pilots', *Journal of Historical Geography*, 46: 93–98.

DeLyser, D., Sheehan, R. and Curtis, A. (2004) 'EBay and research in historical geography', *Journal of Historical Geography*, 30: 764–782.

Denzin, N.K. (1996) *Interpretive ethnography: Ethnographic practices for the 21st century.* Thousand Oaks, CA: SAGE.

Dey, P. and Teasdale, S. (2016) 'The tactical mimicry of social enterprise strategies: Acting "as if" in the everyday life of third sector organizations', *Organization*, 23(4): 485–504.

Dhanani, A. and Connolly, C. (2012) 'Discharging not-for-profit accountability: UK charities and public discourse', *Accounting, Auditing and Accountability Journal*, 25(7): 1140–1169.

Dixon, L. (2016) Exploring the experience of volunteers and paid staff in hospices, using LEGO serious play. *NCVO.* https://blogs.ncvo.org.uk/2016/11/09/exploring-the-experience-of-volunteers-and-paid-staff-in-hospices-using-lego-serious-play/.

Docherty, P. and Shani, A. (2008) 'Learning mechanisms as means and ends in collaborative management research', in A. Shani, S. Mohrman, W. Pasmore, B. Stymne, and N. Adler (eds), *Handbook of collaborative management research*. Thousand Oaks, CA: SAGE, pp 163–182.

Dogra, N. (2012) *Representation of global poverty: Aid, development and international NGOs*. New York, NY: I.B. Tauris.

Duneier, M. (1999) *Sidewalk*. New York, NY: Farrar, Straus and Giroux.

Ecer, S., Magro, M. and Sarpça, S. (2017) 'The relationship between nonprofits' revenue composition and their economic-financial efficiency', *Nonprofit and Voluntary Sector Quarterly*, 46(1): 141–155.

Eckerd, A. (2015) 'Two approaches to nonprofit financial ratios and the implications for managerial incentives', *Nonprofit and Voluntary Sector Quarterly*, 44(3): 437–456.

Edwards, D. and Gibson, L. (2017). 'Counting the pennies: The cultural economy of charity shopping', *Cultural Trends*, 26(1): 70–79.

Eikenberry, A.M. (2009) *Giving circles: Philanthropy, voluntary association, and democracy*. Bloomington, IN: Indiana University Press.

Eikenberry, A.M. (2010) 'Giving circles: Self-help/mutual aid, community philanthropy, or both?', *International Journal of Self Help and Self Care*, 5(3): 249–278.

Eikenberry, A.M. (2017) 'Who benefits from giving circles in the U.S. and UK?', *The Foundation Review*, 9(3): 33–45.

Eikenberry, A.M. and Breeze, B. (2018) 'Growing philanthropy through giving circles: Collective giving and the logic of charity', *Journal of Social Policy & Society*, 17(3): 349–364.

Eliasoph, N. (2013) *The politics of volunteering*. Cambridge: Polity Press.

Ellard-Gray, A., Jeffrey, N., Choubak, M. and Crann, S. (2015) 'Finding the hidden participant: Solutions for recruiting hidden, hard-to-read, and vulnerable populations', *International Journal of Qualitative Methods*, 14(5): 1–10.

Elwood, S. (2006) 'Negotiating knowledge production: The everyday inclusions, exclusions, and contradictions of participatory GIS research', *The Professional Geographer*, 58(2): 197–208.

Feeney, S. (2000) 'Introduction: Symposium: Authority, legitimacy, voice, and the scholar–practice question', *Nonprofit and Voluntary Sector Quarterly*, 29(1): 5–10.

Fielding, N., Lee, M. and Black, G. (2017) *The SAGE handbook of online research*. London: SAGE.

Fitton, T. (2013) 'The "quiet economy": An ethnographic study of the contemporary UK charity shop'. Doctoral dissertation, University of York. http://etheses.whiterose.ac.uk/5639/7/THESIS%20complete%20including%20bibliography.docx.pdf.

Flores, R. (2014) 'From personal troubles to public compassion: Charity shop volunteering as a practice of care', *The Sociological Review*, 62(2): 383–399.

Foster, I., Ghani, R., Jarmin, R.S., Kreuter, F. and Lane, J. (2017) 'Introduction', in I. Foster, R. Ghani, R.S. Jarmin, F. Kreuter and J. Lane (eds), *Big data and social science: A practical guide to methods and tools*. Boca Raton, FL: CRC Press, pp 1–22.

Foucault, M. (1977) *Language, counter-memory, practice: Selected essays and interviews*. Ithaca, NY: Cornell University Press.

Franks, S. (2013) *Reporting disasters: Famine, aid, politics and the media*. London: Hurst.

Fraser, A. (2015) *Urban legends: Gang identity in the post-industrial city*. Oxford: Oxford University Press.

Freshwater, D., Sherwood, G. and Drury, V. (2006) 'International research collaboration: Issues, benefits and challenges of the global network', *Journal of Research in Nursing*, 11(4): 295–303.

Fyfe, N.R. and Milligan, C. (2003) 'Space, citizenship, and voluntarism: Critical reflections on the voluntary welfare sector in Glasgow', *Environment and Planning A*, 35(11): 2069–2086.

Gallagher, M. (2009) 'Data Collection and Analysis', in E. Tisdall, M. Davis and M. Gallagher (eds), *Researching with children and young people: Research design, methods and analysis*. London: SAGE, pp 65–153.

Gauntlett, D. (2007) *Creative explorations: New approaches to identities and audiences*. London: Routledge.

Geertz, C. (1973a) *The interpretation of cultures*. New York, NY: Basic Books.

Geertz, C. (1973b) 'Thick description: Toward an interpretive theory of culture', in *The interpretation of cultures: Selected essays*. New York, NY: Basic Books, pp 3–32.

Gerbner, G., Gross, L., Morgan, M. and Signorielli, N. (1986) 'Living with television: The dynamics of the cultivation process', in J. Bryant and D. Zillman (eds), *Perspectives on media effects*. Hilldale, NJ: Lawrence Erlbaum Associates, pp 17–40.

Giddens, A. (1987) *Social theory and modern sociology*. Stanford, CA: Stanford University Press.

Gillies V. and Edwards R. (2011) 'Working with archived classic family and community studies: Illuminating past and present conventions around acceptable research practice', *International Journal of Social Research Methodology*, 14(4): 321–330.

Goffman, E. (1959) *The presentation of self in everyday life*. London: Penguin.

Goodall, R. (2000) 'Organising cultures: Voluntarism and professionalism in UK charity shops', *Voluntary Action*, 3(1): 43–57.

Götz, N., Brewis, G. and Werther, S. (2020) *Humanitarianism in the modern world: The moral economy of famine relief*. Cambridge: Cambridge University Press.

Granovetter, M. (1983) 'The strength of weak ties: A network theory revisited', *Sociological Theory*, 1: 203–233.

Gregson, N., Brooks, K. and Crewe, L. (2002) 'Discourse, displacement and retail practise: Some pointers from the charity retail project', *Environment and Planning A*, 34(9): 1661–1683.

Guishard, M. (2009) 'The false paths, the endless labors, the turns now this way and now that: Participatory action research, mutual vulnerability, and the politics of inquiry', *The Urban Review*, 41(1): 85–105.

Guta, A., Flicker, S. and Roche, B. (2013) 'Governing through community allegiance: a qualitative examination of peer research in community-based participatory research', *Critical Public Health*, 23(4): 432–451.

Hand, D.J. (2018) 'Statistical challenges of administrative and transaction data', *Journal of the Royal Statistical Society: Series A (Statistics in Society)*, 181(3): 555–605.

Handy, F., Cnaan, R.A., Brudney, J.L., Ascoli, U., Meijs, L.C. and Ranade, S. (2000) 'Public perception of "who is a volunteer": An examination of the net-cost approach from a cross-cultural perspective', *Voluntas*, 11: 45–65.

Harding, S. (1991) *Whose science? Whose knowledge? Thinking from women's lives*. Milton Keynes: Open University Press.

Hariri, J.G. and Lassen, D.D. (2017) 'Income and outcomes: Social desirability bias distorts measurements of the relationship between income and political behavior', *Public Opinion Quarterly*, 81(2): 564–576.

Harper, D. (1988) 'Visual culture: Expanding sociological vision', *The American Sociologist*, 23(1): 54–70.

Harper, D. (2002) 'Talking about pictures: A case for photo elicitation', *Visual Studies*, 17(1): 13–26.

Harris, M. (2001) 'The place of self and reflexivity in third sector scholarship: An exploration', *Nonprofit and Voluntary Sector Quarterly*, 30(4): 747–760.

Harris, M. and Harris, J. (2002) 'Achieving organizational collaboration in the nonprofit sector: An action research approach', *Organization Development Journal*, 20(1): 28–35.

Harvell, J., Kirby, J., Robinson, L., Courage, F., Lamour, S. and Scantlebury, J. (2012) 'Description of the 1980s Mass Observation Directives', http://blogs.sussex.ac.uk/observingthe80s/files/2014/01/DS_Directive_Summary_29_Feb1.pdf

Haski-Leventhal, D. and Foot, C. (2016) 'The relationship between disclosure and household donations to nonprofit organizations in Australia', *Nonprofit and Voluntary Sector Quarterly*, 45(5): 992–1012.

Helmig, B., Ingerfurth, S. and Pinz, A. (2014) 'Success and failure of nonprofit organizations: Theoretical foundations, empirical evidence, and future research', *Voluntas: International Journal of Voluntary and Nonprofit Organizations*, 25(6): 1509–1538.

Hennink, M. and Leavy, P. (2014) *Understanding focus group discussions.* New York, NY: Oxford University Press.

Hermansen, J. (2018) 'Getting it right: Estimating the share of volunteers in Denmark', *Nordic Journal of Social Research*, 9, https://doi.org/10.7577/njsr.2146

Hinton, J. (2013) *The mass observers: A history, 1937–1949.* Oxford: Oxford University Press.

Hodgkinson, V. (2003) 'Volunteering in global perspective', in P. Dekker and L. Halman (eds), *The values of volunteering: Cross-cultural perspectives.* New York, NY: Kluwer Academic/Plenum, pp 35–54.

Hogg, E. (2018) 'What regulation, who pays? Public attitudes to charity regulation in England and Wales', *Nonprofit and Voluntary Sector Quarterly*, 47(1): 72–88.

Horne, S. and Broadbridge, A. (1995) 'Charity shops: A classification by merchandise mix'. *International Journal of Retail and Distribution Management*, 23(7): 17–23.

Horne, S. and Maddrell, A. (2002) *Charity shops: Retailing, consumption and society.* London: Routledge.

Hornung, L., Kane, D. and Jochum, V. (2020) 'Below the radar, exploring grants data for grassroots organisations', *Local Trust*, www.threesixtygiving.org/wp-content/uploads/Charity-regulators-transparency.pdf.

Hustinx, L. and Meijs, L. (2011) 'Re-embedding volunteerism: In search of a new collective ground', *Voluntary Sector Review*, 2: 5–21.

Hyndman, N. and McConville, D. (2016) 'Transparency in reporting on charities' efficiency: A framework for analysis', *Nonprofit and Voluntary Sector Quarterly*, 45(4): 844–865.

Hyndman, N. and McConville, D. (2018) 'Making charity effectiveness transparent: Building a stakeholder-focussed framework of reporting', *Financial Accountability & Management*, 34(1): 133–147.

International Council on Archives (2004) *The records of NGOs, memory to be shared: A practical guide in 60 questions.* Paris: International Council on Archives.

Israel, B.A., Schulz, A.J., Parker, E.A. and Becker, A.B. (1998) 'Review of community-based research: Assessing partnership approaches to improve public health', *Annual Review of Public Health*, 19(1): 173–202.

Janes, J.E. (2016) 'Democratic encounters? Epistemic privilege, power, and community-based participatory action research', *Action Research*, 14(1): 72–87.

Jeffreys, E. (2018) 'Curating philanthropy and socialist governance: The Chinese charity museum', *Museums & Social Issues*, 13(2): 78–93.

Johnsen, S., May, J. and Cloke, P. (2008) 'Imag(in)ing "homeless places": Using auto-photography to (re) examine the geographies of homelessness', *Area*, 40(2): 194–207.

Jones, A. (2004) 'Involving children and young people as researchers', in S. Fraser, V. Lewis, S. Ding, M. Kellett and C. Robinson (eds), *Doing research with children and young people*, London: Sage, pp 113–131.

Kane, D. (2018) 'International comparison of information available from charity regulators', www.threesixtygiving.org/wp-content/uploads/Charity-regulators-transparency.pdf.

Kara, H. (2018) *Research ethics in the real world: Euro-Western and Indigenous perspectives.* Bristol: Policy Press.

Kara, H. and Khoo, S-M. (2020) *Researching in the age of COVID-19.* Bristol: Policy Press.

Kendall, J. and Knapp, M. (1995) 'A loose and baggy monster', in J. Davis Smith, C. Rochester and R. Hedley (eds), *An introduction to the voluntary sector.* London: Routledge, pp 66–95.

Kidd, A. (1996) 'Philanthropy and the social history paradigm', *Social History*, 21(2): 180–192.

Kingston, K., Luke, B., Furneaux, C. and Alderman, L. (2021) 'A reflection on critical methodology: Accountability and beneficiary participative evaluation in third sector research', *Voluntas*, https://doi.org/10.1007/s11266-021-00395-x.

Korelitz, J. (2002) 'Second helpings', *Real Simple*, (August): 85–90.

Kovács, G. and Spens, K.M. (2005) 'Abductive reasoning in logistics research', *International Journal of Physical Distribution & Logistics Management*, 35(2): 132–144.

Krippendorf, K. (2018) *Content analysis: An introduction to its methodology* (4th edn). Thousand Oaks, CA: SAGE.

Krueger, R. and Casey, M. (2000) *Focus groups: A practical guide for applied research.* London: SAGE.

Laqua, D. (2013) *The age of internationalism and Belgium, 1880–1930: Peace, progress and prestige*, Manchester: Manchester University Press.

Laqua, D., Van Acker, W. and Verbruggen, C. (eds) (2019) *International organizations and global civil society: Histories of the Union of International Associations.* London: Bloomsbury.

Law, J. and Urry, J. (2004) 'Enacting the social', *Economy and Society*, 33(3): 390–410.

LeCompte, M.D. and Schensul, J.J. (1999) *Designing and conducting ethnographic research* (Vol. 1). Plymouth: Rowman Altamira.

Lecy, J.D. and Searing, E.A.M. (2015) 'Anatomy of the nonprofit starvation cycle: An analysis of falling overhead ratios in the nonprofit sector', *Nonprofit and Voluntary Sector Quarterly*, 44(3): 539–563.

Lecy, J.D., Ashley, S.R. and Santamarina, F.J. (2019) 'Do nonprofit missions vary by the political ideology of supporting communities? Some preliminary results', *Public Performance & Management Review*, 42(1): 115–141.

Lee, H. (1990) *Critical social research.* London: Unwin Hyman.

Legard, R., Keegan, J. and Ward, K. (2003) 'In-depth interviews', in J. Ritchie and J. Lewis (eds), *Qualitative research*. London: SAGE, pp 138–169.

Li, Y. (2017) 'Is methodology destiny? Religiosity and charitable giving', *International Journal of Social Economics*, 44(9): 1197–1210.

Liamputtong, P. (2011) *Focus group methodology: Principles and practice*. London: SAGE.

Lincoln, Y. and Guba, E. (1986) 'But is it rigorous? Trustworthiness and authenticity in naturalistic evaluation', *New Directions for Evaluation*, 1986(30): 73–84.

Lindsey, R. (2020) 'Sampling the digitised collection of 1980s Mass Observation writing', in *Mass Observation Project 1981–2009*, www. massobservationproject.amdigital.co.uk

Lindsey, R. and Bulloch, S. (2014a) 'A sociologist's field notes to the Mass Observation archive: A consideration of the challenges of 're-using' Mass Observation data in a longitudinal mixed-methods study', *Sociological Research Online*, 19(3): 8.

Lindsey, R. and Bulloch, S. (2014b) 'What the public think of the "Big Society": Mass Observers' views on individual and community capacity for civic engagement', *Third Sector Research Centre (TSRC) Working Paper 95*, Birmingham: TSRC. www.birmingham.ac.uk/Documents/college-social-sciences/social-policy/tsrc/working-papers/working-paper-95.pdf.

Lindsey, R. and Mohan, J. (2018) *Continuity and change in voluntary action: Patterns, trends and understandings*. Bristol: Policy Press.

Lindsey, R., Metcalfe, E. and Edwards R. (2015) 'Time in mixed methods longitudinal research: Working across written narratives and large scale panel survey data to investigate attitudes towards volunteering', in N. Worth and I. Hardill (eds), *Researching the lifecourse: Critical reflections from the social sciences*. Bristol: Policy Press, pp 43–62.

Lingayah, S., Wrixon, K. and Hulbert, M. (2020) *Home truths: Undoing racism and delivering real diversity in the charity sector*. London: Voice4Change/ ACEVO.

Liu, E.S.C., Ching, C.W. and Wu, J. (2017) 'Who is a volunteer? A cultural and temporal exploration of volunteerism', *Journal of Human Behavior in the Social Environment*, 27: 530–545.

Logie, C., James, L., Tharao, W. and Loutfy, M.R. (2012) 'Opportunities, ethical challenges, and lessons learned from working with peer research assistants in a multi-method HIV community-based research study in Ontario, Canada', *Journal of Empirical Research on Human Research Ethics*, 7(4): 10–19.

Lu, J. and Zhao, J. (2019) 'Does government funding make nonprofits administratively inefficient? Revisiting the link', *Nonprofit and Voluntary Sector Quarterly*, 48(6): 1143–1161.

Lucard, M. (2014) 'History in the making', *The Magazine of the International Red Cross and Red Crescent Movement*, 3: 24–35, www.icrc.org/en/doc/assets/files/publications/1143-red-cross-red-crescent-magazine-eng-3-2014.pdf.

Lyons, M., Wijkstrom, P. and Clary, E. (1998) 'Comparative studies of volunteering: What is being studied', *Voluntary Action*, 1(1): 45–54.

Madison, D.S. (2011) 'The labor of reflexivity', *Cultural Studies*, 11(2): 129–138.

Mansfield, C. and Gregory, D. (2019) 'Capitalism in crisis? Transforming our economy for people and planet', *Social Enterprise UK*, https://www.socialenterprise.org.uk/state-of-social-enterprise-reports/capitalism-in-crisis-transforming-our-economy-for-people-and-planet/.

Marriott, J. (2003) *The other empire: Metropolis, India and progress in the colonial imagination.* Manchester: Manchester University Press.

Matson, E. (1996) 'The new face of social capital', *Fast Company*, www.fastcompany.com/27430/new-face-social-capital.

Mauthner N.S., Parry O. and Backett-Milburn K. (1998) 'The data are out there: or are they? Implications for archiving and revisiting qualitative data', *Sociology*, 32: 733–745.

May, J., Cloke, P. and Johnsen, S. (2007) 'Alternative cartographies of homelessness: Rendering visible British women's experiences of "visible" homeless', *Gender, Place and Culture*, 14(2): 121–140.

McAllister, B. and Allen, A. (2017) 'The role of founder and other family participation on US private foundation efficiency', *Financial Accountability & Management*, 33(1): 48–76.

McConville, D. and Cordery, C.J. (2018) 'Charity performance reporting, regulatory policy and standard-setting', *Journal of Accounting and Public Policy*, 37(4): 300–314.

McCulloch, A., Mohan, J. and Smith, P. (2012) 'Patterns of social capital, voluntary activity, and area deprivation in England', *Environment and Planning A*, 44(5): 1130–1147.

McCurley, S. and Vesuvio, D. (1985) 'Brief response: Who is a volunteer?' *Voluntary Action Leadership*, (Summer): 14–15.

McDonnell, D. (2017) 'Improving charity accountability: Lessons from the Scottish experience', *Nonprofit and Voluntary Sector Quarterly*, 46(4): 725–746.

McDonnell, D. and Rutherford, A.C. (2018) 'The determinants of charity misconduct', *Nonprofit and Voluntary Sector Quarterly*, 47(1): 107–125.

McDonnell, D. and Rutherford, A.C. (2019) 'Promoting charity accountability: Understanding disclosure of serious incidents', *Accounting Forum*, 43(1): 42–61.

McDonnell, D. and Rutherford, A.C. (2020a) 'Incentivising charity accountability: Evidence from the Oxfam scandal', *Working Paper*.

McDonnell, D. and Rutherford, A.C. (2020b) 'The impact of Covid-19 on the foundation and dissolution of charitable organisations', https://diarmuidm.github.io/charity-covid19/index.

McDonnell, D., Mohan, J. and Norman, P. (2020) 'Charity density and social need: A longitudinal perspective', *Nonprofit and Voluntary Sector Quarterly*, 49(5): 1082–1104.

McDonnell, D., Rutherford, A.C. and Cordery, C. (forthcoming) 'Mission accomplished? A cross-national examination of charity dissolution', *Voluntas: International Journal of Voluntary and Nonprofit Organizations*.

McDougle, L.M. (2015) 'The accuracy of the core files for studying nonprofit location: How many nonprofits are there?' *Nonprofit and Voluntary Sector Quarterly*, 44(3): 609–624.

McKee, A. (2003) *Textual analysis: A beginner's guide.* Thousand Oaks, CA: SAGE.

McMurray, M. (2014) *Charity archives in the 21st century.* Cardiff: Royal Voluntary Service.

Meijs, L.C., Handy, F., Cnaan, R.A., Brudney, J.L., Ascoli, U., Ranade, S., Hustinx, L., Weber, S. and Weiss, I. (2003) 'All in the eyes of the beholder? Perceptions of volunteering across eight countries', in P. Dekker, and L. Halman (eds), *The values of volunteering: Cross-cultural perspectives.* New York, NY: Kluwer Academic/Plenum, pp 19–34.

Merryweather, D. (2010) 'Using focus group research in exploring the relationships between youth, risk and social position', *Sociological Research Online*, 15(1): 11–23.

Meyer, S. (2020) 'Everything is fine! Using "The Good Place" to teach administrative ethics', *Journal of Public Affairs Education*, 1–15, https://doi.org/10.1080/15236803.2020.1782102.

Michell, L. (1999) 'Combining focus groups and interviews: Telling how it feels', in R. Barbour and J. Kitzinger (eds), *Developing focus group research: Politics, theory and practice*, Thousand Oaks, CA: SAGE, pp 36–46.

Mills, S. (2013a) 'Surprise! Public historical geographies, user engagement and voluntarism', *Area*, 45: 16–22.

Mills, S. (2013b) 'Cultural-historical geographies of the archive: Fragments, objects and ghosts', *Geography Compass*, 7: 701–713.

Møberg, R.J. (2017) 'Muligheder og udfordringer ved kombinationen af survey og registerdata' [Opportunities and challenges related to the combination of survey and register data], in M. Frederiksen, P. Gundelach, and R.S. Nielsen (eds), *Survey: Design, stikprøve, spørgeskema, analyse.* Copenhagen: Hans Reitzels Forlag, pp 337–354.

Mohan, J. (2012a) 'Above and below the radar: Mapping the distribution of civil society associations in England' in D. Halpin and G. Jordan (eds), *The scale of interest organization in democratic politics*. London: Palgrave Macmillan, pp 202–222.

Mohan, J. (2012b) 'Entering the lists: What can we learn about the voluntary sector in England from listings produced by local infrastructure bodies?', *Voluntary Sector Review*, 3(2): 197–215.

Mohan, J. (2015) 'Charity deserts and social justice: Exploring variations in the distribution of charitable organisations and their resources in England', in B. Morvaridi (ed), *New philanthropy and social justice: Debating the conceptual and policy discourse*. Bristol: Policy Press, pp 191–215.

Mohan, J. and Bennett, M.R. (2019) 'Community-level impacts of the third sector: Does the local distribution of voluntary organizations influence the likelihood of volunteering?', *Environment and Planning A: Economy and Space*, 51(4): 950–979.

Mohan, J. and Bulloch, S. (2012) 'The idea of a "civic core": What are the overlaps between charitable giving, volunteering, and civic participation in England and Wales?' *Third Sector Research Centre, Working Paper 73*, www.birmingham.ac.uk/Documents/college-social-sciences/social-policy/tsrc/working-papers/working-paper-73.pdf.

Mohan, J. and Breeze, B. (2016) 'Spatial logics: The geographical distribution of charities and charitable resources', in *The logic of charity: Great expectations in hard times*. London: Palgrave Pivot, pp 43–66.

Moore, S. (2008) *Ribbon culture: Charity, compassion and public awareness*. London: Palgrave Macmillan.

Moran, J. (2007) 'The science of ourselves', *New Statesman*, 29 January.

Morgan, G.G. (2011) 'The use of UK charity accounts data for researching the performance of voluntary organisations', *Voluntary Sector Review*, 2(2): 213–230.

Morgan, G.G. and Fletcher, N.J. (2013) 'Mandatory public benefit reporting as a basis for charity accountability: Findings from England and Wales', *Voluntas: International Journal of Voluntary and Nonprofit Organizations*, 24(3): 805–830.

Morgan, S.L. and Winship, C. (2015) *Counterfactuals and causal inference*. Cambridge: Cambridge University Press.

Musick, M. and Wilson J. (2008) *Volunteers: A social profile*. Bloomington, IN: Indiana University Press.

Nadel, S.F. (1951) *The foundations of social anthropology*. New York, NY: The Free Press.

Nairn, K., Munro, J. and Smith, A. (2005) 'A counter-narrative of a "failed" interview', *Qualitative Research*, 5(2): 221–244.

NCVO (2020) *UK civil society almanac 2020*, https://data.ncvo.org.uk/

Newton, C. (2004) 'Trumpeting the voluntary in the United Kingdom', *Records Management Journal*, 14(3): 107–110.

Nichols, G., Hogg, E., Knight, C. and Storr, R. (2019) 'Selling volunteering or developing volunteers? Approaches to promoting sports volunteering', *Voluntary Sector Review*, 10(1): 3–18.

Nickel, P.M. and Eikenberry, A.M. (2016) 'Knowing and governing: The mapping of the nonprofit and voluntary sector as statecraft', *Voluntas: International Journal of Voluntary and Nonprofit Organizations*, 27(1): 392–408.

Nordbotten, S. (2008) 'The use of administrative data in official statistics – past, present, and future – with special reference to the Nordic countries', in M. Carlson, H. Nyquist and M. Villani (eds), *Official statistics: Methodology and applications in Honour of Daniel Thorburn*. Stockholm: Department of Statistics, Stockholm University, pp 205–223.

O'Neill, A. (2017) 'Hate crime, England and Wales, 2016/17', *Statistical Bulletin 17/17*. London: Home Office.

Onwuegbuzie, A.J. and Leech, N.L. (2007) 'Validity and qualitative research: An oxymoron?', *Quality & Quantity*, 41(2): 233–249.

Open Science Collaboration (2015) 'Estimating the reproducibility of psychological science', *Science* 349(6251): aac4716.

Oppenheimer, M. (2020) 'The historian activist and the Gift to the Nation project: Preserving the records of the Australian Red Cross', *Archives and Manuscripts*, 48: 171–185.

Ospina, S. and Dodge, J. (2005) 'Narrative inquiry and the search for connectedness: Practitioners and academics developing public administration scholarship', *Public Administration Review*, 65(4): 409–423.

Packard, J. (2008) ' "I'm gonna show you what it's really like out here": The power and limitations of participatory visual methods', *Visual Studies*, 23(1): 63–77.

Parsons, E. (2000) 'New goods, old records and second-hand suits: Charity shopping in South-West England', *International Journal of Nonprofit and Voluntary Sector Marketing*, 5(2): 141–151.

Parsons, E. (2004) 'Charity retailing in the UK: A typology', *The Journal of Retailing and Consumer Services*, 11(1): 31–40.

Parsons, E. and Broadbridge, A. (2007) 'Charity, retail or care? Gender and managerialism in the charity retail sector', *Women in Management Review*, 22(7): 552–567.

Parsons, L.M., Pryor, C. and Roberts, A.A. (2017) 'Pressure to manage ratios and willingness to do so: Evidence from nonprofit managers', *Nonprofit and Voluntary Sector Quarterly*, 46(4): 705–724.

Parsons, S. (2013) *Mass Observation archive: How to combine information with the British birth cohort studies*. London: CLOSER.

Patton, M.Q. (2002) *Qualitative research and evaluation methods* (3rd edn). London: SAGE.

Pautz, M.C. (2017) *Civil servants on the silver screen: Hollywood's depiction of government and bureaucrats.* Lanham, MA: Lexington Books.

Payne, G. and Payne, J. (2005) *Key concepts in social research.* London: SAGE.

Payton, R.L. and Moody, M.P. (2008) *Understanding philanthropy: Its meaning and mission.* Indianapolis, IN: Indiana University Press.

Peck, L.R. (2008) 'Do antipoverty nonprofits locate where people need them? Evidence from a spatial analysis of Phoenix', *Nonprofit and Voluntary Sector Quarterly*, 37(1): 138–151.

Pennerstorfer, A. and Rutherford, A.C. (2019) 'Measuring growth of the nonprofit sector: The choice of indicator matters', *Nonprofit and Voluntary Sector Quarterly*, 48(2): 440–456.

Perego, P. and Verbeeten, F. (2015) 'Do "good governance" codes enhance financial accountability? Evidence from managerial pay in Dutch charities', *Financial Accountability & Management*, 31(3): 316–344.

Petrovski, E., Dencker-Larsen, S. and Holm, A. (2017) 'The effect of volunteer work on employability: A study with Danish survey and administrative register data', *European Sociological Review*, 33(3): 349–367.

Picton, J. and Sigafoos, J. (2020) *Debates in charity law.* London: Hart Publishing.

Pink, S. (2007) *Visual interventions: Applied visual anthropology.* Oxford: Berghahn Books.

Pollen, A. (2013) 'Research methodology in Mass Observation past and present: "Scientifically, about as valuable as a chimpanzee's tea party at the zoo"?' *History Workshop Journal*, 75(1): 213–235.

Pollen, A. (2016) 'Who are all these folk dressed in green?', in P. Harper (ed), *A People's history of the Woodcraft Folk.* London: Woodcraft Folk, pp 40–49.

Ponterotto, J.G. (2006) 'Brief note on the origins, evolution and meaning of the qualitative research concept "thick description"', *The Qualitative Report*, 11(3): 538–554.

Porter, A. (2002) 'Church history, history of Christianity, religious history: Some reflections on British missionary enterprise since the late eighteenth century', *Church History*, 71(3): 555–584.

Proctor, T.M. (1998) '(Uni)forming youth: Girl Guides and Boy Scouts in Britain, 1908–39', *History Workshop Journal*, 45: 103–134.

Prosser, J. (1998) *Image-based research: A sourcebook for qualitative researchers.* London: RoutledgeFalmer.

Qvist, H.-P.Y. (2018a) 'Individual and social resources as causes and benefits of volunteering: Evidence from Scandinavia'. Doctoral dissertation, Aalborg University.

Qvist, H.-P.Y. (2018b) 'Secular and religious volunteering among immigrants and natives in Denmark', *Acta Sociologica*, 61(2): 202–218.

Qvist, H.-P.Y. and Munk, M.D. (2018) 'The individual economic returns to volunteering in work life', *European Sociological Review*, 34(2): 198–210.

Qvist, H.-P.Y., Henriksen, L.S. and Fridberg, T. (2018) 'The consequences of weakening organizational attachment for volunteering in Denmark, 2004–2012', *European Sociological Review*, 34(5): 589–601.

Radley, A., Chamberlain, K., Hodgetts, D., Stolle, O. and Groot, S. (2010) 'From means to occasion: Walking in the life of homeless people', *Visual Studies*, 25(1): 36–45.

Robinson, J.A., Block, D. and Rees, A. (2017) 'Community geography: Addressing barriers in public participation GIS', *The Cartographic Journal*, 54(1): 5–13.

Robinson, L. (2012) 'Putting the charity back into charity singles: Charity singles in Britain 1984–1995', *Contemporary British History*, 26(3): 405–425.

Rochester, C., Ellis Paine, A. and Howlett, S. (2010) *Volunteering and society in the 21st century*. Basingstoke: Palgrave Macmillan.

Roddy, S., Strange, J. and Taithe, B. (2019) *The charity market and humanitarianism in Britain, 1870–1912*. London: Bloomsbury.

Rooney, P., Steinberg, K. and Schervish, P.G. (2004) 'Methodology is destiny: The effect of survey prompts on reported levels of giving and volunteering', *Nonprofit and Voluntary Sector Quarterly*, 33(4): 628–654.

Rutherford, A. and Brook, O. (2016) 'Using administrative data to understand civil society organisations in Scotland', Presentation given at Conference of European Statistics Stakeholders, Budapest, 20–21 October 2016.

Ryan, M.R. and Deci, E.L. (2000) 'Intrinsic and extrinsic motivations: Classic definitions and new directions', *Contemporary Educational Psychology*, 25: 54–67.

Rynes, S., Bartunek, J. and Daft, R. (2001) 'Across the great divide: Knowledge creation and transfer between practitioners and academics', *Academy of Management Journal*, 44(2): 340–355.

Saini, A. (2019) *Superior: The return of race science*. London: Fourth Estate.

Saldaña, J. (2015) *The coding manual for qualitative researchers*. Thousand Oaks, CA: SAGE.

Saxton, G.D., Kuo, J.S. and Ho, Y.C. (2012) 'The determinants of voluntary financial disclosure by nonprofit organizations', *Nonprofit and Voluntary Sector Quarterly*, 41(6):1051–1071.

Schreier, M. (2012) *Qualitative content analysis in practice*. London: SAGE.

Schubert, P. and Boenigk, S. (2019) 'The nonprofit starvation cycle: Empirical evidence from a German context', *Nonprofit and Voluntary Sector Quarterly*, 48(3): 467–491.

Shaw, J. (1994) 'Transference and countertransference at the Mass Observation archive: An under-exploited research resource', *Human Relations*, 47(11) 1391–1408.

Sheridan, D. (1996) ' "Damned anecdotes and dangerous confabulations". Mass-Observation as life history', *Mass Observation Occasional Paper No 7*. www.massobs.org.uk/occasional-papers.

Sheridan, D., Street, B. and Bloome, D. (2000) *Writing ourselves: Mass Observation and literary practices*. Cresskill: Hampton Press.

Shrivastava, P. and Mitroff, I. (1984) 'Enhancing organizational research utilization: The role of decision makers' assumptions', *Academy of Management Review*, 9(1): 18–26.

Small, D.A. and Verrochi, N.M. (2009) 'The face of need: Facial emotion expression on charity advertisements', *Journal of Marketing Research*, 46(6): 777–787.

Smith, D.H. and Wang, L. (2016) 'Conducive social roles and demographics influencing volunteering', in D.H. Smith, R.A. Stebbins, and J. Grotz (eds), *The Palgrave handbook of volunteering, civic participation, and nonprofit associations*. Basingstoke: Palgrave Macmillan, pp 632–681.

Smith, G., Noble, M., Anttilla, C., Gill, L., Zaidi, A., Wright, G., Dibben, C. and Barnes, H. (2004) *The value of linked administrative records for longitudinal analysis, Report to the ESRC National Longitudinal Strategy Committee*. Swindon: ESRC.

Smith, L.T. (2013) *Decolonizing methodologies: Research and indigenous peoples*. London: Zed Books.

Song, Y. and Fu, L. (2018) 'Do charitable foundations spend money where people need it most? A spatial analysis of China', *ISPRS International Journal of Geo-Information*, 7(3): 100–116.

Spencer, S. (2011) *Visual research methods in the social sciences: Awakening visions*. London: Routledge.

Spyrou, S. (2016) 'Researching children's silences: Exploring the fullness of voice in childhood', *Childhood*, 23(1): 7–21.

Stanley, D., Marshall, Z., Lazarus, L., LeBlanc, S., Heighton, T., Preater, B. and Tyndall, M. (2015) 'Harnessing the power of community-based participatory research: Examining knowledge, action, and consciousness in the PROUD study', *Social Work in Public Health*, 30(3): 312–323.

Stanley, N. (1981) ' "The extra dimension": A study and assessment of the methods employed by mass-observation in its first period 1937–40'. PhD thesis, City of Birmingham Polytechnic. https://ethos.bl.uk/OrderDetails.do?uin=uk.bl.ethos.257727.

Strangleman, T. (2002) 'Ways of (not) seeing work: The visual as a blind spot in WES?', *Work, Employment, Society*, 18(1): 179–192.

Tandon, R. and Farrell, M. (2008) 'Collaborative participatory research in gender mainstreaming in social change organizations', in A. Shani, S. Mohrman, W. Pasmore, B. Stymne, and N. Adler (eds), *Handbook of collaborative management research*. Thousand Oaks, CA: SAGE, pp 277–292.

Taylor, R., Torugsa, N. and Arundel, A. (2018) 'Leaping into real-world relevance: An "abduction" process for nonprofit research', *Nonprofit and Voluntary Sector Quarterly*, 47(1): 206–227.

The National Archives (2017) *Archives unlocked: Releasing the potential*. London: The National Archives.

Thiery, H., Cook, J., Burchell, J., Ballantyne, E., Walkley, F. and McNeill, J. (2021) '"Never more needed" yet never more stretched: reflections on the role of the voluntary sector during the COVID-19 pandemic', *Voluntary Sector Review*, https://doi.org/10.1332/204080521X16131303365691.

Third Sector Research Forum (2021) *Guide to applying ethical research principles*. Edinburgh: Evaluation Support Scotland.

Thomson, P. (2008) *Doing visual research with children and young people*. Abingdon: Routledge.

Thygesen, L.C., Daasnes, C., Thaulow, I. and Brønnum-Hansen, H. (2011) 'Introduction to Danish (nationwide) registers on health and social issues: Structure, access, legislation, and archiving', *Scandinavian Journal of Public Health*, 39(7): 12–16.

Trickett, E.J. and Beehler, S. (2017) 'Participatory action research and impact: an ecological ripples perspective', *Educational Action Research*, 25(4): 525–540.

van der Heijden, H. (2013) 'Small is beautiful? Financial efficiency of small fundraising charities', *British Accounting Review*, 45(1): 50–57.

Van Eijk, C. and Steen, T. (2016) 'Why engage in co-production of public services? Mixing theory and empirical evidence', *International Review of Administrative Sciences*, 82(1): 28–46.

Vaughn, L.M., Jacquez, F. and Zhen-Duan, J. (2018) 'Perspectives of community co-researchers about group dynamics and equitable partnership within a community–academic research team', *Health Education & Behavior*, 45(5): 682–689.

Vehovar, V. and Beullens, K. (2018) 'Cross-national issues in response rates', in D.L. Vannette and J.A. Krosnick (eds), *The Palgrave handbook of survey research*. Cham: Palgrave Macmillan, pp 29–43.

Verschuere, B., Brandsen, T. and Pestoff, V. (2012) 'Co-production: The state of the art in research and the future agenda', *Voluntas: International Journal of Voluntary and Nonprofit Organizations*, 23(4): 1083–1101.

Walker, E.J., Waterhouse-Bradley, B. and Armour, C. (2020) 'Mapping voluntary sector services for hidden or hard-to-reach populations: Challenges and practice-based lessons for future research', *Voluntary Sector Review*, 11(1): 113–122.

Wallgren, A. and Wallgren, B. (2007) *Register-based statistics: Administrative data for statistical purposes*. New York, NY: John Wiley & Sons.

Warren, C. (2002) 'Qualitative interviewing', in J. Gubrium and J. Holstein (eds), *Handbook of interview research: Context and method*. London: SAGE, pp 83–101.

Weisbrod, B.A. (1975) 'Toward a theory of the voluntary nonprofit sector in a three sector economy', in E.S. Phelps (ed), *Altruism, morality, and economic theory*. New York, NY: Russell Sage Foundation, pp 171–195.

Wellens, L. and Jegers, M. (2016) 'From consultation to participation: The impact of beneficiaries on nonprofit organizations' decision making and output', *Nonprofit Management and Leadership*, 26(3): 295–312.

What is Philanthropy? (2016) Documentary. Produced by Salvatore Alaimo. United States: A Thought Provoking Films Production.

White, R. and Green, A. (2010) 'Opening up or closing down opportunities: The role of social networks and attachment to place in informing young people's attitudes and access to training and employment', *Urban Studies*, 48(1): 41–60.

Whitworth, A. (ed) (2019) *Towards a spatial social policy: Bridging the gap between geography and social policy*. Bristol: Policy Press.

Wilding, K. (2017) 'Data driven social change', *National Statistical*, ONS blog, https://blog.ons.gov.uk/2017/08/24/data-driven-social-change.

Wilkinson, C. (2016) '"Babe, I like your lipstick": Rethinking researcher personality and appearance', *Children's Geographies*, 14(1): 115–123.

Wilson, J. (2005) 'Some things social surveys don't tell us about volunteering', in A.M. Omoto (ed), *Processes of community change and social action*. New Jersey: Lawrence Earlbaum Associates, pp 11–27.

Wilson, J., Mantovan, N. and Sauer, R.M. (2020) 'The economic benefits of volunteering and social class', *Social Science Research*, 85, https://doi.org/10.1016/j.ssresearch.2019.102368.

Wilson, S. (2014) 'Using secondary analysis to maintain a critically reflexive approach to qualitative research', *Sociological Research Online* 19(3). https://doi.org/10.5153%2Fsro.3370

Yin, R.K. (1989) *Case study research: Design and methods* (rev. edn). Newbury Park, CA: SAGE.

Young, D.R. (2009) 'How nonprofit organizations manage risk', in S. Destefanis and M. Musella (eds), *Paid and unpaid labour in the social economy: An international perspective*. Heidelberg: Physica-Verlag, pp 33–46.

Young, L. and Barrett, H. (2001) 'Adapting visual methods: Action research with Kampala street children', *Area*, 33(2): 141–152.

Yu, H.H. and Campbell, T.M. (2020) 'Teaching leadership theory with television: Useful lessons from Game of Thrones', *Journal of Public Affairs Education*, 27(2): 1–35.

Zanetti, L. (1997) 'Advancing praxis: Connecting critical theory with practice in public administration', *The American Review of Public Administration*, 27(2): 145–167.

Index

References to figures and photographs appear in *italic* type; those in **bold** type refer to tables.